Andrew Kennedy Hutchison] [Boyd

The Autumn Holidays of a Country Parson

Andrew Kennedy Hutchison] [Boyd

The Autumn Holidays of a Country Parson

ISBN/EAN: 9783337372255

Printed in Europe, USA, Canada, Australia, Japan

Cover: Foto ©Thomas Meinert / pixelio.de

More available books at **www.hansebooks.com**

THE
AUTUMN HOLIDAYS
OF
A COUNTRY PARSON

BY THE AUTHOR OF

'THE RECREATIONS OF A COUNTRY PARSON'

CONTENTS.

CHAPTER VII.

CHAPTER VIII.

CHAPTER IX.

CHAPTER X.

CHAPTER XI.

CHAPTER XII.

CHAPTER XIII.

CHAPTER XIV.

THE

AUTUMN HOLIDAYS

OF A

COUNTRY PARSON.

CHAPTER I.

BY THE SEASIDE.

E have been here a little more than a week, all of us together. For if you be a man of more than five-and-thirty years, and if you have a wife and children, you have doubtless found out that the true way to enjoy your autumn holidays and to be the better for them, is not to go away by yourself to distant regions where you may climb snowy Alps and traverse glaciers, in the selfish enjoyment of new scenes and faces. These things must be left to younger men, who have not yet formed their home-ties; and who know neither the happiness nor the anxieties of human beings who spread a large surface on any part of which fortune may hit hard and deep. Let us find a quiet place where parents and children may enjoy the

time of rest in company: where you will be free
from the apprehensions of evil which (unless you
be a very selfish person) you will not escape when
the little things are a thousand miles away. And
to this end, one may well do without the sight of
lakes, waterfalls, streets and churches, which it was
pleasant once on a time to see. Upon this day last
year, I ascended the marvellous spire of Strasburg
Cathedral. It was the brightest of all bright days.
You went up and up, by little stairs winding
through a lace-work of stone, which it makes one
somewhat nervous to think of even now, till you
emerged on a platform whence you looked down
dizzily on the market place hundreds of feet below;
upon the town, all whose buildings looked so clean
and well-defined in the smokeless air; upon the
fertile level plain stretching away towards Baden;
and the ugly poplars marking the course of the
Rhine. It was all, to an untravelled man and an
enthusiastic lover of Gothic architecture, interesting
beyond expression: yet I would much rather be here.

For this is Saturday morning; and my parish is
far away. There is no sermon to be thought of for
to-morrow; and no multitude of sick folk to see:
no pressure of manifold parochial cares. This is a
very ugly cottage by a beautiful shore: and through
a simple pecuniary negociation, the cottage is ours
for the months of August and September. Looking
up from this table and looking out of the window,

the first object you would see is a shaggy little fuchsia, covered with red flowers, waving about in a warm western wind. Beyond, there is a small expanse of green grass, in which I see, with entire composure, a good many weeds which would disquiet me much if the grass were my own. The little lawn is bounded by a wall of rough stone, half concealed by shrubs. And on the farther side, the top of the wall cutting sharp against it, weltering and toiling now in shadow, but a minute ago bright in sunshine with the unnumbered dimple of little waves, spreads the sea. Now it has brightened again: and three gleaming sails break the deep blue. Opposite, a few miles off, there are grand Highland hills. Sometimes they look purple: sometimes light blue: sometimes the sunshine shows a yellow patch of corn-field. Never for more than an hour or two do those hills and this sea look the same. They are always changing: and the changes are extreme. You could no more tell a stranger what this place is like by describing it ever so accurately as it is at this moment, than you could worthily represent the most changeful human face by a single photograph. In the sunset, you may often see what will make you understand the imagery of the Revelation, a sea of glass mingled with fire : then the mountains are of a deep purple hue, such as you would think exaggerated if you saw it in a picture. Hardly have the crimson and golden lights faded from the smooth water, when a great moon, nearly full, rises above the trees on this side, and casts a long golden path, flickering and heaving : the stillness is such that you fear to break it by a footfall.   Then there have been times, even within this week, when drenching showers darkened the water and hid the opposite hills : or when white-crested waves made the sea into a wild ridgy plain, and broke on the shingle hard by in foam and thunder.

This is not a fashionable watering-place : you go back to a quiet and simple life, coming here.   No band of music plays upon the black wooden pier where the rare steamboat calls daily.   There is no such thing as a gay promenade, frequented by brightly-dressed people desirous to see and to be seen.   There is no reading room, no billiard room, no circulating library, no hotel, no people who let out boats, no drinking-fountain.   There is a post office; but it is a mile distant.   You would find here no more than a line of detached houses, a few extremely pretty, and more of them extremely ugly, reaching for somewhat more than a mile along the seashore.   The houses, each with its shrubbery and lawn, greater or less, stand on a strip of level ground between the sea and a rocky wall of cliff, which follows the line of the beach at no great distance; doubtless an ancient sea margin.   But now it serves as a beautiful background to the pretty houses, and it almost redeems the ugly ones: it is covered richly with trees, which through ages have rooted themselves in the crevices of the rock; and where the perpendicular wall forbids that vegetation, it is clothed with ivy so luxuriant that you would hardly think those hearty leaves ever knew the blighting salt spray. By the seashore there runs a highway: the waves break within a few yards on a beach of rough shingly gravel. It is to be confessed that this charming place lacks the level sand which the ebbing tide leaves for a firm cool walking space at some time of every day. But your walks are not confined to the path to right and left along the seashore. You will discover pleasant ways, that lead to the country above the wooded and ivied cliff: and there you will find ripening harvest fields, and paths that wind through fragrant woods of birch, oak and pine, and here and there the mountain ash, with its glowing scarlet berries. But it is not what one understands by *a country side*: the whole landscape is gradually but constantly sloping upwards, till it passes into dark heathery hills, solitary as Tadmor in the wilderness. There the sportsman goes in search of grouse and deer; and thence you have views of the level blue water far below you, that are worth going many miles to see.

There are places along this seaside where your only walk is beside the sea. The hills rise almost

from the water, an expanse of shadeless heather.
But we are happier, with our shady woodland
walks. When the glare and heat are oppressive
along the shore in the vacant afternoon, let us turn
away from the road that skirts the beach, up this
thickly-wooded glen, through which a stream brawls
from rock to rock, hardly seen for the leaves. You
will not walk for a few yards under the pleasant
shadow, till you find yourself so environed with ivy-
grown trees, honeysuckle and wild flowers, that
you might fancy the sea many miles off. And the
oppressive light and heat and dust are gone. Let
us go on, following the windings of the path and
the water, till we reach a spot where a clear little
brook, tumbling over rocks from far above us,
crosses the road under a rude arch, to join the
larger stream : and now let us sit down on a great
stone, where the little brook, close by our feet,
makes a leap into the dark entrance of the bridge.
Here let us rest and be thankful. Many people
find this a feverish world : let us rejoice in a nook
so green and quiet. Ferns of many kinds cover the
damp rocks : there is a thick canopy of green leaves
overhead, through which you may see blinks of the
brightest blue sky ; and through which you may see
an intense flickering of light, where the sun is
struggling to pierce the dense shade. The air is
fragrant and cool and moist : all around there is a
thicket of evergreens and underwood, over which

the tall trunks arise whose spreading branches make our grateful shadow.

We have all, young and old, wearied for this time : and here it is at last. The cheerful anticipation of it was something to help one through laborious summer days. For if you are to be in the country no more than two months in the year, the months beyond question should be August and September. Let us keep our cake as long as we can : let us make our holiday season late. June and July are delightful months amid rural scenes : but it would be dismal to go back to the hot town at the end of July and think one had settled down for the winter. But at the beginning of October, a little space of long dark evenings, and the growing crispness of the morning air, help to make one feel ready to take with good heart to the labouring oar again.

Yet, though this holiday-time be so enjoyed by anticipation, I think that when the day comes on which you preach to your own congregation for the last time before leaving, you feel it rather a trial. And you turn your back upon your church with some regret and some misgiving. A clergyman's work is not like any other : you have not quite the schoolboy's feeling when working days are over and holidays begin. For your work is not merely your duty : it is your happiness too. And though some folk may not understand it, you feel it something

of a privation to think on a Sunday in your play-
time that the bells are ringing, and the people
assembling in the familiar place; and you not there.
Happily, there are regions in this world where the
clergyman's last Sunday at church, is likewise the
last Sunday at church of a great part of the congregation. *It* is gathered, as usual, one day: and
the next, scattered far and wide, by the seaside and
among the hills.   And in this uncertain world,
where when many hundreds of human beings are in
one place to-day, no one can say who may be
missing when they meet after some weeks separa-
tion, I think that you, my friend, will preach with
special kindliness and heartiness on your last
Sunday at home; and that you will be heard with
special attention and sympathy.   There will be a
very perfect stillness as you pronounce the blessing
for what may be the last time.   And you will well
remember the words and the music of the parting
hymn.   Taking your final look round your vestry,
and round your emptied church, as you come away,
you will feel the sorrow and anxiety which come of
the vain delusion common to man, that the place
where you worked and laboured your best, will not
go on quite as well in your absence. Ah, my friend,
some day you and I must leave our several churches
for ever: and though we shall be kindly remembered and missed there for a while, they will come
by and by to do without us.   And very fit and

right too. We are not such self-conceited fools as to wish it were otherwise. Yet it is cheering, each Tuesday morning through the holidays, when the letter comes by post, in which a kind friend, whom duty ties to his town work at this season, tells how all went well in the services of the Sunday before.

Then, following that parting day, comes one of confusion and worry and fatigue : the day on which the family accomplishes the journey to the distant resting-place. Would that the age might come when human beings shall be able to do without baggage! Yet even baggage serves good moral ends. You are very thankful indeed when in the quiet evening the cottage, or the more ambitious dwelling, is reached at last : and the manifold packing-cases, being counted up, are found to be all right. During the day, several times, you had quite resigned yourself to the conviction that half of them would never be found more.

There are simple statements which may be repeated many times, while yet no wise man will pull you up by declaring that he has heard the like before. For such simple statements are the irrepressible outflow of the present happy mood and feeling. You could not help uttering such, to any one to whom you might be talking out your heart. Suffer me now to declare, that there is no more precious blessing than Rest. 'The end of work is

to enjoy rest.' 'The end and the reward of toil
is rest.' Yes, it is delightful to rest for a while
from even the most congenial and beloved work.
And rest is not merely delightful: it is needful.
The time comes, when the task drags heavily: when
it is got through heartlessly, and by a painful effort
often renewed. Most busy men, busied with work
that wears the brain and nervous system, have some
little time of rest in their daily round : some precious
hour of quiet. There is generally the short breathing
space between dinner and tea. But as months pass,
the nerves grow so irritable that many sounds and
circumstances worry you : then is the hour when
the organ-grinder painfully thrills you through. At
this stage, busy men find the relief of a little pause :
a day or two away from work, no matter where.
Arnold said that the most restful days of the year
were those spent in the long journeys by coach
between Rugby and Fox How. A very eminent
and over-driven man lately told me, that when he is
being wrought into a fever, he finds rest by going
to London by the express train, and returning the
next day. The distance is four hundred miles going,
and the like returning : eleven hours either way.
But it is enjoyable to lean back in the carriage : to
read and to muse : sure that no one will speak to
him on the business of his profession. I have heard
of a great man who found the like relief in going to
bed for two days or so. There was physical repose :

and even the unreasonable caller and tormentor who would utterly disregard the assurance that the Doctor was weary and could see no one, was beaten by the assurance that the Doctor was in bed. For the average human being, on being told that the Doctor could see no one, would instantly say, ' Oh, but I know he will see ME!' But not even these retreats will stay the gathering weariness which grows on body and mind as the seasons pass. And if you have been at work from the beginning of October to the end of July, ten months with little relaxation, then you have fairly earned the autumn holiday-time. And your rest will be not merely the reward of past work, but the preparation for future. You are laying up the strength, spirit, and patience, needful for the winter months, if you are to see that time. And you must act on the calculation that you are to see it. On dark Sunday afternoons in January, when gas is lit throughout the church, and snow lies in the wintry streets, you may preach your sermon with the greater heart and vigour for the hours you sit now on a stone by the seaside, looking at the waves; and for the bracing breezes that supply the ozone the city lacks. So the diligent clergyman is as much in the way of duty while enjoying his autumn rest, as while fulfilling the work of the remainder of the year.

That you may thoroughly enjoy the autumn holidays, it is essential that you should feel that they

have been fairly earned by long and hard work.
You cannot feel the delight of rest, unless by contrast with toil, hurry, and weariness. All this quiet
and beauty, to you and me grateful as water to the
thirsty, would be to people who habitually live an
idle life, no better than something insufferably dull
and stupid. Let us hope that we have faithfully
gone through the previous discipline, that will make ·
us relish simple quiet and peace. Some people
think it shows humility to say things against themselves which they know are not true. They meekly
confess sins of which they are aware they are not
guilty: saying what they suppose must be true,
instead of what they feel to be true. Let us never
do the like. Few things are more fatal to a true and
honest spirit. For myself, I will say without reserve,
that in these last ten months I have worked to the
very best of my ability and strength, to fulfil my
duty. And if not very much after all, I have done
what I could. I can say the like for certain dear
friends in my own profession. They never wilfully
neglect any work. They never see anything that
ought to be done, without trying to do it. Unpro-
fitable servants, doubtless, in the sight of One above
us: but at least we can look our fellow-men in the
face.

I suppose, my readers, we have all a picture in
our minds of the ideal autumn holidays. They never
have come : they are never to be. Yet we can think

of broad harvest fields, golden in sunshine ; of magnificent trees, the growth of centuries; of green
glades with the startled deer; of the gray Gothic
dwelling, large and hospitable; of a mode of life in
which sickness, anxiety, vague fears, and pinching
efforts to save shillings, are quite unknown. Yes,
it is to be admitted that this ugly little cottage,
and its surroundings physical and moral, are no
more than a makeshift. But then, my friend, what
more is all our life, and all our lot ? We must make
them do : we have great reason to be thankful for
things as they are : but all this is not what we used
to think of, when we were little children or hopeful youths. Let us train ourselves to look at lights
rather than darks. There is such a thing as an eye
for lights, and such a thing as an eye for darks.
You know, when you look at a grand Gothic window, the eastern window of a noble church; and
when you look at a much smaller Gothic window ;
you may look either at the dark tracery of stone, or
at the lights of gorgeous storied glass. Now, in a
physical sense, it is well to look at each in turn.
You may behold a really excellent window by this :
that the darks are beautiful in form if you fix your
attention on them only : and the lights are likewise
beautiful in form if you consider them by themselves. An inferior architect will give you the
tracery beautiful but the lights shapeless; or the lights
pretty but the tracery ugly. But though it is well,

physically, to have an eye for both darks and lights, it is best, usually, to look mainly at lights, as you contemplate the grand Gothic window of your lot, and of circumstances. For many people look at the darks, to the exclusion of the lights. They dwell on the worries of their condition, to the forgetfulness of its blessings and advantages. They contemplate the smoky chimney of their dining-room, to the forgetfulness of a hundred good things. They try to get other people to do the like. My friend Smith told me that once on a time he had Mr. Jones to preach in his church. Smith's church holds fifteen hundred people, and it is perfectly filled by its congregation : of this circumstance Smith is pardonably proud. When Mr. Jones preached, the church was quite crowded, save that three seats (not pews, seats for a single person each) were vacant in a front gallery. But so keen was Mr. Jones's eye for darks, to the oblivion of lights, that after service he merely said to Smith that he had remarked three seats empty in the gallery. Not one thought or word had he for the fourteen hundred and ninety-seven seats that were filled. Smith was a little mortified. But by-and-bye he remembered that the peculiar disposition of Mr. Jones was one that would inflict condign punishment upon itself. Then he was sorry rather than angry. Yes, my friend : let us be glad if we have an eye for the lights of life, rather than for its darks !

It is curious how very soon the burden drops
from one's back, when you come for your holidays
to some place far away from your home and your
duty. The relief is in direct proportion to the distance in miles. A hundred miles will suffice: a
thousand are better. Very lightly does the care of
your parish rest on you, when the parish is a thousand miles distant! Even a tenth part of that
amount makes one feel as a horse must, when its
harness is removed and its shoes taken off and it
is turned out to grass. As you put on a tweed suit,
and adopt a wideawake hat, you forget the responsibilities and labours of past months: you cease to
be the same man. The careful lines are smoothed
out of your face; the hair pauses in growing gray.
It is necessary, indeed, to the true sense of rest,
that you should have the feeling of a good long
horizon of time before you. A few days in the
country, with the feeling that you are just going
back to work, will not do: the feverish pulse
will keep by you. It is quite a different thing,
when you know you have several weeks in prospect.
Then you expatiate: then you truly rest. Those
good men who remain within a few miles of their
parish, and who go back for each Sunday's duty,
do not enjoy the feeling of the holiday-time at all.
And feeling is the reality. It is not what a thing
is in itself, but how it presents itself to you. You
know how different a thing a railway station thirty

miles from home looks to you when you are to stop at it, and when you are to go on three hundred miles further.

It is pleasant, and at first a little perplexing, instead of setting to work after breakfast, to go forth and wander about the shore, or sit on a rock as long as you please, with the sense that you are neglecting nothing that needs to be done. You feel, as regards time, as a poor man who has suddenly inherited a large fortune must feel towards money. Strange, to have so much to spare of the thing of which before one had so little! And how misty and unreal the scenes and the life that are distant and past grow to be! I cannot at this minute, sitting on a warm stone by the sea in the morning sunshine, feel that at the entrance to a certain square, stands in this same sunshine, with a little shrubbery before it, a certain church, Ionic as to its front elevation, which the writer well knows. It is always there when I go back: but I do not know what becomes of it in the meanwhile.

There is nothing more certain than this, that it will not answer to go to your resting-place to spend your holiday-time, without having thought of what you are to do while there. If the truth were told, it would be the confession of many men that the enjoyment of their holidays was all in the anticipation and the retrospect; and that the holidays themselves were a very disappointing and tiresome time,—very listless and weary. All this comes of their vaguely believing that to enjoy the season of rest, all you have to do is to go to some quiet retired place, and then some occupation will suggest itself, some mode of getting the due enjoyment out of the long-expected time. A clergyman might just as wisely ascend his pulpit without having thought of what he is to say from it, of his text and his sermon; and count upon these turning up at the moment they are needed. Before going to the seaside, you should carefully consider what you are to do there, and map out some little plan of life: not adhering to it, of course, should some pleasant deviation suggest itself. And everyone must devise such a plan for himself, according to his own liking. Only let it be remembered, that it will not do to be absolutely vacant. Time will hang heavy; and then enjoyment is at an end. Different men have devised different modes of light occupation for their holiday-time: and that which suited one man might be most unsuitable for another. Mr. Jay, the eminent Nonconformist of Bath, tells us that it helped him to thoroughly enjoy his vacation, to write one little sermon in the morning of each day, and another in the evening. The sermons were certainly very brief: you might read each in five minutes: yet not every preacher would have regarded it as recreation to produce them. There are very many to whom sermon-writing does not come so easily: to whom a sermon is the thought of a week, not the diversion of an hour. Let it be said that Mr. Jay's little sermons now fill four volumes, under the title of *Morning and Evening Exercises*: they provide a little pious reading for the mornings and evenings of a year. The writer is so very warm a Churchman, that he seldom looks at the volumes without regretting that the good man was not one: the more so, as it is plain that no conscientious scruple kept him out of his national Church. Yet let it be said, that if you read the little discourses daily for a year, you will leave off with a very kindly and pleasant impression of their author. It is not that any one discourse is in any way specially brilliant; but that all are so evenly good. And they treat, in the most admirable spirit, not the matters on which good Christians differ; but those on which they all agree.

For men to whom the writing of sermons is not relaxation but rather work, yet whose likings are quiet and scholarly, certain rules may be suggested. In addition to the physical employment of mountain excursions, yachting, riding, shooting and the like, let abundance of reading be provided. Let the *Times* daily tell how the great world goes: let plenty of other newspapers come besides. Thus post-time will be a fresh sensation, even if very few letters appear, and these of very small interest. And besides as many pleasant new books as you can get, let there be some large work, of many volumes, read perhaps long ago, yet worth reading again; and which could not be read satisfactorily amid the pressure of working days and months. And weeks before you come to the seaside, consider what this book shall be. Mine, this year, is Lockhart's *Life of Sir Walter Scott*: an admirable history of a great and good man. If you have read it as a boy, read it once more as a man: and you will find how well you remember it. It is a sad history, certainly: and you will find many things to be thought of with deep regret : yet you will rise from it with a hearty admiration and affection for the greatest Scotchman. And often, as you go on, you will come on passages that will make you pause and muse, with the finger in the half-closed book.

But the writer's special occupation during these holidays, is to revise and consider the essays which make up this volume. He has very little time, now, for writing such; and the little time is growing less. The spare hours of two years have gone to the production of this little book: it will always be pleasant to look back on time so pleasantly spent. And these chapters have already met so kind a reception, as they appeared in that dear old magazine in which the writer saw his earliest article in print and his latest, and in another magazine which professes to publish good words, though some people have declared it to be a bad and dangerous periodical; that the indulgent reader may easily understand how this volume has been added to the list of certain which have gone before. Let me wish for this book that it may fall into as kind hands as the rest; and into as many.

It is a great thing to have some occupation, in a time and place like this, which implies no exertion. It is pleasant, for a very small author, to sit down on a rustic seat under a shady tree, or on a rock by the sea with the murmuring water lapping at one's feet; and there peacefully to read over one's essay. A distinguished American author has put on record the feelings with which he read his own first book: he says frankly, 'I never read a more interesting volume!' Under the shadow of that illustrious precedent it may be confessed, that though when busy with serious work you have something else to do than to read your own compositions, yet in a season of leisure it is light and pleasant employment for an author to do so. Somebody once on a time sent me a lengthened and friendly criticism of these essays, in which it was yet mentioned, as a ground of complaint, that no mental exertion was needful to follow them. That is precisely what their author wished: and he will be too glad to think that it is so. He has pioneered the road, through the jungle and up the pass: he trusts it is smooth and easy. Yet let it be said, that what is easy to read, is for the most part difficult to write.

Let me be allowed a closing word. Why does the writer call himself a *country parson ?* Years have passed since he left that beautiful green valley with the river, the trees and the hills; and went to a great city. But country parson is the name that suits him : and the name by which many kind friends know him. So he calls himself by it, just as his friend Smith calls himself Smith. It is not that that individual is a smith in fact : but that Smith is the name by which people have agreed to call and know him. The ancestor who first bore the name was in fact a smith : and the name of Smith continued to be handed down after the fact of smith ceased. So let it be with the author's cherished designation.

And there is more. Though he now does the duty of a parish in a great city, it is the city in which, above all others, country and town are mingled in the most charming way. In the parish which he serves, you may even find beautiful shady walks, and expanses of grass and flowers, where you might think yourself far from town smoke and bustle. And indeed you are : for in that most beautiful of cities, there is no smoke and little bustle. May it be always so!

CHAPTER II.

CONCERNING UNPRUNED TREES.

N this writing-table, here in a great city, there lie two large pruning-knives, unused for five years. They look inconsistent enough with the usual belongings of the work-room of the incumbent of a town parish; who on weekdays walks about chiefly upon paving-stones, and on Sundays preaches to city folk. But Britons know that there are institutions which the wise man would preserve, though their day and their use have passed away. So is it with these knives : buck-horn as to their handles, and black with rust as to their blades. The writer will never cast them away: will never lock them up in a drawer rarely visited, degrading them from the prominent and easily-reached spot where they lay in years that are gone. Never again, in all likelihood, will those knives be used by the hand that was wont to use them : yet they serve their owner well when they bring back the pleasant picture of days when he was a country parson and pruned many shrubs and trees : walking about leisurely in the enjoyment of snipping off, as a schoolmaster of my youth was accustomed to walk down the rows of boys busy in writing, here and there coming down with a heavy lash on some unlucky back, merely for his own recreation and with no moral aim. Yes, there is a tranquil delight in pruning : to a simple and unfevered mind it is a very fascinating pursuit. And it is a good sign of a man if he finds pleasure in it. Alas, we outgrow the days in which it makes us happy to prune trees !

The reader who is given to pruning, knows how very much some trees need it. You know how horribly awkward and ugly an old bay becomes, after it has been untended for years. It has great branches, which stick out most ungracefully. And it is likely enough that the whole tree is so inextricably grown into that ungainly form, that it is best to saw it off about three or four feet from the ground, and to let it begin to grow anew. Thus starting afresh, you may be able to make it a pretty and graceful object, though of much diminished size. There are trees whose nature is such, that they can do with little or no pruning. They don't need to be watched : they cost no trouble. Such is a Portugal laurel : such is a weeping birch : such is a beech : such is an oak.

But not such is an Irish yew: not such is an apple-tree, nor any kind of fruit-tree. And in the days when you were the possessor of trees, and were sometimes a good deal worried by the charge of them, I know you often thought what a blessing it is that there are some that need no pruning: some that once put in their place, you may let alone. For there were some that needed ceaseless tending: they grew horrible unless you were always watching them, and cutting off this and that little shoot that was growing in a wrong direction. It was an awful thing, standing beside some tree that had given you a great amount of trouble, to think what it would come to if it were just left to itself.

Most human beings are very like the latter order of trees. They need a great deal of pruning. Little odd habits, the rudiments of worse habits, need every now and then to be cut off and corrected. We should all grow very singular, ridiculous, and unamiable creatures, but for the pruning we have got from hands kind and unkind, from our earliest days: but for the pruning we are getting from such hands yet. Perhaps you have known a man who had lived for forty years alone. And you know what odd shoots he had sent out: what strange traits and habits he had acquired: what singular little ways he had got into. There had been no one at home to prune him: and the little shoots of eccentricity, of vanity, of vain self-estimation, that might have easily been cut off when they were green and soft, have now grown into rigidity : woody fibre has been developed : and if you were to try to cut off the oddity now, it would be like trying to lop off a tough oak branch a foot thick with a penknife. You cannot do it : if you were to succeed in doing it, you would thereby change the whole man. Equally grown into rigid awkwardness with the man who has lived a very solitary life, the man is likely to be who for many years has been the Pope of a little circle of admiring disciples, no one of whom would ever contradict him, no one of whom would ever venture to say he judged or did wrong. In such a case, not merely are the angularities, the odd ungainly shoots, not cut off : they are actually fostered. And a really good man grows into a bundle of awkwardnesses and oddities, and stiffens hopelessly into these. And these greatly lessen his influence and usefulness with people who do not know his real excellences. You cannot read the life of Mr. Simeon, of Cambridge, without lamenting that there was not some kind yet firm hand always near him, to prune off the wretched little shoots of self-conceit and silliness which obscured in great measure the sterling qualities of the man. You may remember reading how on an occasion on which some good ladies had collected pieces of needle-work to be sold for a missionary purpose, he came to behold them.

He skipped into the room: held up his hands in a theatrical ecstasy of admiration: and went through various ungainly gambols and uttered various wretched jokes, by way of compliment to the good ladies. I don't tell you the story at length: it is too humiliating. Now do you think the good man would ever have done this, had he lived among people who durst question his infallibility and impeccability? What a blessing it would have been for him had there been some one on such terms with him that he could say, 'Now, Simeon, dear fellow, don't make a fool of yourself!'

It is at once apparent, that when some really kind and judicious friend, or even some judicious person who is not a kind friend, says to you as you are saying something, 'Smith, you're talking nonsense: shut up, and don't make a fool of yourself;' this fact is highly analogous to the fact of a keen pruning-knife snipping off a shoot that is growing in a wrong direction. And you may have seen a good man, accustomed to dwell among those who never dared to differ from him, look as if the world were suddenly coming to an end, when some courageous person said to his face what many persons had frequently said behind his back: to wit, that he was talking nonsense. You may find a house here and there, in which the grey mare is the more energetic if not the better horse: where the husband has been constrained by years of outrageous ill-temper to give the wife her own way: and where, accordingly, the mistress of the house has lived for thirty years without once being told she did wrong. The tree, that is, had never been pruned in all that time: and you may imagine what an ugly and disagreeable tree it had grown. For people who get their own way, have nothing to repress their evil and ridiculous tendencies except their own sense of propriety: and I have little faith in the practical guidance of that sense, unless it be reinforced and directed by the moral and æsthetic sense of other people. A tree, when pruned, suffers in silence: no doubt, it cannot like being pruned: it would like to have its own way. But the pruning of a human being, accustomed to his or her own way, is often accompanied by much moral kicking and howling. Such a person, in those years without pruning, has very likely got confirmed in many ridiculous and disagreeable habits: has learned to sit with his feet upon the mantel-piece: has come to use ungrammatical and ugly forms of speech: has grown into rubbing his nose, or twirling his thumbs, or making pills of paper while conversing with others: indeed there is no reckoning the ugly growths into which unpruned human nature will develop itself; and self-conceited and haughty and petted folk deliberately deprive themselves of that salutary tending and pruning which is needful to keep them in decent shape. There was once a man, who was much given to advocating the admission of fresh air: an excellent end.   But of course in advocating it, the word *Ventilation* had frequently to be used; and that man made himself ridiculous in the eyes of all educated people by invariably pronouncing the word as *Ventulation.*   For a long time, a youthful relative of that man suffered in silence the terrible annoyance of listening to the word, thus rendered: and there are few more irritating things among the minor vexations of life, than to be compelled habitually to listen to some vulgar and illiterate error in speech.   Perhaps you have felt a burning desire to prune a person, who talked of some trouble being *tremenduous*; or who said he would rather go to Jericho *as* hear Dr. Log preach; or who declared the day to be *that* hot that he was nearly killed. Oh, the thought of such expressions makes one's nerves tingle, and one's hand steal towards the pruning-knife.   But after long endurance, the youthful relative of the man who talked about *Ventulation,* could stand it no longer: and ventured humbly to suggest that *Ventilation* was the preferable way of setting forth the word.   Ah, the tree did not take the pruning peaceably!   Wasn't there an explosion of vanity and spite and stupidity!   Was not the youthful individual scorched with furious sarcasm, for pretending to know better than his seniors, and for venturing to think that his betters could go wrong!   From that day forward, he resolved that however hideous the shoots of ignorance and conceit his seniors put forth, *he* would not venture to correct them. For there is nothing that so infuriates an uneducated and self-sufficient man of more than middle age, as the faintest and best-disguised attempt to prune him. 'Are you sure that your *data* is correct?' said a vulgar rich man to an educated poor man. '*Data* ARE correct, I think you mean,' said the poor man (rather hastily), before going on to answer the question. The rich man's face reddened like an infuriated turkeycock; and had there been a cudgel in his hand, he would have beaten the pruner upon the head. Yes: it is thankless work to wield the moral pruning-knife.

Probably among the class of old bachelors you may find the most signal instances of the evil consequence of going through life with nobody to prune one. I could easily record such manifestations of silliness and absurdity in the case of such men as would be incredible. Of course, I am not going to do so. An old bachelor of some standing, living in a solitary house, with servants who dare not prune him, and with acquaintances who will not take the trouble to prune him, must necessarily, unless he be a very wise and good man, grow into a most amorphous shape. I beg the reader to mark the exception I make: for I presume he will agree with me when I say, that in the class of old bachelors and old maids, may be found some of the noblest specimens of the human race. A judicious wife is always snipping off from her husband's moral nature, little twigs that are growing in wrong directions. She keeps him in shape, by continual pruning. If you say anything silly, she will affectionately tell you so. If you declare that you will do some absurd thing, she will find means of preventing your doing it./ And by far the chief part of all the common sense there is in this world, belongs unquestionably to women. The wisest things a man commonly does, are those which his wife counsels him to do. It is not always so. You may have known a man do, at the instigation of his wife, things so malicious, petty, and stupid, that it is inconceivable any man should ever do them at all. But such cases are exceptional.

My friend Jones, when a boy of fourteen, went to visit a relative, a rich old bachelor. That relative was substantially a very kind person : that is, he gave Jones lots of money, and the like. But Jones, an observant lad, speedily took his relative's measure. The first evening Jones was with him, the old bachelor said, in a very cordial way, ' Now Tom, my boy, it is my duty to tell you something. You have been trained up to believe that your father' (a clergyman) ' is an able and dignified person. It is right that you should know that he is a very poor stick.'

Jones listened, without remark, but with rather a

scared face. It was a trial to the young fellow. It was a shock to his belief in things in general, to hear his father thus spoken of. And Jones, who is now a man, tells me that though he said nothing, he inwardly groaned, looking at his wealthy relative, 'You're a horrid old fool.' And in all the years that have passed since then, Jones assures me he has not in the least modified that early opinion.

Now, don't you feel that no married man would have so behaved? Even if he were such an ass as to begin to say such a thing to a little boy, don't you feel his wife (if present) would have taken care that the sentence was never finished?

The same person began to tell Jones about the Opera. And all of a sudden, to the lad's consternation, he burst out into some awful roars. Jones was terrified. He thought his relative had gone mad, or was suddenly seized by some unusual and terrible disease. But the old gentleman said, with great self-complacency, 'That's just to give you some idea what the human voice is capable of!' Jones secretly thought that it gave him some idea what a fool an old gentleman might make of himself.

I have heard of an extremely commonplace man, who lived an utterly solitary life in London. He had gained considerable wealth : but he had nothing else to stand on ; and he was not rich enough to stand on that alone. The worthy man has been in his grave for many years. Having heard that

Mr. Brown had stated that he did not know him, he exclaimed : ‘ He does not know ME !   Well, there is no Act of Parliament to make people know about me.   All I can say is, that if he does not know about me, he is an ill-informed man!’   This was not a joke.   It was said in bitter earnest.   For when a young fellow who was present showed a tendency to smile at this outburst of self-conceit nursed in solitude, the young fellow was furiously ordered out of the room.

Doubtless you have remarked, with satisfaction, how the little oddities of men who marry rather late in life, are pruned away speedily after their marriage.   You have found a man who used to be shabbily and carelessly dressed, with a huge shirt-collar frayed at the edges, and a glaring yellow silk pocket handkerchief, broken of these things, and become a pattern of neatness.   You have seen a man whose hair and whiskers were ridiculously cut, speedily become like other human beings.   You have seen a clergyman who wore a long beard, in a little while appear without one.   You have seen a man who used to sing ridiculous sentimental songs, leave them off.   You have seen a man who took snuff copiously, and who generally had his breast covered with snuff, abandon the vile habit. | A wife is the grand wielder of the moral pruning-knife. | If Johnson’s wife had lived, there would have been no hoarding up of bits of orange peel : no touching all the posts in walking along the street : no eating and drinking with a disgusting voracity. If Oliver Goldsmith had been married, he would never have worn that memorable and ridiculous coat. Whenever you find a man whom you know little about, oddly dressed, or talking absurdly, or exhibiting any eccentricity of manner, you may be tolerably sure that he is not a married man. For the little corners are rounded off, the little shoots are pruned away, in married men. Wives generally have much more sense than their husbands, especially when the husbands are clever men. /The wife's advices are like the ballast, that keeps the ship steady. They are like the wholesome though painful shears, snipping off little growths of self-conceit and folly./

So you may see, that it is not good for man to be alone. For he will put out various shoots at his own sour will, which will grow into monstrously ugly and absurd branches unless they are pruned away while they are young. But it is quite as bad, perhaps it is worse, to live among people with whom you are an Oracle. There are many good Protestants who, by a long continuance of such a life, have come to believe their own infallibility much more strongly than the Pope believes his. An only brother amid a large family of sisters, is in a perilous position. There is a risk of his coming to think himself the greatest, wisest, and best of men : the most graceful dancer, the most melodious singer, the sweetest poet, the most unerring shot: also the best-dressed man, and the possessor of the most beautiful hands, feet, eyes, and whiskers. And as the outer world is sure not to accept this estimate, the only brother is apt to be soured by the sharp contrast between the adulation at home and the snubbing abroad. A popular clergyman, with a congregation somewhat lacking in intelligence, is exposed to a prejudicial moral atmosphere. It is a dreadful sight, to see some clergymen surrounded by the members of their flock. You see them, with dilated nostrils, inhaling the incense, directly and indirectly offered. It irritates one, to hear such a person spoken of (as I have heard in my youth) as ' the dear man,' ' the precious man,' or even, in some cases, ' the sweet man.' It is a great deal too much for average human nature to live among people who agree with all one says, and think it very fine. We all need ' the animated No:' a forest tree will not grow up healthy and strong unless you let the rude blasts wrestle with it and root it firmer. It is insufferable, when any mortal lives in a moral hot-house. And if there be anything for which a clergyman ought to be thankful, it is if his congregation, though duly esteeming him for his office and for his work, have so much good sense as to refrain from spoiling him by deferring unduly to all his crotchets. Let there be as few worsted slippers as possible sent him: no bouquets laid on his

study table by youthful hands before he comes
down stairs in the morning : no young women pre-
serving under a glass shade the glove they wore in
shaking hands with him, that it may be profaned
by no inferior touch.   Let the phrase *dear man* be
utterly excluded.   A manly person does not want
to be made a pet of.   And if there be any occasion
on which a man of sense, bishop or not, ought to
be filled with shame and confusion, it is when man
or woman kneels down and asks his blessing. Pray,
how much is the blessing worth ? What good will it
do anybody ?   Most educated men have a very decided estimate of its value, which would be expressed
in figures by a round o.

One great good of a great public school, is the
way in which the moral pruning-knife is wielded
there.   I do not mean by the masters, but by the
republic of boys. Many a lad of rank and fortune,
in whom the evil shoots of arrogance, self-conceit,
contempt for his fellow-creatures, and a notion that
he himself is the mightiest of mortals, have been
fostered at home by the adulation of servants and
cottagers and tenantry, has these evil shoots
effectually shred away. You have heard, of course,
how the Duke of Middlesex and Southwark came
to his title as a baby : and grew up under the care
of obsequious tutors and governors till he had
attained the age to go to school. The first evening
he was there, he was standing at a corner of the

playground with a supercilious air, surveying the sports that were proceeding. A boy about his own size perceived him : and running up, said, with some curiosity, ' Who are you ? ' ' The Duke of Middlesex and Southwark,' was the reply. ' Oh,' said the other boy, with awakened interest, ' There's one kick for the Duke of Middlesex and another for the Duke of Southwark; ' and having thus delivered himself, he ran away. O what a sharp pair of shears in that moment pruned off certain shoots which had been growing in that little peer's nature ever since the dawn of intelligence ! The awful yet salutary truth was impressed, by a single lesson, that there were places in this world where nobody cared for the Duke of Middlesex and Southwark. And perhaps that painful pruning was the beginning of the discipline which made that duke, as long as he lived, the most unpretending, admirable, and truly noble of men.

There are few people in public life who in this age are not promptly pruned, where needful, by ever-ready shears. If the shoots of bumptiousness appear in a Chief Justice, they are instantly cut short by the tongue of some resolute barrister. If a Prime Minister, or even a loftier personage, evinces a disposition to neglect his or her duty, that disposition is speedily pruned by the *Times*; speaking in the name of the general sense of what is fit. And indeed the newspapers and reviews are the universal shears. If any outgrowth of folly, error, or conceit, appear in a political man, or in a writer of even moderate standing, some clever article comes down upon it, and shows it up if it cannot snip it off. And if a wise man desires that he may keep, intellectually and æsthetically, in becoming shape, he will attentively consider whatever may be said or written about him by people who dislike him. For, as a general rule, people who don't like you come down sharply upon your real faults: they tell you things which it is very fit that you should know; and which nobody is likely to tell you but them. I have heard of one or two distinguished authors who made it a rule never to read anything that was written about themselves. Probably they erred in this. They missed many hints for which they might have been the better. And mannerisms and eccentricities developed into rigid boughs, which might have been readily removed as growing twigs.

A vain self-confidence is very likely to grow up in a man who is never subjected to the moral pruning-knife. The greatest men (in their own judgment) that you have ever known, have probably been the magnates of some little village, far from neighbours. Probably the bully is never developed more offensively than in some village dealer, who has accumulated a good deal of money, and who has got a number of the surrounding cottages mortgaged to him. Such is the man who is likely to insult the Conservative candidate, when he comes to make a speech before an election. Such is the man to lead the opposition to any good work proposed by the parish clergyman. Such is the man to become a church-rate martyr, or an especially offensive manager of Salem Chapel. Such is the kind of man who, if he has children growing up, will refuse to let them express their opinion on any sub-ject. A parent can fall into no greater mistake than to take the ground that he will never argue with his children, nor hear what they may have to suggest in opposition to any plan he may have pro-posed. For children very speedily take the measure of their parents; and have a perfectly clear idea how far their ability, judgment, and education, justify their assuming the rank of infallible oracles. And it is infinitely better to let a lad of eighteen speak out his mind, than to have him like a boiler ready to burst with repressed views and feelings, and with the bitter sense of a petty and contempti-ble tyranny. Something has already been said of women who acquire the chief power in their own houses : whose husbands are cowed into cyphers : and whose infallibility is to be recognized through-out the establishment, under pain of some ferocious explosion. At last, some son grows up; and resists the established despotism. Infallibility and impeccability are conceded no longer. And the thick branches, consolidated by many years' growth, are lopped off painfully, which should have gone when they were slender shoots. Rely upon it, the man or woman who refuses to be peaceably and kindly pruned, will some day have to bear being rudely lopped.

There is one shoot which human nature keeps putting forth again, however frequently it is pruned away. It is self-conceit. *That* would grow into a terrible unwieldy branch, if it were not so often shred away by circumstances: that is, by God's Providence. Everybody needs to be frequently taken down: which means, to have his self-conceit pruned away. And what everybody needs, most people (in this case) get. Most people are very frequently taken down.

I mean, even modest and sensible people. This wretched little shoot keeps growing again, however hard we try to keep it down. There is a tendency in each of us to be growing up into a higher opinion of ourself: and then, all of a sudden, that higher estimate is cut down to the very earth. You are like a sheep suddenly shorn: a thick fleece of self-complacency had developed itself: something comes and all at once shears it off, and leaves you shivering in the frosty air. You are like a lawn, where the grass had grown some inches in length; till some dewy morning it is mown just as close as may be. You had gradually and insensibly come to think rather well of yourself, and your doings.

You had grown to think your position in life a rather respectable or even eminent one; and to fancy that those around estimated you rather highly. But all of a sudden, some slight, some mortification, some disappointment comes : something is said or done that shows you how far you had been deceiving yourself. Some considerable place in your profession becomes vacant, and nobody thinks of naming you for it. You are in company with two or three men who think themselves specially charged with finding a suitable person for the vacant office : they name a score of possible people to fill it : but not you. They never have thought of you : or possibly they refrain from naming you, with the design of mortifying you. And so you are pruned close. For the moment, it is painful. You are ready to sink down, disheartened and beaten. You have no energy to do anything. You sit down blankly by the fire, and acknowledge yourself a failure in life. It is not so much that you are beaten, as that you are set in a lower place than you hoped. Yet it is all good for us, doubtless. Few men can say they are too humble with it all. And, as even after all our mowings, prunings, and shearings we are sometimes so conceited and self-satisfied as we are, what should we have been had those things not befallen us ? The elf-locks of wool would have been feet in length. The grass would have been six feet high, like that of the prairies.

And the shoot of vanity would have grown and consolidated into a branch, that would have given a lopsided aspect to the whole tree.

Happily, there is no chance of these things occurring. We seldom grow for more than a few days, without being pruned, mown, and shorn afresh. And all this will continue to the end. It is not pleasant; but we need it all. And we are all profiting by it. Possibly no one will read this page, who does not know that he thinks more humbly of himself now than he did ten years since. And ten years hence, if we live, we shall think of ourselves more humbly still.

Yes : we have all been severely pruned, in many ways. Perhaps our sprays and blossoms have been shred away by a knife so unsparing, that we are cut very much into the form of a pollarded tree. Perhaps we have been pruned too much; and the spring and the nonsense taken out of us only too effectually. Certain awkward knots are left in the wood, where some cherished hope was snipped off by the fatal shears, or some youthful affection (in the case of sentimental people) came to nothing; and it was like cutting a tree over, not far above the roots, when a man was made to feel that his entire aim in life was no better than a dismal failure. But it was all for the best; and (defeat, bravely borne, is the noblest of victories.) What an overbearing, insolent person you would have been, if you had always got your own way; if your boyish fancies had come true! What an odd stick you would have become, had you been one of the Unpruned Trees!

CHAPTER III.

CONCERNING UGLY DUCKS:

BEING SOME THOUGHTS ON MISPLACED MEN.

OME men's geese, it has occasionally been said, are all swans. Dr. Newman declares that this was so with the great Archbishop Whately of Dublin. Read this page, intelligent person; and you shall be informed about an Ugly Duck, and what it proved in truth to be.

·Rather, you shall be reminded of what you doubtless know already. The story is not mine: it was originally devised by somebody much wiser and possibly somewhat better. I propose to do no more than tell afresh, and briefly, what has been told at much greater length before. No doubt it has touched and comforted many to read it. For there may be much wisdom and great consolation in a Fairy Tale.

Amid a family of little ducks, there was one, very big, ugly, and awkward. He looked so odd and uncouth, that those who beheld him generally felt that he wanted a thrashing. And in truth, he frequently got one. He was bitten, pushed about, and laughed at, by all the ducks, and even by the hens, of the house to which he belonged. Thus the poor creature was quite cast down under the depressing sense of his ugliness. And the members of his own family used him worst of all. He ran away from home: and lived for a while in a cottage with a cat and an old woman. Here, likewise, he failed to be appreciated. For chancing to tell them how he liked to dive under the water and feel it closing over his head, they laughed at him, and said he was a fool. All he could say in reply was, 'You can't understand me!' 'Not understand you, indeed,' they replied in wrath; and thrashed him.

But he gradually grew older and stronger. One day he saw at a distance certain beautiful birds, snow-white, with magnificent wings. Impelled by something within him, he could not but fly towards them: though expecting to be repulsed and perhaps killed for his presumption. But suddenly looking into the lake below him, he beheld not the old ugly reflection; but something large, white, graceful. The beautiful birds hailed him as a companion. The stupid people had thought him an ugly duck, because he was too good for them. They could not understand him: nor see the great promise of that uncouth aspect. The ugly duck proved to be a Swan!

He was not proud, that wise bird: but he was very happy. Now, everybody said he was the most beautiful of all beautiful birds: and he remembered how, once upon a time, everybody had laughed at him and thrashed him. Yes: he was appreciated at his true value at last !

Possibly, my friendly reader, you have known various Ugly Ducks. Men who were held in little esteem, because they were too good for the people among whom they lived. Men who were held in little esteem, because it needed more wit than those around them possessed, to discern the makings of great and good things under their first unpromising aspect. When John Foster, many years ago, preaching to little pragmatic communities of uneducated, stupid, and self-conceited sectaries, was declared by old women and young whipper-snappers, to be A PERFECT FOOL ; he was an Ugly Duck of the first kind. When Keats published his earliest poetry; and when Mr. Gifford bitterly showed up all its extravagance and mawkishness, and positively refused to discern under all that, the faculties which would be matured and tamed into those of a true poet; Keats was an Ugly Duck of the second kind. John Foster was esteemed an Ugly Duck at the time when he actually was a Swan, because the people who estimated him were such blockheads that they did not know a swan when they saw one

Keats was esteemed an Ugly Duck, because he really was an awkward, shambling, odd animal; and his critic had not patience, or had not insight, to discern something about him that promised he would yet grow into that which a mere Duck could never be. For the creature which is by nature a Swan, and which will some day be known for such by all, may in truth be, at an early stage in its development, an uglier, more offensive, more impudent and forward, more awkward and more insufferable animal, than the creature which is by nature a Duck, and which will never be taken for anything more.

Yes, many men, with the gift of genius in them: and many more, with no gift of genius but with a little more industry and ability than their fellows: are regarded as little better than fools by the people among whom they live; more especially if they live in remote places in the country, or in little country towns. Some day, the Swans acknowledge the Ugly Duck for their kinsman: and *then* all the quacking tribe around him recognize him as a Swan. Possibly, indeed, even then, some of the neighbouring ducks who knew him all his life, and accordingly held him cheap till the world fixed his mark, will still insist that he is no more than an extremely Ugly Duck, whom people (mainly out of spite against the ducks who were his early acquaintances) persist in absurdly calling a Swan. I have beheld a Duck absolutely foam at the mouth, when I said something implying that another bird (whose name you would know if I mentioned it) was a Swan. For the Duck, at College, had been a contemporary of the Swan : he had even played at marbles with the Swan, in boyhood : and so, though the Swan was quite fixed as being a Swan, the Duck never could bear to recognize him as such. On the contrary, he held him as an overrated, impudent, purseproud, conceited, disagreeable, and hideously Ugly Duck. I remember, too, a very venomous and malicious old Duck, who never had done anything but quack (in an envious and uncharitable way, too) through all the years which made him very old and exceedingly tough, giving an account of the extravagances and bombastic flights of a young Swan. The Duck vilely exaggerated the sayings of that youthful Swan. He put into the Swan's mouth words which the Swan had never uttered : and ascribed to the Swan sentiments (of a heretical character) which he very well knew the Swan abhorred. But even upon the Duck's own showing, there was the promise of something fine about the injudicious and warm-hearted young Swan : and a little candour and a little honesty might have acknowledged this. And it appeared to me a poor sight, to behold the ancient Duck, with all his feathers turned the wrong way with spite, standing beside a dirty puddle, and stretching his neck, and gobbling and quacking out his impotent malice, as

the beautiful Swan sailed gracefully overhead, perfectly unaware of the malignity he was exciting in
the muscle which served the Duck for a heart.

It makes me ferocious, I confess it, to hear a
Duck, or a company of Ducks, abusing and vilifying
a Swan. And a good many Ducks have a tendency
so to do. If you ask one of very many Ducks,
' What kind of a bird is A ? ' (A being a Swan), the
answer will be, ' Oh, a very Ugly Duck ! ' If the
present writer had the faintest pretension to be
esteemed a Swan, he would not say this. But he
knows, very well indeed, that he can pretend to no
more than to plod humbly and laboriously along
upon the earth, while other creatures sail through
the empyrean. He has seen, with wonder, several
ill-natured attacks upon himself in print, the *grava-
men* of the charge against him being that he does
not and cannot write like A, B, and C, who are great
geniuses. Pray, Mr. Snarling, did he ever pretend
to write like A, B, and C ? No : he pretends to nothing more than to produce a homely material (with
something real about it) that may suit homely folk.
And so long as a great number of people are content to read what he is able to write, you may rely
upon it he will go on writing. As for you, Mr.
Snarling, of course *you* can write like A, B, and C.
And in that case, your obvious course is to proceed
to do so. And when you do so, you may be sure
of this : that the present writer will never twist nor

misrepresent your words, nor tell lies to your prejudice.

It is a curious and interesting spectacle, to witness two Ducks discussing the merits of a Swan. I have known a Duck attack a Swan in print. The Swan was an author. The Duck attacked the Swan on the ground that his style wanted elegance. And I assure you the attack, for want of elegance of style, was made in language not decently grammatical. You may have heard a Duck attack a Swan in conversation. The Swan was a pretty girl. The charge was that the Swan's taste in dress was bad. You looked at the Duck, and were aware that the Duck's taste was execrable. Would that we could 'see ourselves as others see us!' Then you would no longer see such sights as this, which we may have witnessed in our youth. Two Ducks viciously abusing a Swan, flying by: and pointing out that the Swan had lost an eye, also a foot : and with wearisome iteration, dwelling on those enormities. And when you looked carefully at the spiteful creatures, wagging their heads together, hissing and quacking, you were aware that (strange to say) each of them had but one foot and one eye, and that, in short, in every respect in which the Swan was bad, the Ducks were about fifty times worse. Thus you may have known a very small and shabby Duck, who scoffed at a noble Swan, because (as he said) the Swan had no logic. Yet whenever that Duck himself attempted to argue any question, he had but one course : which was, scandalously to misrepresent and distort something said by the man maintaining the other opinion ; and then to try to raise against that man a howl of heresy. Not indeed that that man, or any one of his friends, cared a brass farthing for what the shabby little Duck thought or said of him. Yet the Duck showed all the will to be a viper, though nature had constrained him to abide a Duck. And this was the Duck's peculiar logic.

At this point the reader may pause, and ponder what has been said. If exhausted by the mental effort of attention, he may take a glass of wine. And then he is requested to observe, that the writer considers himself to have made but one step in advance since he finished the legend of the Ugly Duck, with which the present work commenced. That step in advance was to the Principle :

THAT SOME MEN ARE HELD IN LITTLE ESTI- MATION BECAUSE THEY ARE TOO GOOD FOR THE PEOPLE AMONG WHOM THEY LIVE. These are my MISPLACED MEN.

Of course, not all misplaced men are what I understand by Ugly Ducks. For there are men who are misplaced by being put in places a great deal too good for them. You may have known individuals who could not open their mouths but you heard the unmistakeable *quack-quack*, who yet gave themselves all the airs of Swans. And probably a good many people honestly took them for Swans : and other people, prudent, safe, and somewhat sneaky people, pretended that they took them for Swans, while in fact they did not. And when perspicacious persons privately whispered to one another, 'That fellow Stuckup is only a duck,' it was because in fact he was no more. Yet Stuckup did not think himself so. I have not seen many remarkable human beings ; but I have studied a few with attention : and I can say, with sincerity, that the peculiar animal known as the *Beggar on Horseback* is by far the greatest and most important human being I have ever known. Probably, my reader, you still hold your breath with awe, as you remember your first admission to the presence of a person whom you saw to be on horseback, but did not know to be a beggar who had attained that eminence. You afterwards learned the fact ; and then you wondered you did not see it sooner. For now the beggar's dignity appeared to you to bear the like relation to that of the true man in such a place, that the strut of a king with a tinsel crown in a booth at a fair bears to the quiet assured air of Queen Victoria walking into the House of Lords to open Parliament.

It is an unspeakable blessing for a man, that he should be put down among people who can understand him. For no matter whether a man is thought

a fool by his neighbours because he is too good for
them, or because he is really a fool, the depressing
effect upon his own mind is the same ; unless indeed
he have the confidence which we might suppose
would have gone with the head and heart of
Shakspeare, if Shakspeare appreciated himself
justly. Very likely he did not. John Foster, great
man as he was, could not have liked to see the little
meeting-houses at which he held forth gradually
getting empty, as the people of the congregation
went off to some fluent blockhead with powerful
lungs and a vacuous head. For many a day Archbishop Whately of Dublin was a misplaced man :
feared and suspected just because that clear head
and noble heart were so high above the sympathy
or even the comprehension of many of those over
whom he was set. A bitter little sectary would
have been, at first, an infinitely more popular Prelate.
And the writer cannot refrain from saying with
what delight, but a few months before that great
man died, he saw, by the enthusiastic reception
which the archbishop met, rising to make a short
speech at a public meeting in Dublin of three
thousand people, that justice was done him at last.
He had found the place which was his due. They
knew the noble Swan they had got : and knew that
the honour he derived from the archiepiscopal
throne, was as a sand-grain when compared with
the honour which he reflected on it. Yet he found

the time hard to bear, when he was undervalued because he was too good : when men vilified him because they could not understand him. 'I have tried to look as if I did not feel it,' he said ; 'but it has shortened my life.' Whereas our friend Carper, who for ten years past has held an eminent place for which he is about as fit as a cow, and which he has made ridiculous through his incompetence,—the wrong man in the wrong place, if such a thing ever was,—is entirely pleased with himself, and will never have his life shortened by any consideration of his outrageous incapacity. There were years of Arnold's life at Rugby during which he was an unappreciated man, just because he rose so high above the ordinary standard. If the sun were something new, and if you showed it for the first time to a company of blear-eyed men, they would doubtless say it was a most disagreeable object. And if there were no people of thoughtful hearts and of refined culture in the world, the author of *In Memoriam* would no doubt pass among mankind for a fool. There are people who, through a large part of their life, are above the high-water-mark of popular appreciation. Wordsworth was so. He needed 'an audience fit ;' and it for many a day was 'few.' The popular taste had to be educated into caring for him : it was as if you had commanded a band of children to drink bitter ale and to like it. Even Jeffrey could write, 'This will never do !'

And you miss people as completely by shooting over their heads, as by hitting the ground a dozen yards on this side of them. A donkey, in all honesty, prefers thistles to pine-apple. Yet the poor pine-apple is ready to feel aggrieved.

This misjudging of people, because they rise above the sphere of your judgment, begins early and lasts late. I have known a clever boy, under the authority of a tyrannical and uncultivated governor, who was savagely bullied and ignominiously ordered out of the room, because he declared that he admired the *Hartleap Well.* His governor declared that he was a fool, a false pretender, a villain. His governor sketched his future career by declaring that he would be hanged in this world, and sent to perdition in the next. All this was because he possessed faculties which his uncultivated tyrant did not possess. It was as if a stone-deaf man should torture a lover of music because he ventured to maintain that there is such a thing as sound. It was as if a man whose musical taste was educated up to the point of admiring the *Rat-catcher's Daughter*, should vilipend and suspend by hemp a human being who should declare there was something beyond *that* in Beethoven and Mendelssohn. And I believe that very often, thoughtful little children are subjected to the great trial of being brought up in a house where they are utterly misunderstood, by guardians and even by parents quite unequal to understanding them. And this has a very souring effect on the little heart. There are boys and girls, living under their fathers' roof, who in their deepest thoughts are as thoroughly alone as if they dwelt at Tadmor in the Wilderness. There are children who would sooner go and tell their donkey what was most in their mind, than they would tell it to their father or their mother. In some cases, the lack of power to understand or appreciate becomes still more marked as childhood advances to maturity. You may have known a man, recognized by the world as a very wise man, for expressing to the world the self-same views and opinions whose expression had caused him to be adjudged a fool at home. ' Do you know, Charlotte has written a book; and it's better than likely:' was all the father of its author had to say about *Jane Eyre.* What a picture of a searing, blighting home atmosphere! You cannot read the story without thinking of evergreens crisping up under a withering east wind of three weeks' duration. And I could point to a country, in Africa, where men, who would be recognized as great men elsewhere, are thought very little of: because there is hardly anybody who can appreciate them and their attainments. I have known, there, an accomplished scholar, who in the neighbouring kingdom of Biafra would be made a *clefrag* (corresponding to our Bishop), who, living where he does, when spoken of at all, is usually spoken of contemptuously as A DOMINIE; corresponding to our schoolmaster or College tutor, but the undignified way of stating the fact.   Such a man is a great Greek scholar: but if he dwell among Africans who know nothing earthly about Greek, and who care even less for it, what does it profit him? Alas, for that misplaced man! Thought an Ugly Duck because he lives at Heliopolis: while four hundred miles off, in the great University of Biafra, he would be hailed as a noble Swan, by kindred Swans!

Almost the only order of educated men who have it not in their power to live among educated folk, are the clergy.   Almost all other cultivated men may choose for their daily companions people like themselves.   But in the Church, you have doubtless known innumerable instances in which men of very high culture were set down in remote rural districts, where there was not a soul with whom they had a thought in common within a dozen miles.   It is all right, of course: in that broader sense in which everything is so: and doubtless the cure of souls, however rude and ignorant, is a work worthy of the best human heart and head that God ever made.   Still, it is sad to see a razor somewhat inefficiently cutting a block, for which a great axe with a notched edge is the right thing.   It is sad to see a cultivated, sensitive man, in the kind of parish where I have several times seen such.   You may be able to think of one, an elegant scholar, a profound theologian, a man of most refined taste, taken unhappily from the common-room of a College, and set down in a cold upland district, where there were no trees and where the wind almost invariably blew from the east : among people with high cheek-bones and dried-up complexions, of Radical politics and Dissenting tendencies, dense in ignorance and stupidity, and impregnable in self-confidence and self-conceit : and just as capable of appreciating their clergyman's graceful genius as an equal number of cod-fish would be. And what was a yet more melancholy sight than even the sight of the first inconsistency between the man and his place, was the sight of the way in which the man year by year degenerated till he grew just the man for the place ; and only a middling man for it. Yes, it was miserable to see how the Swan gradually degenerated into an Ugly Duck : how his views got morbid, and his temper ungenial, how his accomplishments rusted, and his conversational powers died through utter lack of exercise : till after a good many years you beheld him a soured, wrongheaded, cantankerous, petty, disappointed man. For luck was against him : and he had no prospect but that of remaining in the bleak upland parish, swept by the east wind, as long as he might live. And after a little while, he ceased entirely to go back to the University where he would have found fit associates:

and he grew so disagreeable that his old friends did
not care to visit him, and listen to his moaning.
Now, you cannot long keep much above what you
are rated at. At least, you must have an iron constitution of mind if you do. I daresay sometimes
in old days an honourable and good man was constrained by circumstances to become a Publican : I
mean, of course, a Jewish Publican. He meant to
be honest and kind, even in that unpopular sphere
of life. But when all men shied him : when his old
friends cut him: when he was made to feel, daily,
that in the common estimation Publicans and Sinners
ranked together: I have no doubt earthly but he
would sink to the average of his class. Or, as the
sweetest wine becomes the sourest vinegar, he
might not impossibly prove a sinner above all the
other Publicans of the district.

But not merely do ignorant and vulgar persons
fail to appreciate at his true value a cultivated man :
more than this: the fact of his cultivation may
positively go to make vulgar and ignorant persons
dislike and underrate him. My friend Brown is a
clergyman of the Scotch Church, and a man who
has seen a little of the world. Like most educated
Scotchmen now-a-days, he speaks the English language if not with an English accent, at least with
an accent which is not disagreeably Scotch. He
does not call a boat a bott; nor a horse a hoarrse ;
nor philosophy philozzophy; nor a road a rodd.

He does not pronounce the word *is* as if it were spelt eez, nor talk of a lad of speerit. Still less does he talk of salvahtion, justificahtion, sanctificahtion, and the like. He does not begin his church service by giving out either a *sawm* or a *samm* : in which two disgusting forms I have sometimes known the word *psalm* disguised. Brown told me that once on a time he preached in the church of a remote country parish, where parson and people were equally uncivilized. And after service the minister confided to him that he did not think the congregation could have liked his sermon. '·Ye see,' said the minister, ' thawt's no the style o' langidge they're used wi'!' My friend replied, not without asperity, that he trusted it was not. But I could see, when he told me the story, that he did not quite like to be an Ugly Duck: that it irked him to think that, in fact, some vulgar boor with a different style o' langidge would have been much more acceptable to the people of Muffburgh. I am very happy to believe that such parishes as Muffburgh are becoming few : and that a scholar and a gentleman will rarely indeed find that he had better, for immediate popularity, have been a clodhopper and an ignoramus. You have heard, no doubt, how a dissenting preacher in England demolished the parish clergyman, in a discourse against worldly learning. The clergyman, newly come, was an eminent scholar. ' Do ye think Powle knew Greek?' said his opponent, perspiring all over. And the people saw how useless and indeed prejudicial was the knowledge of that heathen tongue.

And this reminds me that it will certainly make a man an Ugly Duck to be, in knowledge or learning, in advance of the people among whom he lives. A very wise man, if he lives among people who are all fools, may find it expedient, like Brutus, to pass for a fool too. And if he knows two things or three which they don't know, he had better keep his information to himself. Even the possession of a single exclusive piece of knowledge may be a dangerous thing. Long ago, in an ancient University near the source of the Nile, the professors of Divinity regarded not the quantity of Greek or Latin words. The length of the vowels they decided in each case according to the idea of the moment. And their pronunciation of Scripture proper names, if it went upon any principle at all, went on a wrong one. A youthful student, named McLamroch, was reading an essay in the class of one of these respectable but antediluvian professors. And coming to the word *Thessalonica*, he pronounced it, as all mortals do, with the accent on the last syllable but one, and giving the vowel as long. 'Say Thessaloanica,' said the venerable professor, with emphasis. 'I think, *doctissime professor* (for all professors in that University were *most learned* by courtesy) that Thessalonica is the right way,' replied poor

McLamroch. 'I tell you it is wrong,' shrilly shouted the good professor: 'Say Thessaloanĭca! and let me tell you, Mr. McLamroch, you are most aboaminably affectit!' So poor McLamroch was put down. He was an Ugly Duck. And he found by sad experience, that it is not safe to know more than your professor. And I verily believe, that the solitary thing that McLamroch knew and his professor did not know, was the way to pronounce Thessalonica. I have heard, indeed, of a theological professor of that ancient day, who bitterly lamented the introduction of new fashions of pronouncing Scriptural proper names. However, he said, he could stand all the rest : but there were two renderings he would never give up but with life. These were Kapper-nawm, by which he meant Capernaum : and Levvy-awthan, by which he meant Leviathan. And if you, my learned friend, had been a student under that good man, and had pronounced these words as scholars and all others do, you would have found yourself no better than an Ugly Duck, and a fearfully misplaced man. A torrent of *wut*, sarcasm at new lights, and indignation at people who were not content to pronounce words (wrong) like their fathers before them, would have made you sink through the floor.

To be in advance of your fellow-mortals in taste, too, is as dangerous as to be in advance of them in the pronunciation of Thessalonica. When Mr. Jones

built his beautiful Gothic house, in a district where
all other houses belonged to no architectural school
at all, all his neighbours laughed at him. A genial
friend, in a letter in a newspaper, spoke of his
peculiar taste, and called him *the preposterous Jones*.
And it was a current joke in the neighbourhood,
when you met a friend, to say, 'Have you seen
Jones's house?' You then held up both hands, or
exclaimed 'Well, I never!' Then your friend burst
into a loud roar of laughter. In a severer mood, you
would say, 'That fellow! Can't he build like his
fathers before him? Indeed he never had a grand-
father: I remember how he was brought up by his
aunt, that kept a cat's-meat shop in Muffburgh,'
and the like. All this evil came upon Jones, because he was a little in advance of his neighbours
in taste. For in ten years, hardly a house round
but had some steep gables, several bay windows,
and a little stained glass. Their owners esteemed
them Gothic. And in one sense, undoubtedly some
of them were Gothic enough. In Scotland, now,
people build handsome churches, and pay all due
respect to ecclesiastical propriety. But it is not
very long since a parish clergyman proposed to the
authorities that a proper font should be provided for
baptisms, because the only vessel heretofore used
for that purpose was a crockery basin, used for washing hands. And one of the authorities exclaimed
indignantly, 'We are not going to have any gew-

gaws in our church:' by gewgaws meaning a decorous font. What could be done with such a man?
Violently to knock his head against a wall would
have been wrong: for no man should be visited
with temporal penalties on account of his honest
opinions. Yet any less decided treatment would
have been of no avail.

We ought all to be very thankful, if we are in our
right place : if we are set among people whom we
suit, and who suit us : and among whom we need
neither to practise a dishonest concealment of our
views, nor to stand in the painful position of Ugly
Ducks and Misplaced Men. Yes, a man may well
be glad, if he is the square man in the square hole.
For he might have been a round man in a square
hole : and then he would have been unhappy in the
hole, and the hole would have hated him. I know
a place where a man who should say that he thought
Catholic Emancipation common justice and common sense, would be hooted down, even yet: would
be told he was a villain, blinded by Satan. There
is a locality, where morality indeed is very low, but
where a valued friend of mine was held up to
reprobation as a dangerous and insidious man, because he declared in print that he did not think it
sinful to take a quiet walk on Sunday. In that
locality, one birth in every three is illegitimate : but
it was pleasant and easy, by abuse of the Rector of

a London parish, and by abuse of others like him, to compound for the neglect of the duty of trying to break Hodge and Bill, Kate and Sally, of their evil ways. I know a place where you may find an intelligent man, out of a lunatic asylum too, who will tell you that to have an organ in church is to set up images and go back to Judaism. I have lately heard it seriously maintained that to make a decorous pause for a minute after service in church is over, and pray for God's blessing on the worship in which you have joined, is 'contrary to reason and to Scripture!' I know places where any one of the plainest canons of taste, being expressed by a man, would be taken as stamping him a fool. Now what would you do, my friend, if you found yourself set down among people with whom you were utterly out of sympathy: whose first principles appeared to you the prejudices of pragmatic block-heads, and to whom your first principles appeared those of a silly and Ugly Duck? One would say, If you don't want to dwarf and distort your whole moral nature, get out of that situation. But then some poor fellows cannot. And then they must either take rank as Misplaced Men; or go through life hypocritically pretending to share views which they despise. The latter alternative is inadmissible in any circumstances. Be honest, whatever you do. Take your place boldly, as an Ugly Duck, if God has appointed that to be your portion in this life.

Doubtless, it will be a great trial. But you and I, friendly reader, set by Providence among people who understand us and whom we understand: among whom we may talk out our honest heart, and (let us hope) do so: in talking to whom we don't need to be on our guard, and every now and then to pull up, thinking to ourselves, ' Now this sneaking fellow is lying on the catch for my saying something he may go and repeat to my prejudice behind my back:' how thankful we should be! I declare, looking back on days that have been, in this very country, I cannot understand how manly, enlightened, and honest men lived then at all! You must either have been a savage bigot, or a wretched sneak, or a martyr. The alternative is an awful one: but let us trust, my friend, that if you and I had lived then, we should by God's grace have been equal to it. Yes, I humbly trust that if we had lived then, we should either have been burned, hanged, or shot. For the days have been, in which *that* must have been the portion of an honest man, who thought for himself: and who would be dragooned by neither Pope, Prelate, nor Presbyter.

But now, having written myself into a heat of indignation, I think it inexpedient to write more. For it appears to me that to write or to read an essay like this, ought always to be a relief and recreation. And those grave matters, which stir the heart too deeply, and tingle painfully through the nervous system, are best treated at other times, in other ways. Many men find it advisable to keep to themselves the subjects on which they feel most keenly. As for me, I dare not allow myself to think of certain evils of whose existence I know. Sometimes they drive one to some quiet spot, where you can walk up and down a little path with grass and evergreens on either hand, and try to forget the sin and misery you cannot mend: looking at the dappled shades of colour on the grass; taking hold of a little spray of holly and poring upon its leaves; stopping beside a great fir-tree, and diligently perusing the wrinkles of its bark.

So we shut up. So we cave in. Oh the beauty of these simple phrases, so purely classic!

CHAPTER IV.

OF THE SUDDEN SWEETENING OF CERTAIN GRAPES.

MANY years since, on a sunshiny autumn day, a gentleman named Mr. Charles James Fox, a lawyer of eminence, was walking with his friend Mr. Mantrap through a vineyard near Melipotamus. A vineyard in that region of the earth is not the shabby field of what look like stunted gooseberry bushes which you may see on the Rhine. For trellised on high from tree to tree there hung the ripe clusters, rich and red. One cluster, of especial size and beauty, attracted the attention of Mr. Fox. He had in his hand a walking-stick (made of oak, varnished to a yellow hue) with a hook at its superior end. With this implement he sought to reach that cluster of grapes, with the view of appropriating it to his personal consumption, possibly upon the spot. But after repeated attempts, he found he could not in any way attain it. Upon this Mr. Fox, a man of ready wit intellectually, but morally no more than an average human being, turned off the little disappointment by saying to his friend, 'Oh, bother: I believe the grapes are as sour as the disposition of Mr. Snarling.' The friends prosecuted their walk. But after they had proceeded a few miles, it occurred to Mr. Mantrap that Mr. Fox had depreciated the grapes because he could not reach them. Mr. Mantrap mentioned the occurrence to various acquaintances : and gradually it came to be, that in the circle of Mr. Fox's friends SOUR GRAPES grew a proverbial phrase, signifying anything a human being would like to get ; and, failing to get, cried down.

These facts, now given to the public in an accurate fashion, were lately made the subject of a short narrative in a little volume of moral stories published by an individual whose name I do not mention. But by one of those misapprehensions which naturally occur when a story is conveyed by oral tradition, that gentleman (of whom I desire to speak with the utmost respect) represented that the person who acted in the way briefly described, was not Mr. C. J. Fox the eminent lawyer : but the well-known inferior animal which is termed a fox. A moment's thought may show how impossible it is to receive such a representation. For it is extremely doubtful whether a fox would care to eat grapes, even if he could get a cluster of the very finest: while the notion that such an animal could express his ideas in articulate language, is one which could not possibly be received unless by illiterate persons residing at a great distance from a University town.

Should the reader have had any difficulty in grasping the full meaning of what has been said, it is requested that he should pause at this point, and read the preceding paragraphs a second or even a third time, before proceeding further.

Sometimes, in this world, people dishonestly say that the grapes they have failed to reach are sour, though knowing quite well that the grapes are sweet. In this case, these people desire to conceal their own disappointment; and (if possible) to make the value of the grapes less to such as may ultimately get them. Sometimes, in this world, when people have done their best to reach the grapes and failed, they come to honestly believe that the grapes *are* sour. They do, in good faith, cease to care for them: and resign their mind quite cheerfully to doing without them. But there is no reckoning up the odd ways in which the machinery of thought and feeling within human beings works: and it is the purpose of the present dissertation to notice two of these.

One is, that when you get the grapes, and specially if you get them too easily, the grapes are apt, if not exactly to grow sour, yet in great measure to lose their flavour. When you fairly get a thing, you do not care for it so much. Many people have lately been interested and touched by a truthful representation in the pages of a very graceful, natural, and pure writer of fiction, whose pages (I have learned with some surprise) various worthy people think it wrong to read. That graceful and excellent writer shows us how a certain young man sought the love of a certain young woman: and how when that young man (not a noble or worthy man indeed) found the love of that poor girl given him so fully and unreservedly, he came not to care for it, and to think he might have done better. Lead him out and chastise him, my friend: and having done so, look into your own heart, and see whether there be anything like him. If you be a wise person, you may find reason severely to flagellate yourself. For it is the ungrateful and unworthy way of average human nature, to undervalue the blessings God gives us, if they come too cheaply and easily. Even Bruce, at the source of the Nile, thought to himself, ' Is this all ? ' And Gibbon, looking out upon the Lake of Geneva after writing the last lines of the *Decline and Fall*, tells us how he thought and felt in like manner.

This, however, is not my special subject. My subject is also connected with grapes: but it is a different phenomenon to which I solicit the reader's rapt and delighted attention. It is, how suddenly certain grapes grow sweet, when you find you can get them. You had no estimate at all of these grapes before : or you even thought them sour. But suddenly you find the hook at the end of your walking-stick can reach them : suddenly you find you can get them : and now you judge of them quite differently.

Many young women have thought, quite honestly : and perhaps have said, in the injudicious way in which inexperienced people talk : that they would not marry such and such a man upon any account. But some fine afternoon, the man in question asked them : and to the astonishment of their friends (some of whom would have been glad to do the like themselves), the young ladies gladly accepted the human being, held in such unfavourable estimation before. It just made all the difference, to find that the thing could be got. They began, all at once, to have quite a different estimate of the man : to think of him and of his qualifications in quite a different way. The grapes suddenly grew sweet. And instead of being contumeliously cast into the ditch, they were eaten with considerable satisfaction.

Even so have young clergymen, fresh from the University, thought that they would not on any account take such a small living, or such a shabby church : and in a little while been very thankful to get one not so good. And I do not mean at present, in the case of either the young women or the young

preachers, that they learn humbler ideas of themselves as time goes on, and come to lowlier expectations. *That*, of course, is true : but my present
assertion is, that in truth when the thing is put
within their reach, they come to think more highly
of it : they come to see all its advantages and
merits : they are not merely resigned to take it:
they are glad to get it. Many a man is now in a
place in life, and very content and thankful to be
there, which he would have repudiated the notion
of his accepting, very shortly before he accepted it
with thankfulness.

The truth is, that if you look carefully, and look
for some length of time, into the character of almost
anything that is not positively bad, you will see a
great deal of good about it. Friends in my own
calling, do you not remember how, in your student
days, you used to look at the shabby churches of
our native land, when shabby churches are (alas !)
the rule, and decorous ones the exception : and how
you wondered then how their incumbents could
stand them ? You thought how much it would
add to the difficulty of conducting public worship
worthily, to be obliged to do it under the cross-
influence of a dirty dilapidated barn, with a mass
of rickety pews, where every arrangement would
jar distressingly upon the whole nervous system of
every man with a vestige of taste. You remember
how your heart sunk as you looked at the vile

waggon-roofed meeting-house in a dirty village
street, with no churchyard at all round it; or with
the mangy, weedy, miserable-looking pound which
even twenty years since was in many places thought
good enough for the solemn sleep of the redeemed
body, still united to the Saviour. And you remember how earnestly you hoped that you might be
favoured so highly as to attain a parish where the
church was a building at least decent; and if possible fairly ecclesiastical. And yet, it is extremely
likely you got a remarkably shabby church for
your first one: and it is in the highest degree probable that in a little you got quite interested in it,
and thought it really very good. Of course, when
my friend Mr. Snarling reads this, he will exclaim,
What, is not the clergyman's work so weighty, that
it ought not to matter to him in the least what the
mere outward building is like? Is not the spiritual
church the great thing: may not God be worshipped
in the humblest place as heartily as in the noblest?
And I reply to that candid person, who never mis-
represented anyone, and who never said a good word
of anyone,—Yes, my acquaintance: I remember all
that. But still I hold that little vexatious external
circumstances have a great effect in producing a
feeling of irritation the reverse of devotional: and
I believe that we poor creatures, with our wandering thoughts and our cold hearts, are much more
likely to worship in spirit, if we are kept free from

such unfriendly influences: and if our worship be surrounded by all the outward decency and solemnity which are attainable. Give us a decorous building, I don't ask for a grand one: give us quietude and order in all its arrangements: give us church music that soothes and cheers and brings us fresh heart: give us an assemblage of seemingly devout worshippers. And these things being present, I do not hesitate to say that the average worshipper will be far more likely to offer true spiritual worship, than in places to which I could easily point, where the discreditable building and the slovenly service are an offence and a mortification to everyone with any sense of what is fit.

This, however, is by the bye. I could say much more on the subject. But I remember, thankfully, that it is a subject on which all educated persons now think alike, everywhere. It did not use to be so, once.

But not merely as regards churches, but as regards most other things: my principle holds true, that if you look carefully and for some time into the qualifications of almost anything not positively bad, you will discern a great deal of good about it. Take a very ordinary-looking bunch of grapes: take even a bunch of grapes which appears sour at a cursory glance: look at it carefully for a good while, with the sense that it is your own; and it will sweeten before your eyes. You pass a seedy little country house, looking like a fourth-rate farm-house: you think, and possibly say, (if the man who lives in it be a friend of your own,) that it is a wretched hole. The man who lives in it has very likely persuaded himself that it is a very handsome and attractive place. 'What kind of manse have you got?' said my friend Smith to a certain worthy clergyman. 'Oh, it is a beautiful place,' was the prompt reply. It was in fact a dismal weather-stained whitewashed erection, without an architectural feature, with hardly a tree or an evergreen near it, standing on a bleak hill-side. Smith heard the reply with great pleasure; feeling thankful that by God's kind appointment a sensible man's own grapes seem sweet to him, which appear sour to everybody else; and to nobody sourer than to himself, before they became his own. The only wonder Smith felt was, that the good minister's reply had not been stronger. He was prepared to hear the good man say, 'Oh, it is the most beautiful place in Scotland!' For people in general cannot express their appreciation of things, without introducing comparisons; and indeed superlatives. If a man's window commands a fine view, he is not content to say that it does command a fine view: No, it commands 'the finest view in Britain.' If a human being has an attack of illness, about a hundredth part as bad as hundreds of people endure every day, that human being will probably be quite indignant unless you recognize it as a

fact, that nobody ever suffered so much before.
Take an undistinguished volume from your shelves:
read it carefully in your leisure hours for several
evenings : and that undistinguished volume will become (in your estimation) an important one. My
friend Smith, when he went to his country parish,
was obliged for several months to have his books in
large packing-boxes, his study not being ready to
receive them. He lived in a lonely rural spot, for
many wintry weeks, all alone. It was a charming
scene around, indeed : warm with green ivy and
yews and hollies through the brief daylight: but
dreary and solitary through the long dark evenings
to a man accustomed to gas-lit streets. Soon after
settling there, Smith chanced to draw forth from a
box a certain volume, which had remained for
months in his bookcase unnoted: one among many
more, all very like. And on every Sunday evening
of that solitary time, Smith read in that volume.
He read with pleasure and profit. Ever since then,
he has thought the book a valuable and excellent
one. It is distinguished among his books as the
Bishop of Anywhere is among five hundred other
clergymen : not that he is a whit wiser or better,
but that he has been accidentally made more conspicuous. When Smith turns over its leaves now,
the moaning of January winds through the pine
wood comes back ; and the brawl of a brook, winter-
flooded. In brief, that cluster of grapes suddenly

sweetened, because its merits were fairly weighed. If a thing be good at all, look at it and examine it, and it will seem better.

Now, a thing you have no chance of getting, you never seriously weigh the merits of. When you receive a half offer of a place in life, it is quite fair for you to say, 'Offer it fairly, and I shall think of it.' You cannot take the trouble of estimating it now. It is a laborious and anxious thing to make up your mind in such a case. You must consider, and count up, and weigh, possibly a great number of circumstances. You do not choose to undergo that fatigue, perhaps for no result. And if you be in perplexity what to do, the balance may be turned just by the fact that the thing is attainable. Hence the truth of that true proverb, that *Faint heart never won fair lady.* If you are fond of Miss Smith, and wish to marry her, don't speculate at home whether or not she will have you. Go and ask her. Your asking may be the very thing that will decide her to have you. And you, patron or electors of some little country parish which is vacant, don't say ' We need never offer it to such and such an eminent preacher: he would never think of it!' Go and try him. Perhaps he may. Perhaps you may catch him just at a time when he is feeling weary and exhausted: when he is growing old: when your offer may recall with fresh beauty the green fields and trees amid which he once was young: when he is sighing for a little rest.   I could point out instances, more than one or two, in England and in Scotland, in which a bold offering of a bunch of grapes to a distinguished human being, induced him to accept the grapes: though you would have fancied, beforehand, that they would have been no temptation to him.   I have known a man who (in a moral sense) refused a pine-apple, afterwards accept a turnip; and like it. We have all heard of a good man who might have lived in a palace, holding a position of great rank and gain, and of very easy duty; who put that golden cluster of grapes aside : and by his own free choice went to a place of hard work and little fame or profit, to remain there one of the happiest as well as one of the noblest and most useful of humankind ! And the only way in which I can account for various marriages, is by supposing that the grapes suddenly grew irresistibly sweet, just when it appeared that they could be had.   You may have known a fair young girl quite willingly and happily marry a good old creature, whom you would have said *à priori* she was quite sure to refuse.   But when the old creature made offer of his faded self (and his unfaded possessions), the whole thing offered acquired a sudden value and beauty.   He might be an odd stick; but then his estate had most beautiful timber.   Intellectually and morally he might be inferior, or even deficient : but then his three per cents. formed a positive quantity, of enormous amount. The whole thing offered had to be regarded as one bunch of grapes. And if some of the grapes were sour and shrivelled, a greater number of them was plump and juicy.

Nobody who reads this page really knows whether he would like to be Lord Chancellor, or to live in a house like Windsor Castle. The writer has not the faintest idea whether he would like to be Archbishop of Canterbury. We never even ourselves to such things as these. We don't seriously consider whether the grapes are sweet or sour, which there is not the faintest possibility of our ever reaching. When Mr. Disraeli (as he himself said in Parliament) 'would have been very thankful for some small place,' he had never lifted his eyes to the leadership of a certain great political party. Of that lofty cluster he had no estimate *then*: but the modest little bunch of twelve hundred a-year seemed attainable, and so seemed sweet. But he was a great man when he said 'I am very glad now I did not get it!' He was destined to something bigger, and loftier. And when that greater position at last loomed in view, and became possible, became likely, —we can well believe that the great orator began to estimate it: and that it became an object of honourable ambition when it was very near, and was all but grasped. When the prize is within reach, it becomes precious. When the Atlantic cable was being laid, you can think how precious it would seem when the vessels which were laying it had got within a mile or two of land. Yes, success, just within our grasp, grows inestimably valuable. The cluster of grapes, long striven after, and now at length just got hold of,—how sweet it seems!

My friend Mr. Brown had often remarked to me, ' If ever there was a hideous erection on the face of the earth, it is that St. Sophia's Church: and I don't know a man less to be envied than the incumbent of so laborious and troublesome a parish.' Brown and I were sitting on the wall of his beautiful churchyard in the country, one fine summer day, when he made this remark; adding, ' How much happier a life we have here in this pure air and among these sweet fields ' (and indeed the fragrance of the clover was very delightful that day): ' and with our kindly, well-behaved country people!' I need hardly mention, that Mr. Brown shortly afterwards succeeded to the vacant charge of St. Sophia's, a huge church in a great city. He was offered it in a kind way: saw its claims and advantages in a new light: accepted it, and is very happy in it. And recently he recalled to my memory his former estimate of it, and said how mistaken it was. He even added, that although the architecture of St. Sophia's was not the purest Gothic (it is in fact not Gothic at all), still there is a simple grandeur about it, which produces a great effect upon the mind when you grow accustomed to it. ' I used to laugh,' he said, 'at poor old Dr. Log when he declared it was the finest church in Britain : but, do you know, some of its proportions are really unrivalled. Here, for instance, look at that arch,'—and then he went on at considerable length. The truth was, that the grapes had suddenly sweetened. The position, never thought of, or thought of only as quite unattainable, was a very different thing now.

I do not for a moment suppose any insincerity on the part of my friend. He quite sincerely esteemed the grapes as sour, when they hung beyond his reach. He quite sincerely esteemed them as sweet, when he came to know them better. But, as a general rule, whenever any man or woman undervalues and despises something which average human nature prizes and enjoys, we may say that if the grapes are fairly put within reach, they would suddenly and greatly sweeten. I speak of average human nature. There are exceptional cases. There is a great and good man who did not choose to be a Bishop; who did not choose to be an Archbishop. The test is, that he was offered these places and refused them. But there are a great many men, who could quite honestly say that they don't want to be Bishops or Archbishops. But then they have not been tried : and there are some that I should not like to try. I believe the lawn would brighten into effulgence, when it was offered. The opportunity of usefulness would appear so great, that it

G

could not in conscience be refused. The grapes being within reach, would grow so sweet, that those good men would forget their old professions, and (in the words of Lord Castlereagh) turn their backs upon themselves.

Perhaps you have known a refined young lady of thirty-nine years, who looked with disdain at her younger female friends when they got married. She wondered at their weakness in getting spoony about any man: and despised their flutter of interest in the immediate prospect of the wedding-day and all its little arrangements. The whole thing—trousseau, cards, favours, cake—was contemptible. Perhaps you have known such a mature young lady get married herself at last: and evince a pride and an exhilaration in the prospect such as are rarely seen. It was delightful to witness the maidenly airs of the individual to whom the bunch of grapes had finally become attainable: the enthusiastic affection she testified towards the romantic hero (weighing sixteen stone) to whom she had given her young affections: the anguish of perplexity as to the material and fashion of the wedding-dress: in short, the sudden sweetening of the grapes which had previously been so remarkably sour. There is nothing here to laugh at: it is a beneficent providential arrangement. In all walks of life you may have remarked the same. You may have known a hard-featured and well-principled servant, who, having no admirer, gave herself out as a man-hater, and believed herself to be one. But some one turning up who (let us hope) admired and appreciated her real excellence, that admirable young woman grew quite tremendous : first, in her pride and exultation that she had a beau ; and secondly, in her admiration and fondness for him. Yes : turn out human nature with a pitch-fork ; and it will come back again.

Perhaps you have known a wealthy old gentleman, living quietly somewhere in the City (let the word be understood in its Cockney sense), and going into no society whatever ; who frequently professed to despise the vanities to which other folk attach importance. He utterly contemned such things as a fine house, a fashionable neighbourhood, titled acquaintances and the like. And he did it all, quite sincerely. But nature had her way at last. That wealthy gentleman bought a house in an aristocratic West End square. His elation at finding himself there was pleasing, yet a little irritating. He could not refrain from telling everyone that he lived there. Occasionally he would cut short a conversation with a City acquaintance, by stating that he 'must be home to dinner at half-past seven in Berkeley Square.' He speedily informed himself of the precise social standing of every inhabitant of that handsome quadrangle : and would even produce the 'Court Guide' and tell an occasional visitor about the rank and connections of each name in the square. The delight with which he beheld a peer at his dinner-table may be conceived but not described. The grapes, in fact, had in all sincerity been esteemed as sour till he got possession of them. Then, all of a sudden, they became inconceivably sweet. So you may have beheld a plain respectable man, who had made a considerable fortune in the oil trade, buy a property in the country and settle there. ' I want nothing to do with your stuck-up gentry,' said that respectable man: 'I shall keep by my old friends Smith, Brown, and Robinson, who were apprentices with old McOily along with me, forty years ago.' But when the carriage of the neighbouring baronet drove up to the worthy man's door to call, it and its inmates were received with enthusiasm. There was, after all, a refinement of manner and feeling about gentle blood, not possessed by Smith and the others: and after a little intercourse with the family of the baronet and with other similar families, poor Smith, Brown, and Robinson got so chilly a reception at the country house, and were so infuriated by the frequent mention and the high laudation of the landed families about (whom Smith and his friends did not know at all), that these old acquaintances quite dropped off; and the good old oil-merchant was left to the enjoyment of the grapes, formerly so sour and now so sweet. It is all in human nature. You may have known a cultivated man, with a small income, living in a city of very rich and not remarkably cultivated men. You may have heard him speak with much contempt of mere vulgar wealth, and of certain neighbours who possessed it. And you felt how easily that cultivated man might be led to change his tune. I have witnessed a parallel case. Once upon a time, the writer was walking along a certain country road ; a walk of nine miles. He overtook a little boy, walking along manfully by himself : a little fellow of seven years old. The two wayfarers proceeded together for several miles, conversing of various subjects. It appeared in the course of conversation, that the little boy, whose parents are very poor, never had any pocket-money. I don't believe he ever had a penny to spend, in all his life. He stated that he did not care for money; nor for the good things (in a child's sense of that phrase) which might be bought with it. And parting from the little man, I could not but tip him a shilling. Every human being who will ever read this page would of course have done the same. It was his very first shilling. He tried to receive it with philosophic composure, as if he did not care a bit about it. But he tried with little success. It was easy to see how different a thing a shilling had suddenly grown. The grapes had all at once sweetened.

But it is the same way everywhere. An author

without popular estimation thinks he can do quite well without it : he does not care for it. 'The world knows nothing of its greatest men ;' nor, let us add, of its best. Yet popular favour proves very pleasant, when it comes at last. So a barrister without briefs does not want them or value them; till they come. So with the schoolboy who does not care for prizes : so with the student at college whose prize essays fail, through the incompetence of the judges. So (I fear) with the very intellectual preacher who would rather have his church empty than full : and who (at present) thinks that only the stupid and blinded are likely to attend a church where all the seats are occupied. I have known clever young fellows, more than two or three, who at a very early age had outgrown all ambition : men who had in them the makings of great things, but by free choice took to a quiet and unnoted life : men whose University standing had been un-rivalled, but who instead of aiming at like eminence afterwards, took to gardening, to evergreens and grass and trees : to contented walks through winter fields : to preaching to fifty rustic labourers : to reading black letter books in chambers at the Temple, instead of trying for the Great Seal : quite happy, and quite sincere in thinking and saying they did not care for more eminent places. But at length, perhaps, success and eminence come : and they are very glad and pleased. Their views of these things are quite changed. They see that they can be more useful than they are. They feel that there was a good deal of indolent self-indulgence in the life they had been leading: that there is more in this life than to practise a refined Epicureanism,—at least while strength and spirits suffice for more. The day may come, when these shall be worn out: and then the old thing will again be pleasant.

Let us hear the sum of the whole matter. If there be anything in this world, which is in its nature agreeable to average humanity, yet which you think sour; the likelihood is that if you got it it would grow sweet. You cannot finally turn out nature. Though you may mow it down very tightly, it will grow again, as grass does in the like contingency. And if there be in you evil and unworthy tendencies which by God's grace you have resolved to extirpate, you must keep a constant eye upon them. You must knock them on the head not once for all; but daily and hourly.

There are things, perhaps, which you know you would like so much, yet which are so unattainable, that you will not allow yourself to think of them. *That* way lies your safety. If you allowed yourself to dwell upon them, and upon their pleasures and advantages, you would grow discontented with what you have. So, though you cannot help sometimes casting a hasty glance at the cluster of grapes, hanging high, which you would like, but which you will never have,—yet don't look long at it.   Don't sit down, and contemplate it for a good while from various points of view, and think how much you would like it.   *That* will only make you unhappy. And if you have known this world long, then you know this about it : that the thing you would like best is just the last you are ever likely to get.   But of this I shall say no more.   I said something like it once before : and got a shower of long letters controverting it.

If a young fellow fails in his profession : and then say he did not want to succeed; let us believe him. He is entitled to this.   We do him, in most cases, no more than justice.   The grapes have indeed grown sour : and it is a kind appointment of Providence that it is so.   But if success should come yet, you will find them sweeten again, surprisingly.

In writing upon this subject, I have been led to think of many things : and to think of many old acquaintances.   Not very cheerfully did the writer trace out the first page : still less so the last.   How sadly short has many a one of whom we expected great things, fallen of those expectations !   Is there one, of the clever boys and thoughtful lads, that has done as much as we looked for ?   Not one.

The great thing, of course, that resigns one to this, and to anything else, is the firm belief that

God orders all. 'IT HAD PLEASED GOD to form poor Ned, A thing of idiot mind,' wrote Southey. There the matter is settled. We have not a word more to say. 'I was dumb; I opened not my mouth: BECAUSE THOU DIDST IT!'

We have all smiled at the fable of Æsop, of which the writer has given you the accurate version: and smiled at many manifestations we have seen in life, showing its truth; and showing us how human nature age after age abides the self-same thing. I believe it is one of the most beneficent arrangements of God's providential government, that the grapes we cannot reach grow sour. But for *that*, this would be a world of turned heads and broken hearts. Who has got the purple clusters he in his childhood thought to get? Yet who (if a sensible mortal) cares? You were to have been a laurelled hero: you are in fact a half-pay captain, glad to be made adjutant of a militia regiment. You were to have been Lord Chancellor of Great Britain: you are in fact parish minister of Drumsleekie, with a smoky manse, and heritors who oppose the augmentation of your living. You were to have lived in a grand castle, possibly built of alternate blocks of gold and silver: you live, in fact, in a plain house in a street, and find it hard enough to pay the Christmas bills. And you were to have been buried, at last, in Westminster Abbey: while in fact you won't. But the beauty has faded off the things never to be attained; and the humble grapes you could reach have sweetened : and you are content. Yet there are grapes which, if submitted to your close inspection, would seem so sweet that in comparison with them those you have would seem very insipid : so you may be glad you will never see those grapes too near nor too long.

CHAPTER V.

CONCERNING THE ESTIMATE OF HUMAN BEINGS.

HE other day, talking with my friend Smith, I incidentally said something which implied that a certain individual, who may be denoted as Mr. X, was a distinguished and influential man. 'Nonsense!' was Smith's prompt reply. 'I saw Mr. X,' continued Smith, 'at a public meeting yesterday. He is a gorilla—a yahoo. He is a dirty and ugly party. I heard him make a speech. He has a horribly vulgar accent, and an awkward cubbish manner. In short, he is not a gentleman; nor the least like one!'

And having said this, my friend Smith thought he had finally disposed of X.

But I replied, 'I grant all that. All you have said about X is true. But still I say he is a distinguished and influential man; a very able man— almost a great man.'

Smith was not convinced. He departed. I fear

I have gone down in his estimation. I have not seen him since. Perhaps he does not want to see me. I don't care.

But my friend Smith's observations have made me think a good deal of a tendency which is in human nature. It is very natural, if we find a man grossly deficient in something about which we are able to judge—and perhaps in the thing about which we are able best to judge—to conclude that he must be all bad. In the judgment of many, it is quite enough to condemn a man, to show that he is a low fellow, with an extremely vulgar accent. We forget how much good may go with these evil things; good more than enough to outweigh all these and more. There is great difficulty in bringing men heartily to admit the great principle which may be expressed in the familiar words—FOR BETTER FOR WORSE. There is great difficulty in bringing men really to see that excellent qualities may coexist with grave faults; and that a man, with very glaring defects, may have so many great and good qualities, as serve to make him a good and eminent man, upon the balance of the whole account. Though you can show that A owes a hundred thousand pounds, this does not certainly show that A is a poor man. Possibly A may possess five hundred thousand pounds; and so the balance may be greatly in his favour.

We all need to be reminded of this. It is very

plain; but it is just very plain things that most of us practically forget. There are many folk who instantly on discovering that A owes the hundred thousand pounds, proceed to declare him a bankrupt without further enquiry. Possibly the debt A owes is constantly and strongly pressed on your attention; while it costs some investigation to be assured of the large capital he possesses. There is one debt in particular, which if we find owed by any man, it is hard to prevent ourselves declaring him a bankrupt, without more investigation. Great vulgarity will commonly stamp a man in the estimation of refined people, whatever his merits may be. *That* is a thing not to be got over. If a man be deficient by *that* hundred thousand pounds, all the gold of Ophir will (in the judgment of many) leave him poor. Once, in my youth, I beheld an eminent preacher of a certain small Christian sect. I knew he was an eloquent orator, and that he was greatly and justly esteemed by the members of his own little communion. I never heard him speak, and never beheld him save on that one occasion. But, sitting near him at a certain public meeting, I judged, from obvious indications, that he never had brushed his nails in his life. I remember well how disgusted I was; and how hastily I rushed to the conclusion that there was no good about him at all. Those territorial and immemorial nails hid from my youthful eyes all his excellent qualities. Of course, this was because I was very foolish and inexperienced. Men with worse defects may be great and good upon the whole. Or, to return to my analogy, no matter how great a man's debts may be, you must not conclude he is poor till you ascertain what his assets are. These may be so great as to leave him a rich man, though he owes a hundred thousand pounds.

The principle which I desire to enforce is briefly this :—that men must be taken *for better for worse.* There may be great drawbacks about a thing, and yet the thing may be good. Many people think, in a confused sort of way, that if you can mention several serious objections to taking a certain course, this shows you should not take that course. Not at all. Look to the other side of the account. Possibly there are twice as many and twice as weighty objections to your not taking that course. There are things about your friend Smith that you don't like. They worry you. They point to a conclusion which might be expressed in the following proposition :—

SMITH IS BAD.

But if you desire to arrive at a just and sound estimate of Smith, your course will be to think of other things about Smith, which speak in a different strain. There are things about Smith you cannot help liking and respecting him for. And these point to a conclusion which a man of a comprehensive mind and of considerable knowledge of the language might express as follows :—

SMITH IS GOOD.

And having before you the things which may be said *pro* and *con*, it will be your duty first to count them, and then to weigh them. Counting alone will not suffice. For there may be six things which tell against Smith, and only three in his favour; and yet the three may be justly entitled to be held as outweighing the six. For instance, the six things counting against Smith may be these :—

1. He has a red nose.
2. He carries an extremely baggy cotton umbrella.
3. He wears a shocking bad hat.
4. When you make any statement whatever in his hearing, he immediately begins to prove, by argument, that your statement cannot possibly be true.
5. He says *tremenduous* when he means *tremendous*; and talks of a *prizenter* when he means a *precentor*.
6. He is constantly saying 'How very curious!' also 'Goodness gracious!'

Whereas the three things making in Smith's favour may be these :—

1. He has the kindest of hearts.
2. He has the clearest of heads.
3. He is truth and honour impersonate.

Now, if the account stand thus, the balance is unquestionably in Smith's favour. And it is so with everything else as well as with Smith. When you change to a new and better house, it is not all gain. It is gain on the whole; but there may be some respects in which the old house was better than the new. And when you are getting on in life, it is not all going forward. In some respects it may be going back. It is an advance, on the whole, when the attorney-general becomes chancellor; yet there were pleasant things about the other way too, which the chancellor misses. It is, to most men, a gain on the whole to leave a beautiful rectory for a bishop's palace; yet the change has its disadvantages too; and some pleasant things are lost. When Bishop Poore, who founded Salisbury Cathedral in the thirteenth century, left his magnificent church amid its sweet English scenery, to be bishop of the bleak northern diocese of Durham, he must have felt he was sacrificing a great deal. Yet to be Bishop of Durham in those days was to be a Prince of the Church, with a Prince's revenue: and so Bishop Poore was on the whole content to go. I daresay in the thirteen years he lived at Durham before he died, he often wondered whether he had not done wrong.

You will find men who are good classical scholars ready to think it extinguishes a man wholly to show that he is grossly ignorant of Latin and Greek.

It is to be granted, no doubt, that as a classical training is an essential part of a liberal education, the lack of it is a symptomatic thing, like a man's dropping his h's. He must be a vulgar man who talks about his Ouse and his Hoaks. And even so, to write about *rem, quomodo rem*, as an eminent divine has done, raises awful suspicions. So it is with *macte estote puer*. Still, we may build too much on such things. By a careful study of English models a man may come to have a certain measure of classical taste and sensibility, though he could not construe a chance page of Æschylus or Thucydides, or even an ode of Horace. Yet you will never prevent many scholars from sometimes throwing in such a man's face his lack of Latin and Greek; as though that utterly wiped him out. I cannot but confess, indeed, that there is no single fact which goes more fatally to the question, whether a man can claim to be a really educated person, than the manifest want of scholarship; all I say is, that too much may be made of even this. You know that a false quantity in a Latin quotation in a speech in Parliament can never be quite got over. It stamps the unfortunate individual who makes it. He may have many excellent qualities; many things of much more substantial worth than the power of writing alcaics ever so fluently; yet the suspicion of the want of the education of a gentleman will brand him. Yet Paley was a great man, though when he went to

H

Cambridge to take his degree of Doctor of Divinity, in the *Concio ad Clerum* he preached on that occasion, he pronounced *profŭgus, profŭgus.* A shower of epigrams followed. Many a man, incomparably inferior to Paley on the whole, felt his superiority to Paley in the one matter of scholarship. Here was a joint in the great man's armour, at which it was easy to stick in a pin. Lockhart, too, was a very fair scholar; though you read at Abbotsford, above the great dog's grave, certain lines which he wrote:—

> Maidæ marmoreâ dormis sub imagine, Maida,
> Ad januam Domini. Sit tibi terra levis !

You will find it difficult, if you possess a fair acquaintance with the literature of your own country, to suppress some little feeling of contempt for a man whose place in life should be warrant that he is an educated man, yet who is blankly ignorant of the worthy books in even his own language. Yet you may find highly respectable folk in that condition of ignorance:—medical men in large practice; country attorneys, growing yearly in wealth as their clients are growing poorer; clergymen, very diligent as parish priests, and not unversed in theology, if versed in little else. I have heard of a highly respectable divine, of no small standing as a preacher, who never had heard of the *Spectator* (I mean, of course, Steele and Addison's *Spectator*), at a period very near the close of his life. And certain of his neighbours who willingly laughed at that good man's ignorance were but one degree ahead of him in literary information. They knew the *Spectator*, but they had never heard of Mr. Ruskin nor of Lord Macaulay. Still, they could do the work which it was their business to do very reputably. And *that* is the great thing, after all.

The truth is, that the tendency in a good scholar to despise a man devoid of scholarship, and the tendency in a well-read man to despise one who has read little or nothing besides the newspapers, is just a more dignified development of that impulse which is in all human beings to think A or B very ignorant, if A or B be unacquainted with things which the human beings first named know well. I have heard a gardener say, with no small contempt, of a certain eminent scholar—'Ah, *he* knows nothing: *he* does not know the difference between an arbutus and a juniper.' Possibly you have heard a sailor say of some indefinite person—'*He* knows nothing : *he* does not know the fore-top from the binnacle.' I have heard an architect say of a certain man, to whom he had shown a certain noble church— 'Why, the fellow did not know the chancel from the transept.' And although the architect, being an educated man, did not add that the fellow knew nothing, *that* was certainly vaguely suggested by what he said. A musician tells you, as something which finally disposes of a fellow-creature, that he does not know the difference between a fugue and a madrigal.   I remember somewhat despising a distinguished classical professor, who read out a passage of Milton to be turned into heroic Latin verse.   One line was,

Fled and pursued transverse the resonant fugue :

which the eminent man made an Alexandrine, by pronouncing fugue in two syllables, as FEWGEW. In fact, if you find a man decidedly below you in any one thing, if it were only in the knowledge how to pronounce fugue, you feel a strong impulse to despise him on the whole, and to judge that he stands below you altogether.

Probably the most common error in the estimate of human beings, is one already named: it is, to think meanly of a man if you find him plainly not a gentleman.   And I have present to my mind now, a case which we have all probably witnessed: namely, a set of empty-headed puppies, of distinguished aspect and languid address, imperfectly able to spell the English language, and incapable of anything but the emptiest badinage in the respect of conversation ; yet expressing their supreme contempt for a truly good man, who may have shown himself ignorant of the usages of society. You remember how Brummell mentioned it as a fact quite sufficient to extinguish a man, that he was 'a person who would send his plate twice for soup.' The judgment entertained by Brummell, or by anyone like Brummell, is really not worth a moment's consideration. I think of the difficulty which good and sensible people feel, in believing the existence of sterling merit along with offensive ignorance and vulgarity. Yet a man whom no one could mistake for a gentleman, may have great ability, great eloquence in his own way, great influence with the people, great weight even with cultivated folk. I am not going to indicate localities or mention names; though I very easily could. No doubt, it is irritating to meet a member of the House of Commons, and to find him a vulgar vapourer. Yet, with all that, he may be a very fit man to be in Parliament; and he may have considerable authority there, when he sticks to matters he can understand. And if refined and scholarly folk think to set such a one aside, by mentioning that he cannot read Thucydides, they will find themselves mistaken.

It is, to many, a very bitter pill to swallow; a very disagreeable thing to make up one's mind to; yet a thing to which the logic of facts compels every wise man to make up his mind: that in these days men whose features, manner, accent, entire ways of thinking and speaking, testify to their extreme vulgarity, have yet great influence with large masses of mankind. And it is quite vain for cultivated folk

to think to ignore such. Men grossly ignorant of
history, of literature, of the classics : men who
never brushed their nails : men who don't know
when to wear a dress coat and when a frock: may
gain great popularity and standing with a great
part of the population of Great Britain. Their
vulgarity may form a high recommendation to the
people with whom they are popular. It would be
easy to point out places where anything like refinement or cultivation would be a positive hind-
rance to a man. Let not blocks be cut with razors.
Let not coals be carried in gilded chariots. Rougher
means will be more serviceable. And if people of
great cultivation say—'A set of vulgar fellows;
not worth thinking of;' and refuse to see the work
such men are doing, and to counteract it where its
effects are evil : those cultivated people will some
day regret it. I occasionally see a periodical publication, containing the portraits of men who are
esteemed eminent by a certain class of human
beings. Most of those men are extremely ugly and
all of them extremely vulgar-looking. The natural
impulse is to throw the coarse effigies aside, and to
judge that such persons can do but little, either for
good or ill. But if you enquire, you will find they
are doing a great work, and wielding a great influence with a very large section of the population;
the work and influence, being, in my judgment, of
the most mischievous and perilous character.

Then a truth very much to be remembered, is, that the fact of a man's doing something conspicuously and extremely ill, is no proof whatsoever that he is a stupid man. To many people it appears as if it were such a proof, simply because their ideas are so ill-defined. If a clergyman ride on horseback very badly, he had much better not do so in the presence of his humbler parishioners. The esteem in which they hold his sermons will be sensibly diminished, by the recollection of having seen him roll ignominiously out of the saddle, and into the ditch. Still, in severe logic, it must be apparent that if the sermons be good in themselves, the bad horsemanship touches them not at all. It comes merely to this: that if you take a man off his proper ground, he may make a very poor appearance; while on his proper ground, he would make a very good one. A swan is extremely graceful in the water; the same animal is extremely awkward on land. I have thought of a swan, clumsily waddling along on legs that cannot support its weight, when I have witnessed a great scholar trying to make a speech on a platform, and speaking miserably ill. The great scholar had left his own element, where he was graceful and at ease; he had come to another, which did not by any means suit him. And while he floundered and stammered through his wretched little speech, I have beheld fluent empty-pates grinning with joy at the badness of his appearance. They had got the great scholar to race with them: they in their own element, and he out of his. They had got him into a duel, giving them the choice of weapons. And having beat him (as logicians say), *secundum quid*, they plainly thought they had beat him *simpliciter*. You may have been amused at the artifices by which men, not good at anything but very fluent speaking, try to induce people infinitely superior to them in every respect save that one, to make fools of themselves by miserable attempts at that one thing they could not do. The fluent speakers thought, in fact, to tempt the swan out of the water. The swan, if wise, will decline to come out of the water.

I have beheld a famous anatomist carving a goose. He did it very ill. And the faith of the assembled company in his knowledge of anatomy was manifestly shaken. You may have seen a great and solemn philosopher, seeking to make himself agreeable to a knot of pretty young girls in a drawing-room. The great philosopher failed in his anxious endeavours; while a brainless cornet succeeded to perfection. Yet though the cornet eclipsed the philosopher in this one respect, it would be unjust to say that, on the whole, the cornet was the philosopher's superior. I have beheld a pious and amiable man playing at croquet. He played frightfully ill. He made himself an object of universal derision. And he brought all his good qualities into grave suspicion, in the estimation of the gay young people with whom he played. Yes, let me recur to my great principle: no clergyman should ever hazard his general usefulness, by doing anything whatsoever signally ill in the presence of his parishioners. If he have not a good horse, and do not ride well, let him not ride at all. And if, living in Scotland, he be a curler; or living in England, join in the sports of his people; though it be not desirable that he should display pre-eminent skill or agility, he ought to be a good player; above the average.

It is an interesting thing, to see how habitually, in this world, excellence in one respect is balanced by inferiority in another: how needful it is, if you desire to form a fair judgment, to take men for better for worse. I have oftentimes beheld the ecclesiastics of a certain renowned country, assembled in their great council to legislate on church affairs. And—sitting mute on back benches, never dreaming of opening their lips—pictures of helplessness and sheepishness — I have beheld the best preachers of that renowned country: I am not going to mention their names. Meanwhile— sitting in prominent places, speaking frequently and lengthily, speaking in one or two cases with great pith and eloquence—I have beheld other preachers, whose power of emptying the pews of whatever church they might serve had been established beyond question by repeated trials. Yet, by tacit consent, these dreary orators were admitted as the church's legislators ; and, in many cases, not unjustly. There is a grander church, in a larger country, in which the like balance of faculties may be perceived to exist. The greater clergymen of that church are entitled *bishops*. Now, by the public at large, the bishops are regarded in the broad light of the chief men of the church ; that is, the greatest and most distinguished men. Next, the thing as regards which the general public can best judge of a clergyman is his preaching. The general public, therefore, regard the best preachers as the most eminent clergymen. But the qualities which go to make a good bishop are quite different from those which go to make a great preacher. Prudence, administrative tact, kindliness, wide sympathies, are desirable in a bishop. None of these things can be brought to the simple test of the goodness of a man's sermon. Indeed, the fiery qualities which go to make a great preacher, do positively unfit a man for being a bishop. From all this comes an un-happy antagonism between the general way of thinking as to who should be bishops, and the way in which the people who select bishops think. And the general public is often scandalized by hearing that this man and the other, whom they never heard of, or whom they know to be a very dull preacher, is made a bishop ; while this or that man who charms and edifies them by his admirable sermons is passed over. For the tendency is inveterate with ill-cultivated folk, to think that if a man be very good at anything, he must be very good at everything. And with uneducated folk, the disposition is almost ineradicable, to conclude that if you are very ignorant on some subject they know, you know nothing; and that if you do very ill something as to which they can judge, you can do nothing at all well. Pitt said of Lord Nelson, that the great admiral was the greatest fool he ever knew, when on shore. A less wise man than Pitt, judging Nelson a very great fool on shore, would have hurried to the conclusion that Nelson was a fool everywhere and altogether. And Nelson himself showed his wisdom, when informed of what Pitt had said. 'Quite true,' said Nelson; 'but I should soon prove Pitt a fool if I had him on board a ship.' It may, indeed, be esteemed as certain that Pitt's strong common sense would not have failed him, even at sea; but when he, was rolling about in deadly sea-sickness, and testifying twenty times in an hour his ignorance of nautical affairs, it may be esteemed as equally certain that the sailors would have regarded him as a fool.

I have heard vulgar, self-sufficient people in a country parish, relate with great delight instances of absence of mind and of lack of ordinary sense, on the part of a good old clergyman of great theological learning, who was for many years the incumbent of that parish. A thoughtful person would be interested in remarking instances in which an able and learned man proved himself little better than a baby. But it was not for the psychological interest that those people related their wretched little bits of ill-set gossip. It was for the purpose of conveying, by inuendo, that there was no good about that simple old man at all; that he was, in fact, a fool *simpliciter*. But if you, learned reader, had taken that old man on his own ground, you would have discovered that he was anything but a fool. 'What's the use of all your learning,' his vulgar and ignorant wife was wont to say to him, 'if you don't know how to ride on horseback, and how turnips should be sown after wheat?'

You may remember an interesting instance, in the *Life of George Stephenson*, of two great men supplementing each the other's defects. George Stephenson was arguing a scientific point with a fluent talker who knew very little about the matter: but though Stephenson's knowledge of the subject was great, and his opinions sound, he was thoroughly reduced to silence. He had no command of language or argument: he had a good case, but he did not know how to conduct it. But all this happened at a country-house, where Sir William Follett was likewise staying. Follett saw that Stephenson was right; and he was impatient of the triumph of the fluent talker. Follett, of course, had magnificent powers of argument; but he had no knowledge whatever of the matter under discussion. But, privately getting hold of Stephenson, Follett got Stephenson to coach him up in the facts of the case. Next day, the great advocate led the conversation once more to the disputed question: and now Stephenson's knowledge and Follett's logic combined, smashed the fluent talker of yesterday to atoms.

Themistocles, every one knows, could not fiddle; but he could make a little city a big one. Yet the people who distinctly saw he could not fiddle were many, while those who discerned his competence in the other direction were few. So, it is not unlikely that many people despised him for his bad fiddling, failing to remark that it was not his vocation to fiddle. Goldsmith wrote *The Vicar of Wakefield* and *The Goodnatured Man*; yet he felt indignant at the admiration bestowed by a company of his acquaintances upon the agility of a monkey; and, starting up in anger and impatience, exclaimed—'I could do all that myself.' I have heard of a very great logician and divine, who was dissatisfied that a trained gymnast should excel him in feats of strength, and who insisted on doing the gymnast's feats himself; and, strange to say, he actually did them. Wise men would not have thought the less of him though he had failed; but it is certain that many average people thought the more of him because he succeeded.

There are single acts which may justly be held as symptomatic of a man's whole nature; for, though done in a short time, they are the manifestation of ways of thinking and feeling which have lasted through a long time. To have written two or three malignant anonymous letters may be regarded as branding a man finally. To have only once tried to stab a man in the back may justly raise some suspicion of a man's candour and honesty ever after. You know, my reader, that if A poisons only one fellow-creature, the laws of our country esteem that single deed as so symptomatic of A's whole character that they found upon it the general conclusion that A is not a safe member of society; and so, with all but universal approval, they hang A. Still the doing of one or two very malicious and dishonourable actions may not indicate that a man is wholly dishonourable and malicious. These may be no more than an outburst of the bad which is in every man—cleared off thus, as electricity is taken out of the atmosphere by a good thunderstorm. I am not sure what I ought, in fairness, to think of a certain individual, describing himself as a clergyman of the Church of England, who has formed an unfavourable opinion of the compositions of the present writer; and who, every now and then,

sends me an anonymous letter. It is, indeed, a
curious question, how a human being can deliberately sit down and spend a good deal of time in
writing eight rather close pages of anonymous matter of an unfriendly, not to say abusive, character,
and then send it off to a man who is a total stranger.
What are we to think of this individual ? Are we
to think favourably of him as a clergyman and as a
gentleman ? He has sent me a good many letters ;
and I shall give you some extracts from the last.
For the sake of argument, let it be said that my
name is Jones. I am a clergyman of the Established Church in a certain country. But my correspondent plainly thinks it a strong point to call
me a Dissenter, which he does several times in each
of his letters. Of course, he knows that I am not
a Dissenter; but this mode of address seems to
please him. I give you the passages from his last
letter *verbatim*, only substituting Jones for another
name, of no interest to anybody :—

Rev. Jones (Dissenting Preacher),

I have read your *Sermons* from *curiosity*. They exhibit
your invincible conceit, like all your other works. Your notion
as to the resurrection of the *old body* is utterly *exploded*, except amongst such divines as Dr. Cumming (who is *not* eminent, as you assert), and similar riff-raff.

There is now-a-days no Sabbath. The Scotch, who talk of
a ' sabbath,' are fools and ignorant fanatics. I am glad to
see that *you*, Jones, were well castigated by a London paper
for lending your name to a hateful crusade of certain fanatics
in Edinburgh (including the odious Guthrie), against opening

the *parks* to the people on Sunday. I intend to visit Edinburgh or Glasgow some *Sunday*, and to walk about, *as a clergyman*, between the services, with some little ostentation, in order to show my contempt of the local custom. Let any low Scotch Presbyterian lay hands on me at his peril! Ah, Jones, you evidently dare not say your soul is your own in Scotland!

Neither Caird nor Cumming are men of first-rate ability. Cumming is a mere dunce, not even *literate*. How *can* you talk of understanding the works of Mr. Maurice? Of course not : you are too low-minded, and narrow-souled! But do not dare to disparage such exalted merit. Say you are a fool, and blind, and we may excuse you.

You are clearly unable to appreciate excellence of any kind. Your assertion, that the doctrines of *the* Church, *our* Church, are *Calvinistic*, is a *false* one. *Calvinism* is now confined to illiterate tinkers, Dissenters, Puritans, and low Scotch Presbyterians.

Your constant use of the phrase, ' My friends,' in your sermons, is bad and affected. We are not your ' friends :' and you care nothing for your hearers, except to gain their applause!

I remain, Sir Jones,
With no *very great* respect,
Your obedient servant,
P. A.

(P. S.) Poor A. K. H. B. Why not A. S. S. !

Now, my reader, how shall we estimate the man that wrote this? Can he be a gentleman? Can he be a clergyman? I have received from him a good many letters of the same kind, which I have destroyed, or I might have culled from them still more remarkable flowers of rhetoric. In a recent letter he drew a very unfavourable comparison between the present writer and the author of *Friends in*

Council. In that unfavourable comparison I heartily concur; but it may be satisfactory to Mr. P. A. to know that immediately after receiving his letter I was conversing with the author of *Friends in Council*; and that I read his letter to my revered friend. And I do not think Mr. P. A. would have been gratified if he had heard the opinion which the author of *Friends in Council* expressed of P. A. upon the strength of that one letter. Let us do P. A. justice. For a long time he sent his anonymous letters unpaid, and each of them cost me twopence. For some time past he has paid his postages. Now this is an improvement. The next step in advance which remains for P. A., is to cease wholly from writing anonymous letters.

Now to conclude:

There is great difficulty in estimating human beings: that is, in *placing* them (in the racing sense) in your own mind. And the difficulty comes of this, that you have to take a conjunct view of a man's deservings and ill-deservings: the man's merit is the resultant of all his qualities, good and bad. In a race the comparison is brought to the single point of speed; or, more accurately speaking, to the test, which horse shall, on a given day, pass the winning-post first. Everyone understands the issue; and the prize goes on just the one consideration. Great confusion and difficulty would

I

arise if other issues were brought in: as for instance, if a man were permitted to say to the owner of the winner, 'You have passed the post first, but then my horse has the longest tail; and, upon the strength of that fact, I claim the cup.' Yet, in placing human beings (mentally) for the race of life, the case is just so. You are making up your mind—'Is this man eminent or obscure? is he deserving or not?—is he good or bad?' But there is no one issue to which you can rightly bring his merits. He may exhibit extraordinary skill and ability in doing some one thing; but a host of little disturbing circumstances may come to perplex your judgment. Mr. Green was a good scholar and a clever fellow, yet I have heard Mr. Brown say—'Green! ah, he's a beast! Do you know, he told me he always studies without shoes and stockings!' And then there is a difficulty in saying what importance ought to be attached to those disturbing causes, as well as whether they exist or not. One man thinks a long tail a great beauty, another attaches no consequence to a long tail. One man concludes that Mr. Green is a beast because he studies without shoes or stockings; another holds *that* as an indifferent circumstance, not affecting his estimate of Green. I fear we can come to no more satisfactory conclusion than this—that of Green, and of each human being, there are likely to be just as many different estimates as there are people who will take the trouble of forming an estimate of them at all.

You will remark, I have been speaking of estimates, honestly formed and honestly expressed. No doubt we often hear, and often read, estimates of men, which estimates have plainly been disturbed by other forces. No wise man will attach much weight to the estimate of a successful man, which is expressed by a not very magnanimous man whom he has beaten. If A sends an article to a magazine, and has it rejected, he is not a competent judge of the merit of the articles which appear in that number in which he wished his to be. You would not ask for a fair estimate of Miss Y's singing from a young lady who tries to sing as well, and fails. You would not expect a very reliable estimate of a young barrister, getting into great practice, of poor Mr. Briefless, mortified at his own ill-success. You would not look for a very flattering estimate of Mr. Melvill or Bishop Wilberforce from a preacher who esteems himself as a great man, but who somehow gets only empty pews and bare walls to hear him preach. Sometimes, in such estimates, there are real envy and malice, as shown by intentional misrepresentation and mere abuse. More frequently, we willingly believe, there is no intention to estimate unfairly; the bias against the man is strong, but it is not designed. A writer cut off from the staff of a periodical, though really an honest man, has been known to attack another writer retained on that staff. Let me say that, in such a case, a very high-minded man would decline to express publicly any estimate, being aware that he could not help being somewhat biassed.

Let this be a rule :—

If we think highly of one who has beaten us, let us say out our estimate warmly and heartily.

If we think ill of one who has beaten us, let us keep our estimate to ourselves. It is probably unjust. And even if it be a just estimate, few men of experience will think it so.

CHAPTER VI.

REMEMBRANCE.

HALL I, because I have seen the subject which has been simmering in my mind for several past days, treated beautifully by another hand, resolve not to touch that subject, and to let my thoughts about it go? No, I will not.

It was a little disheartening, no doubt, when I looked yesterday at a certain Magazine, to find what I had designed to say, said far better by somebody else. But then Dean Alford said it in graceful and touching verse: I aimed no higher than at homely prose.

Sitting, my friend, by the evening fireside: sitting in your easy chair, at rest: and looking at the warm light on the rosy face of your little boy or girl, sitting on the rug by you: do you ever wonder what kind of remembrance these little ones will have of you, if God spares them to grow old?

Look into the years to come : think of that smooth face lined and roughened ; that curly hair gray ; that expression, now so bright and happy, grown careworn and sad ; and you long in your grave. Of course, your son will not have quite forgot you : he will sometimes think and speak of his father who is gone. What kind of remembrance will he have of you ? Probably very dim and vague.

You know for yourself, that when you look at your little boy in the light of the fire, who is now a good deal bigger than in the days when he first was able to put a soft hand in yours and to walk by your side, you have but an indistinct remembrance of what he used to be then. Knowing how much you would come to value the remembrance of those days, you have done what you could to perpetuate it. As you turn over the leaves of your diary, you find recorded with care many of that little man's wonderful sayings : though, being well aware that these are infinitely more interesting to you than to other people, you have sufficient sense to keep them to yourself. There are those of your fellow-creatures to whom you would just as soon think of speaking about these things, as you would think of speaking about them to a jackass. And you have aided your memory by yearly photographs : thankful that such invaluable memorials are now possible ; and lamenting bitterly that they came so late. Yet, with all this help : and though the years are very few; your remembrance of the first summer that your little boy was able to run about on the grass in the green light of leaves, and to go with you to the stable-yard and look with admiration at the horse, and with alarm at the pig, voraciously devouring its breakfast; is far less vivid and distinct than you would wish it to be. Taught by experience, you have striven with the effacing power of time: yet assuredly not with entire success. Yes; your little boy of three years old has faded somewhat from your memory: and you may discern in all this the way in which you will gradually fade from his. Never forgotten, if you have been the parent you ought to be, you will be remembered vaguely. And you think to yourself, in the restful evening, looking at the rosy face, Now, when he has grown old, how will he remember me? I shall have been gone, for many a day and year; all my work, all my cares and troubles, will be over: all those little things will be past and forgot, which went to make up my life, and about which nobody quite knew but myself. The table at which I write, the inkstand, all my little arrangements, will be swept aside. That little man will have come a long, long way, since he saw me last. How will he think of me? Will he sometimes recall my voice, and the stories I told, and the races I used to run? Will he sometimes say to a stranger, ' That's his picture: not very like him;' will he sometimes think to himself, 'There is the corner where he used to sit: I wonder where his chair is now?'

Cowper, writing at the age of fifty-eight, says of his mother: 'She died when I had completed my sixth year, yet I remember her well. I remember too a multitude of maternal tendernesses which I received from her, and which have endeared her memory to me beyond expression.' For fifty-two years the over-sensitive poet had come on his earthly pilgrimage, since the little boy of six last saw his mother's face. Of course, at that age, he could understand very little of what is meant by death; and very little of that great truth, which Gray tells us he discovered for himself, and which very few people learn till they find it by experience, that in this world a human being never can have more than one mother. Yet we can think of the poor little man, finding daily that no one cared for him now as he used to be cared for: finding that the kindest face he could remember was now seen no more. And doubtless there was a vague, overwhelming sorrow at his heart, which lay there unexpressed for half a century, till his mother's picture sent him by a relative touched the fount of feeling, and inspired the words we all know:

> I heard the bell toll'd on thy burial day:
> I saw the hearse that bore thee slow away:
> And turning from my nursery window, drew
> A long, long sigh, and wept a last adieu!

But was it such ?—It was.—Where thou art gone,
Adieus and farewells are a sound unknown.
May I but meet thee on that peaceful shore,
The parting word shall pass my lips no more !

Nobody likes the idea of being quite forgot. Yet sensible people have to make up their mind to it. And you do not care so much about being forgotten by those beyond your own family circle. But you shrink from the thought that your children may never sit down alone, and in a kindly way think for a little of you after you are dead. And all the little details and interests which now make up your habitude of life seem so real, that there is a certain difficulty in bringing it home to one that they are all to go completely out, leaving no trace behind. Of course they must. Our little ways, my friend, will pass from this earth : and you and I will be like the brave men who lived before Agamemnon. A clergyman who is doing his duty diligently, does not like to think that when he goes, he will be so soon forgotten in his old parish and his old church. Bigger folk, no doubt, have the same feeling. A certain great man has been entirely successful in carrying out his purpose; which was, he said, to leave something so written that men should not easily let it die. But that which is nearest us, touches us most. We sympathise most readily with little men. Perhaps you preached yesterday in your own church, to a large congregation of

Christian people. Perhaps they were very silent
and attentive. Perhaps the music was very beautiful,
and its heartiness touched your heart. The service
was soon over: it may have seemed long to some.
Then the great tide of life that had filled the church
ebbed away, and left it to its week-day loneliness.
The like happens each Sunday. And many years
hence, after you are dead, some old people will say,
Mr. Smith was minister of this parish for so many
years. That is all. And looking back for even five
or ten years, a common Sunday's service is as undistinguished in remembrance as a green leaf on a
great beech-tree now in June, or as a single flake in
a thick fall of snow.

Probably you have seen a picture by Mr. Noel
Paton, called *The Silver Cord Loosed.* It is one of
the most beautiful and touching of the pictures of
that great painter. I saw it the day before yesterday: not for the first or second time. People came
into the place where it was exhibited, talking and
laughing: but as they stood before that canvas, a
hush fell on all. On a couch, there is a female
figure, lying dead. Death is unmistakeably there,
but only in its beauty. And beyond, through a
great window, there is a glorious sunset sky. 'Thy
sun shall no more go down; neither shall thy moon
withdraw herself: for the Lord shall be thine everlasting light, and the days of thy mourning shall
be ended.' Seated by the bed, there is a mourner,

with hidden face, in his first overwhelming grief. Looking at that picture in former days, I had thought how 'at evening time there shall be light:' but looking at it now, with the subject of this essay in my mind, I thought how that man, so crushed meanwhile, if the first grief do not kill him (and the greatest grief rarely kills the man of sound physical frame), would get over it: and after some years would find it hard to revive the feelings and thoughts of this day. People in actual modern life are not attired in the picturesque fashion of the mourner in Mr. Noel Paton's picture: but it is because many can from their own experience tell what a human being in like circumstances would be feeling, that this detail of the picture is so touching. And the saddest thing about it is not the present grief: it is the fact that the grief will so certainly fade and go. And no human power can prevent it. 'The low beginnings of content' will force themselves into conscious existence, even in the heart that is most unwilling to recognize them. You will chide yourself that you are able so soon to get over that which you once fancied would darken all your after days. And all your efforts will not bring back the first sorrow: nor recall the thoughts and the atmosphere of that time. When you were a little boy, and a little brother pinched your arm so that a red mark was left, you hastened downstairs to make your complaint to the proper authority. On your way down, fast as you went, you perceived that the red mark was fading out, and becoming invisible. And did you not secretly give the place another pinch to keep up the colour till the injury should be exhibited ? Well, there are mourners who do just the like. I think I can see some traces of *that* in *In Memoriam.* In sorrow that the wound is healing, you are ready to tear it open afresh. And by observing anniversaries : by going to places surrounded by sad associations : some human beings strive to keep up their feeling to the sensitive point of former days. But it will not do. The surface, often spurred, gets indurated : sensation leaves it. And after a while, you might as well think to excite sensation in a piece of India rubber by pricking it with a pin, as think to waken any real feeling in the heart which has indeed met a terrible wound, but whose wound is cicatrized. All this is very sad to think of. Indeed I confess to thinking it the very sorest point about the average human being. Great grief may leave us : but it should not leave us the men we were. There are people in whose faces I always look with wonder ; thinking of what they have come through, and of how little trace it has left. I have gone into a certain room, where everything recalled vividly to me one who was dead. Furniture, books, pictures, piano : how plainly they brought back the face of one, far away ! But the regular inmates of the house had no such feeling :

had it not, at least, in any painful degree. No
doubt, they had felt it for awhile, and outgrown it :
whereas, to me it came fresh. And after a time it
went from me too.

You know how we linger on the words and looks
of the dead after they are gone. It is our sorrowful protest against the power of Time, which we
know is taking these things from us. We try to
bring back the features and the tones : and we are
angry with ourselves that we cannot do so more
clearly. 'Such a day,' we think, 'we saw them
last : so they looked : and such words they said.'
We do *that* about people for whom we did not
especially care while they lived : a certain conse-
cration is breathed about them now. But how much
more as to those who did not need this to endear
them ! You ought to know the lines of a true and
beautiful poet, about his little brother who died :—

> And when at last he was borne afar
>   From the world's weary strife,
> How oft in thought did we again
>   Live o'er his little life !
>
> His every look, his every word,—
>   His very voice's tone,—
> Came back to us like things whose worth
>   Is only prized when gone !

I wish I could tell Mr. Hedderwick how many
scores of times I have repeated to myself that most
touching poem in which these verses stand. But I
know (for human nature is always the same) that,

when the poet grew to middle age and more, those tones and looks that came so vividly back in the first days of bereavement, would grow indistinct and faint. And now, when he sits by the fire at evening, or when he goes out for a solitary walk, and tries to recall his little brother's face, he will grieve to feel that it seems misty and far away.

> I cannot see the features right,
>   When on the gloom I strive to paint
>   The face I knew ; the hues are faint,
> And mix with hollow masks of night.

And you will remember how Mr. Hawthorne, with his sharp discernment of the subtle phenomena of the mind, speaking in the name of one who re-called the form and aspect of a beautiful woman not seen for years, says something like this : When I shut my eyes, I see her yet, but a little wanner than when I saw her in fact.

Yes ; and as time goes on, a great deal wanner. I have remarked that even when the outlines remain in our remembrance, the colours fade away.

Thus true is it, that as for the long absent, and the long dead, their remembrance fails. Their faces, and the tones of their voice, grow dim. And some-times we have all thought what a great thing it would be to be able at will to bring all these back with the vividness of reality. What a great thing it would be if we could keep them on with us, clearly and vividly as we had them at the first! When your young sister died, oh how distinctly you could hear, for many days, some chance sentence as spoken by her gentle voice! When your little child was taken, how plainly you could feel, for awhile, the fat little cheek laid against your own, as it was for the last time! But there is no precious possession we have which wears out so fast as the remembrance of those who are gone. There never was but one case where that was not so. Let us remember it as we are told of it in the never-failing Record: there are not many kindlier words, even there:

'But the Comforter, which is the Holy Ghost, whom the Father will send in My name, He shall teach you all things, and bring all things to your remembrance, whatsoever I have said unto you.'

So you see in *that* case the dear remembrance would never wear out but with life. The Blessed Spirit would bring back the words, the tones, the looks, of the Blessed Redeemer, as long as those lived who had heard and seen Him. He was to do other things, still more important; but you will probably feel what a wonderfully kindly and encouraging view it gives us of that Divine Person, to think of Him as doing all that. And while we have often to grieve that our best feelings and impulses die away so fast, think how the Apostles, everywhere, through all their after years, would have recalled to them when needful, *all things* that the Saviour had said to them; and how He said those things; and how He looked as He said them. *They* had not to wait for seasons when the old time came over them; when through a rift in the cloud, as it were, they discerned for a minute the face they used to know; and heard the voice again, like distant bells borne in upon the breeze. No: the look was always on St. Peter, that brought him back from his miserable wander: and St. John could recall the words of that parting discourse so accurately, after fifty years.

The poet Motherwell begins a little poem with this verse: —

> When I beneath the cold red earth am sleeping,
>   Life's fever o'er,—
> Will there for me be any bright eye weeping
>   That I'm no more?
> Will there be any heart sad memory keeping
>   Of heretofore?

Now that is a pretty verse; but to my taste it seems tainted with sentimentalism. No man really in earnest could have written these lines. And I feel not the slightest respect for the desire to have 'bright eyes weeping' for you; or to have some vague indefinite 'heart' remembering you. Mr. Augustus Moddle, or any empty-headed lackadaisical lad, writing morbid verses in imitation of Byron, could do that kind of thing. The man whose desire of remembrance takes the shape of a wish to have some pretty girl crying for him (which is the thing aimed at in the mention of the 'bright eye weeping') is on precisely the same level, in regard to taste and sense, with the silly conceited blockhead who struts about in some place of fashionable resort, and fancies all the young women are looking at him. Why should people with whom you have nothing to do weep for you after you are dead, any more than look at you or think of you while you are living? But it is a very different feeling, and an infinitely more respectable one, that dwells with the man who has outgrown silly sentimentalism; yet who looks at those whom he holds dearest; at those whose stay he is, and who make up his great interest in life; at those whom *he* will remember, and never forget, no matter where he may go in God's universe: and who thinks, Now, when the impassable river runs between,—when I am an old remembrance, unseen for many years,—and when they are surrounded by the interests of their after life, and daily see many faces but never mine; how will they think of me? Do not forget me, my little children whom I loved so much, when I shall go from you. I do not wish you (a wise good man might say) to vex yourselves, little things; I do not wish you to be gloomy or sad: but sometimes think of your father and mother when they are far away. You may be sure that, wherever they are, they will not be forgetting you.

K

CHAPTER VII.

ON THE FOREST HILL:

WITH SOME THOUGHTS TOUCHING DREAM-LIFE.

HY is it that that purple hill will not get out of my mind to-night ? I am sure it is not that I cared for it so much when I could see it as often as I pleased. I suppose, my reader, that you know the painful vividness with which distant scenes and times will sometimes come back, unbidden and unwished. No one can tell why. And now, at 11.25 P.M., when I have gone up to my room far away from home, and ought to go to bed, that hill will not go away. There is no use in trying. And nothing can be more certain than that if I went to bed now, I should toss about in a fever till 4 or 5 A.M. Well, as a smart gallop takes the nonsense out of an aged horse, which has shown an unwonted friskiness, there is something which will quiet this present writer's pulse : and it shall be tried. Come out, you writing case. Come forth,

the foolscap, the ink-bottle, the little quill that has
written many pages. And now you may come
back again before the mind's eye, purple hill not
seen for years.

I shut my eyes, which if opened would behold
many things not needful to be noted; and then the
scene arises. In actual fact, the writer is surrounded
by the usual furniture of a bedroom in a great railway hotel in a certain ancient city : and occasional
thundering sounds, and awful piercing screeches,
speak of arriving and departing trains somewhat
too near. I have walked round the city, upon the
wall. And reaching a certain spot, I sat down in
the summer twilight, and looked for a long time at
the old cathedral, which is not grey with age. On
the contrary, it is red; as though there lingered
about its crumbling stones the sunsets of seven
hundred summers. The day was, as we learn from
Bishop Blomfield's *Life*, wherein to be the chief
minister of that noble church was esteemed as a
very poor preferment. And this estimation is
justified by the statement that the annual revenue
of the bishop was not so very many hundred pounds.
But who shall calculate the money value of the
privilege of living in this quaint old city, whose
streets carry you back for centuries; and of worship-
ping, as often as you please, under that sublime
roof: of breathing the moral atmosphere of the
ancient place; and of looking from its walls upon

those blue hills and over those rich plains? Surely one might here live a peaceful life of worship, thought, and study: amid Gothic walls and carved oak and church music. And if any ordinary man should declare that he could not be content with all this, just let me get him by the ears. Wouldn't I shake him!

But all this is a deviation. And if there is anything on which the writer prides himself, it is the severity of his logic. You will not find in his pages those desultory and wandering passages which attract the unthinking to the works of Archbishop Whately and Mr. John Stuart Mill. And from this brief excursion he returns, to the severe order of thought which is natural to him.

I shut my eyes, as has been already remarked. The railway hotel, the thundering trains, and the yelling engines vanish; and the old scene arises. It is a bright autumn afternoon. The air is very still. The sun is very warm, and makes the swept corn-fields golden. The trees are crimson and brown; and crisp leaves rustle beneath your foot. It is a long valley, with hills on either side; and a river flowing down it. A path winds by the river side, through the fields; and there, in front, is the purple hill. An Englishman would think it pretty high. It is more than twelve hundred feet in height. The upper part of it is covered with heather. It rises like a great pyramid, closing in the valley. There are two or three little farm-houses half way up it. Above these, it is solitary and still.

I wonder, this evening, being so far away, yet with painful distinctness seeing all that, whether I am there in fact as well as feeling? Would some country lad, returning late from market, discern a shadowy figure walking slowly along the path; and bawl out and run away, recognizing me?

If you believe various recent books, you will understand that when you think very intently of a place or person, it is not improbable that some misty eidolon of yourself is present to the person or at the place. I cannot say that I think this fact well authenticated.

I walk on, not in the summer night, but in the autumn afternoon. I want to climb the hill, as I have done so often in departed days. So I lay aside the pen, and bend down my head on my hands.

I have been there, if ever I was in my life. It is not every day one can sit in a very hard easy chair; and take such a walk, nearly two hundred miles off.

Through the long grass, with a dry rustle under one's feet, by the river side: up through a little wood of firs, till the highway is gained: over a one-arched bridge, that spans a little rocky gorge, where a stream, smaller than the river, tumbles over a shelf of rock, making a noisy waterfall, now white as country snow that has lain but a night : up a steep and rough road, with birches on either hand, and a brook flowing down on one side, that brawls in rainy weather, but only murmurs on the still autumn day : up and up till the hedges give place to walls of rude stones, built without mortar ; and till rough slopes of heather spread away on either side : up and up till the path ceases, and you sit down on a great boulder of granite in the lonely bosom of the hill : through all that I have been. A long way below this, but a longer way above the wooded valley, which you now see in its whole extent, you may discern the smoke rising from a farm-house, screened a little by a clump of rather scraggy pines. There is a sick man there : an aged man whom I go to see frequently. I went to the farm-house door, a black and white dog barking furiously : there a pleasant comely young face welcomed me : I went in and found my old friend sitting by his warm fireside, which was, indeed, a great deal too warm for anyone who had been striving up that stiff ascent. I saw his face, and heard his voice : though he has been dead for years. I saw the sheep feeding on the hill around : I heard a cart passing noisily along a road far below : I saw the long gleam of the river, down in the valley : and the horizon of encircling hills : saw and heard all these things as really as though they had been present. Memory is certainly a most wonderful thing. It is very capricious. Sometimes it recalls things very faintly and dimly: sometimes with a vividness that makes one start. Can it be so long ago! And it selects, in a very arbitrary fashion, what it will choose to remember. The faces and voices we would most desire to recall, it allows to fade away: and scenes and people we did not particularly care for, it now and then sets before us with this strange vividness of force and colour. I did not cherish any special regard for the old farmer: and the walk up the hill was not a very great favourite. Yet to-night something took me by the collar, and walked me up that path, and set me down beside the old man's chair.

I have come back. It has exorcised the hill, to write all this about it. I had an eerie feeling, like that which De Quincey tells he had for many nights about the Malay to whom he gave the great piece of opium. But now the hill is appeased. All these odd, inexplicable states of thought and feeling are transitory. And it is much better that they should be so. Hard work crowds them out: it is only in comparative leisure they come at all.

But we are not to suppose that only weak and fanciful persons know by experience these mental phenomena. What may be called *Dream-life*, that is, spending some part of one's time in an imaginary world; is a thing in which some of the hardest-headed of human beings have had their share. And this little walk which the writer has had to-night, in a place far away, and as upon a day that is left far behind, helps him to understand some of those singular things which are recorded of the extent to which many men have spent their time in castles in the air; and of the persistency with which they have dwelt there, to the forgetfulness of more tangible interests. If ever there was a man who was not a morbid day-dreamer, it was Sir James Mackintosh, Sir James Mackintosh was known to mankind in general as an acute metaphysician: a forcible political writer: a brilliant talker. The greatest place he ever held, to the common eye, was that of Recorder of Bombay. And he held that place just the shortest time he possibly could to earn his pension. How many men knew, looking at the homely Scotchman, what his true place in life was? Had he not told us himself, we should hardly have believed it. He was Emperor of Constantinople! And a laborious and anxious position he found it. He (mentally) promoted many of his friends to important offices of state: and his friends, by their indiscretion and incompetence, caused him an immense deal of trouble. Then the empire was always getting involved in the most vexatious complications, which seriously affected the Emperor's sleep and general health. He always felt like a man playing a very intricate game at chess. No wonder he was sometimes very absent and distracted. You would say he might have escaped all this by resigning his crown : but he could not arrange satisfactorily to do that. A thoughtless person smiles at these things : but to Mackintosh they were among the most serious things of his life. A man of bread-and-butter understanding would explain it by saying that Mackintosh was cracked ; but then we all know that he was not cracked. Yet, in his disengaged hours, regularly as they came, was the thread of his history taken up where it had been dropped last time : and he was the Emperor, laden with an Emperor's cares. It was not as with the actor Elliston, received with great applause on the stage at Drury Lane, and fancying himself a king just long enough to bestow a blessing upon the audience, till he was pulled up by a burst of laughter. Nor was it like Alexander the Great, according to Dryden, who 'assumed the god' for only a very limited period. Neither was the astute philosopher's notion of an Emperor the childish one. He was not Emperor, to sit on a throne, and receive homage, and make a grand appearance on grand occasions : but to go through intricate calculations and hard work, and to undergo great anxiety.

In short, Sir James Mackintosh, being a great man, indulged in dream-life on a great scale. But commonplace human beings do it in a way that suits themselves, and their moderate aspirations.

The poor consumptive girl, who on a dark December evening is propped up with pillows, and gets you to sit beside her while she tells you how much stronger and better she feels; how by spring she will be quite well again; and how delightful the long walks will be in the summer evenings, while you know she will never see the black-thorn in blossom, nor the green leaves on the tree: she is doing just what the great metaphysician used to do. And the little schoolboy, far away from home, a thoughtful, bullied little fellow, does it too, when he pictures out the next holiday-time, and his getting away from all this to be with those who care for him. Possibly more people than you would think make up for the dulness of their actual life in some such way. They take pleasure in fancying what they would like, in their vacant hours. And unless you wish your mind to become very small and dry, you will have such hours. No matter how hard-worked you may be, they are attainable. You remember what Charles Lamb once wrote to a friend: ' If you have but five consolatory minutes, between the desk and the bed, make much of them, and live a century in them.' Human beings, living even the most prosaic lives, have sometimes their enchanted palace, and live in it a great deal. Have you not sometimes, my reader, pictured out the life you would like: not in the least expecting it, or even really wishing it, any more than Mackintosh really

looked to be made Emperor of Constantinople?
And when you have set your heart on something
happening, which is very likely not to happen, it is
quite right to please yourself by picturing out the
best: all the more that this is all the enjoyment of
it you are likely to have. If we have all suffered a
great deal of pain, through the anticipation of evils
which never came; we have all probably enjoyed a
great deal of pleasure, through the anticipation of
pleasant things which were never to be. We have
lived a good deal in castles which were never to be
built, but in the air. When we tried for something
we did not get, you remember well how we used, in
vacant hours, to plan out all the mode of life, even
to its minute details: enjoying it only the more
keenly through the intrusion of the fear that only
in this airy fashion should we ever lead that life
which we should have enjoyed so much. Of course,
it is not expedient to waste in dreaming over noble
plans, the precious hours which might have gone
far to turn our dreams into serviceable realities. It
is foolish for the lad at college to spend, in thinking
how proud his parents would be, and how pleased
all his friends, if he were to carry off all the ho-
nours that were to be had, the time which if devoted to hard work might have gained at least some
of those soon-forgotten laurels. It may be said
here, by way of parenthesis, that one of the very
last visions in which ambitious youth need indulge,

is the vision of being recognized as great and distinguished in the place of your birth or your early days. A prophet has no honour in his own country. I have a friend, greatly revered, who expresses an opposite opinion. He maintains, in a charming volume, that if you rise to decent eminence in life, the people who knew you as a boy will be proud of you, and will help to push you on farther. ‘I see, with my mind’s eye,’ says my friend, ‘a statue of Dunsford erected in Tollerporcorum.’ Dunsford was a native of Tollerporcorum : and having recorded the conversation of his *Friends in Council,* would probably be thus distinguished. There are portions of this earth where the fact is just the contrary. Tollerporcorum is just the last place where certain Dunsfords I know are likely to have a statue. Dunsford’s early acquaintances cannot bear the moderate success which has attended Dunsford in life : they regard *Friends in Council* as a very poor work ; and a college acquaintance, who never forgave Dunsford the medals he won there, now and then abuses Dunsford in the Tollerporcorum newspaper. I lately visited a certain Tollerporcorum : an ancient town in a fair tract of country. That Tollerporcorum had its Dunsford. Dunsford started from small beginnings ; but gradually rose about as high as a human being well can in a certain portion of Scandinavia. But the fashionable and intellectual thing, in Tollerporcorum, was to ignore Dunsford and his career altogether. Nobody cared about him or it. Dunsford sometimes went back to Tollerporcorum; and the Tollerporcorum people diligently shut their eyes to his existence. Every envious little wretch who had stuck in the mud, thus avenged himself on Dunsford for having got on so far. In the latter years of his honoured life, Dunsford hardly ever visited Tollerporcorum: and when the great man died, it was never proposed at Tollerporcorum to erect so much as a drinking-fountain to his memory.

Here ends the parenthesis. Take up the broken thread of thought. It is right and pleasant to gain at least the pleasure of anticipation out of happy things that are not to be. And when you see a sanguine person in a state of great enjoyment through such anticipation, you will not, unless you have in you the spirit of my old friend Mr. Snarling, try to throw a damp upon all this innocent happiness by pointing out, with great force of logic, how very little chance there is of the anticipation being realized. That is only the stronger reason for enjoying in this way that which you are not likely to enjoy in any other. There is hardly a more touching sight, than the sight of a human being, old or young, happy in the anticipation of any pleasant thing which he will never reach. With what a rosy face and what bright eyes your little boy of five years old confides to you all he is to do when he is

a man! Great are the grandeur and fame in which
he is to live: many are to be his horses and nume-
rous his dogs; but a great feature in his plan always is, how happy he is to make his father and
mother.   Ah, little man, before those days come,
your father and mother will be far away.

And a reason why a wise man, desirous to eco-
nomize the enjoyment there is in this life, and to
make it go as far as possible, will often quietly
luxuriate in the prospect of what he secretly knows
is not likely to happen, is this certain fact: that in
this world the thing you would like best, is the
thing you are least likely to get.   *That* is a fact
which, as we get on through life, we come to know
extremely well.   Yes: if you set your heart on a
thing, whoever gets it, *you* won't.   You may get
something else: perhaps something better: but not
that.   If you have such an enthusiasm for Gothic
architecture, that you sometimes think no one could
enjoy it so much: if you feel that it would sensibly
flavour all your life, to live in a Gothic house, or to
worship in a Gothic church: then, though everything else about them be all you could wish, rely
on it, your church and house will be Palladian.
And you will often meet men whose belongings are
Gothic: who tell you they are very beautiful, very
uncomfortable; that the church is destroying their
lungs, and the house giving them perpetual cold in
their heads: and who greatly envy you.   Of course,

all this is gratifying, to a certain degree. It serves to make you content.

I have known a man who lived in a house which was extremely comfortable, and extremely ugly. No one could ever say to what school of architecture, in particular, his residence was to be referred. And the country round was very ugly and bare. But, like the farmer in Virgil, in that exquisite passage in one of the *Georgics, regum æquabat opes animo :* he could picture out, at will, a charming English manor-house, of hospitable-looking red brick with stone dressings; oriel-windowed, steep-gabled, with great wreathed chimneys, with environing terraces, with magnificent horse-chestnuts ever blazing in the glory of June. You thought he was walking a bleak moorland road, dreary and dismal; but in truth the warm breeze was shaking the blossoms overhead, and making a chequered dancing shade on soft green turf below. And there yearly comes a certain season, when very many human beings practise on themselves a delusion something like his. I mean Christmas-time. Who ever spent the ideal Christmas ? I should like very greatly to behold that person. I have never done so yet : never spent a Christmas in all my life in the ideal way. You ought to be living in a noble Gothic house, somewhere in the Midland Counties of England. There ought to be a large and gay party, spending the holidays there. There ought

to be an exquisite old church near. There ought
to be bracing frost, and cheerful snow. All hearts
should seem touched and warmed by the sacred
associations of the season. There should be an
oaken hall, and a vast wood-fire: holly and mistle-
toe; and of course roast beef and plum pudding
and strong ale for every poor person near. You
should be living, in short, at Bracebridge Hall,
exactly as it was when Washington Irving described
it: and with all the same people. It need not be
said that in fact, the Christmas time and its surroundings are quite different from all this. You
sit down by yourself, and try to get up the feeling
of the time by reading Washington Irving and Mr.
Dickens' *Christmas Carol.* The *Illustrated London
News* is a great help to ordinary imaginations at
that season. On the actual Christmas-day, rainy,
muddy, tooth-aching, ill-tempered, you turn over
the pictures in that excellent journal; and you find
the ideal Christmas there. My friend Smith once
told how he spent his first Christmas-day in his
little country parsonage. Luckily, there was snow.
He provided that his servants, three in number,
should have the means of a little enjoyment. He
worked hard all the forenoon writing a sermon,
whose subject was not the Nativity. And for an
hour before dinner he walked, alone, up and down
a little gravelled walk with evergreens on each side,
looking at the leaden sky, and the solitary fields;

and trying to feel as if he were at Bracebridge Hall. He tried with small success. Then, having dined in solitude on turkey and plum-pudding, he read the pleasant Christmas chapter in *Pickwick*: and tried to get up an enthusiasm about the enjoyment which, for the sake of argument, might be conceived as existing in many houses that night. Finally, he concluded that he was unsuccessfully trying to humbug himself; and ended by reading Butler's *Analogy* in a good deal of bitterness of heart.

Very early in our intelligent life, our personality begins to cut us off from those nearest to us. Unless a parent have a much deeper insight and sympathy than most parents have, he loses knowledge, very early, of the real inward life of his children. At first, it is like wading in shallow water; but it is not long till it shelves down into depths beyond your diving. The little thoughtful face you see every day; the little heart within you know just as much as you know the outer side of the moon. No doubt, if this be so, it is in a great measure your own fault. There are many parents to whom their children, young or old, would no more confide the things they really care for and think about, than they would confide these to the first cabman at the next stand. But beyond this, the little things soon begin to have a world of their own, not known to any but themselves. You may have known young children who wearied for the hour when they might get to bed, and begin to think again: take up the history where they left it off last night. Of course, the history and the world were very different from the fact. Kings and queens, heroes and giants, elves and fairies, palaces and castles, these being oftentimes enchanted, were common there. Also clear views of the kind of life they would live when they grew up: a life in which coaches and six, suits of armour, and the like, were not unknown.

It is a mercy for some people, that circumstances keep them down. Their lot circumscribes their opportunity of making fools of themselves. My friend Smith, already named, is a clergyman. His church is a plain one. Such is his craze for Gothic architecture, that I tremble to think what would have become of him if he had chanced to attain a magnificent church dating from the eleventh century: a church with stately ranks of shafts, echoing aisles, storied window, crusaders' statues, rich oak carving and monumental brasses, standing amid grand old trees. I fear he would have spent great part of his time in admiring and enjoying the structure: in sitting on a gravestone outside and looking at it: in walking up and down inside it: and the like. It would have been a great feature in his life. It is much safer and better that he has been spared that temptation. The grand building, of course, has fallen to somebody who does not care for it at all. In a former age, there was a barrister who would have keenly enjoyed being made a judge. Probably no man ever made a judge would have delighted so much in the little accessories of that eminent position : the curious garb, and the varied dignity wherewith the administrators of the law are surrounded. How tremendously set up he would have been if he could once have sentenced a man to be hanged! The writer was present when the name of that person was suggested to an individual who could have made him what he wished to be. That individual was asked whether he might not do. That individual did not open his lips; but he shook his head slowly from side to side, several times. For thus goes on this world.

Probably most human beings, now and then, have short glimpses of cheerfulness and light-heartedness, which make them think how much more and better might be made of this life. You have seen a charming scene, bathed in a glorious sunshine ; and you have thought, Now, it might always be like this. Sometimes there comes a hopefulness of spirit in which all difficulties and perplexities vanish : in which everything seems delightful, and all creatures good. This is the potential of happiness in man. Of course, it is seldom reached, and never for long. Most people are more familiar with the converse case, in which everything looks dark and amiss : the season of perplexity, despondency, depression. Probably this comes many times more frequently than the other. Let me say, my reader, that we know the reason why.

The truth is, it is not needful to our enjoyment of many things, that we should fancy any connexion between ourselves and them. You read a pleasant story, and like it, without fancying yourself its hero or heroine. Never in your life, perhaps, have you spent a week in a house like Bracebridge Hall: and you are never likely to do that. Yet you enjoy the sunshiny volume; and you thank its author for many hours of quiet, thoughtful enjoyment, for which you felt the better. And indeed, much of what is pleasing and beautiful you enjoy most, when you never think of it in relation to yourself. Take the most pleasing development of human comeliness: which is doubtless in the case of young women. Let it be admitted, that there are few things more pleasing and interesting to the rightly-constituted mind, than the sight of sweet girlish faces and graceful girlish forms, and the tones of the pleasant voices that generally go with them. But there is no doubt earthly, that in grave middle age, you have much more real pleasure in these things, than in feverish youth. Let us suppose, my reader, that you are a man in years. Those who were young girls in your day, are middle-aged women now: they are past. But you look with the kindest interest on the fair young faces of another generation. A young lad is eager to commend himself to the notice and admiration of these agreeable human beings. He is filled with bitter enmity at other lads, more successful than himself in gaining their favour. His whole state of mind, in the circumstances, leads him into a host of absurdities: the contemplative mind sees him in the light of an ass. Now, you are beyond and above all these things. You look with pure pleasure and kindness at the fairest beings of God's creation. And you look at the fair sight and enjoy it, as you look at Ben Lomond or at the setting sun, without the faintest wish to make it your own. It is the entire absence of personal interest, that makes your interest so pleasant, and so unmingled with any disagreeable feeling. I remember to have read, in a religious biography, a statement made by a very clever and good man, about a certain beautiful girl, called away in early youth. 'I found myself,' he said, 'looking at her with an interest for which I could not account.' Was that unsophisticated simplicity real? Not able to account for the interest with which you look at a pleasant sight! I think it might be accounted for. Though indeed when we go to first principles, we get beyond the reach of logical explanation. In strictness, you may not be able to say why the tear comes to your eye, when you look at a number of little children and think what is before them. In strictness, you may not be able to say why it was that so many people found themselves shedding tears, on a day in Westminster Abbey, when they saw the Crown placed on the head of a certain young girl, who in after years was destined to gain the love of most hearts in Britain as the best of Queens. Yet a great many thoughtful persons have recorded that they were affected alike, in beholding that sight. So there must have been something in the sight, to awaken the emotion.

These are the things of which the writer thought, in the circumstances already set out. Probably it has made you sleepy to read all this. It had the contrary effect to write it : for when the writer at length wearily sought his couch, he could not sleep at all.

CHAPTER VIII.

CONCERNING RESIGNATION.

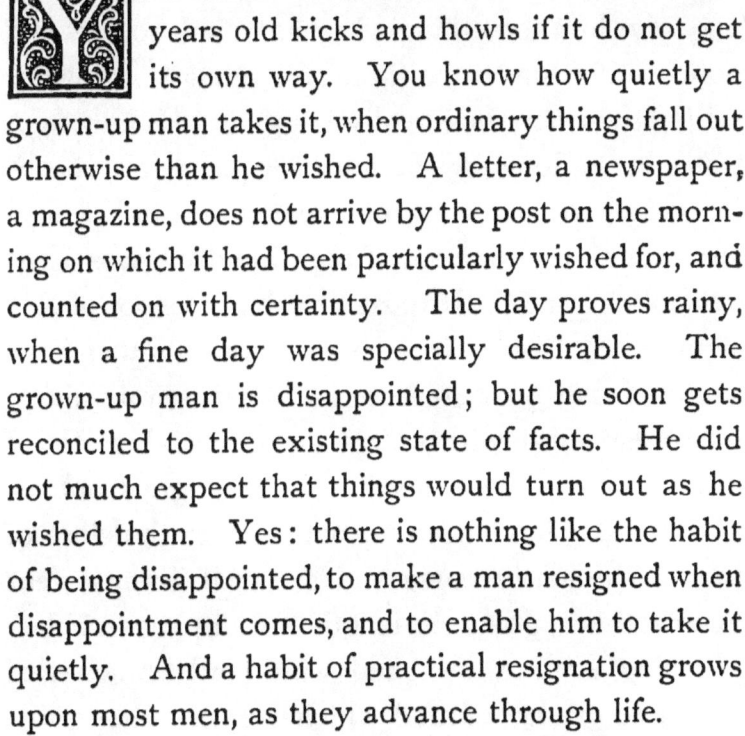

YOU know how a little child of three or four years old kicks and howls if it do not get its own way. You know how quietly a grown-up man takes it, when ordinary things fall out otherwise than he wished. A letter, a newspaper, a magazine, does not arrive by the post on the morning on which it had been particularly wished for, and counted on with certainty. The day proves rainy, when a fine day was specially desirable. The grown-up man is disappointed; but he soon gets reconciled to the existing state of facts. He did not much expect that things would turn out as he wished them. Yes: there is nothing like the habit of being disappointed, to make a man resigned when disappointment comes, and to enable him to take it quietly. And a habit of practical resignation grows upon most men, as they advance through life.

You have often seen a poor beggar, most probably an old man, with some lingering remains of respect-

ability in his faded appearance, half ask an alms
of a passer-by: and you have seen him, at a word
of repulse, or even on finding no notice taken of his
request, meekly turn away: too beaten and sick at
heart for energy: drilled into a dreary resignation by
the long custom of finding everything go against him
in this world. You may have known a poor cripple,
who sits all day by the side of the pavement of a certain street, with a little bundle of tracts in his hand,
watching those who pass by, in the hope that they
may give him something. I wonder, indeed, how the
police suffer him to be there: for though ostensibly
selling the tracts, he is really begging. Hundreds of
times in the long day, he must see people approaching; and hope that they may spare him a halfpenny;
and find ninety-nine out of each hundred pass without noticing him. It must be a hard school of Resignation. Disappointments without number have
subdued that poor creature into bearing one disappointment more with scarce an appreciable stir of
heart. But on the other hand, kings, great nobles,
and the like, have been known, even to the close of
life, to violently curse and swear if things went
against them; going the length of stamping and blas-
pheming even at rain and wind, and branches of
trees and plashes of mud, which were of course guilt-
less of any design of giving offence to these eminent
individuals. There was a great monarch, who when
any little cross-accident befell him, was wont to fling

himself upon the floor; and there to kick and scream and tear his hair. And around him, meanwhile, stood his awe-stricken attendants: all doubtless ready to assure him that there was something noble and graceful in his kicking and screaming: and that no human being had ever before with such dignity and magnanimity torn his hair. My friend Mr. Smith tells me that in his early youth he had a (very slight) acquaintance with a great Prince, of elevated rank and of vast estates. That great Prince came very early to his greatness; and no one had ever ventured, since he could remember, to tell him he had ever said or done wrong. Accordingly, the Prince had never learned to control himself; nor grown acustomed to bear quietly what he did not like. And when any one, in conversation, related to him something which he disapproved, he used to start from his chair, and rush up and down the apartment, furiously flapping his hands together, till he had thus blown off the steam produced by the irritation of his nervous system. That Prince was a good man: and so aware was he of his infirmity, that when in these fits of passion, he never suffered himself to say a single word: being aware that he might say what he would afterwards regret. And though he could not wholly restrain himself, the entire wrath he felt passed off in flapping. And after flapping for a few minutes, he sat down again, a reasonable man once more. All honour to him! For my friend

Smith tells me that that Prince was surrounded by toadies, who were ready to praise everything he might do; even to his flapping. And in particular, there was one humble retainer, who whenever his master flapped, was wont to hold up his hands in an ecstacy of admiration: exclaiming, 'It is the flapping of a god, and not of a man!'

Now all this lack of Resignation on the part of princes and kings comes of the fact, that they are so far like children, that they have not become accustomed to be resisted; and to be obliged to forego what they would like. Resignation comes by the habit of being disappointed; and of finding things go against you. It is, in the case of ordinary human beings, just what they expect. Of course, you remember the adage: 'Blessed is he who expecteth nothing, for he shall not be disappointed.' I have a good deal to say about that adage. Reasonableness of expectation is a great and good thing: despondency is a thing to be discouraged and put down as far as may be. But meanwhile let me say, that the corollary drawn from that dismal beatitude seems to me unfounded in fact. I should say just the contrary. I should say, 'Blessed is he who expecteth nothing, for he will very likely be disappointed.' You know, my reader, whether things do not generally happen the opposite way from that which you expected. Did you ever try to keep off an evil you dreaded, by interposing this buffer? Did you ever think you might perhaps prevent a trouble from coming, by constantly anticipating it: keeping meanwhile an under-thought that things rarely happened as you anticipate them: and thus that your anticipation of the thing might possibly keep it away? Of course you have: for you are a human being. And in all common cases, a watch might as well think to keep a skilful watchmaker in ignorance of the way in which its movements are produced, as a human being think to prevent another human being from knowing exactly how he will think and feel in given circumstances. We have watched the working of our own watches far too closely and long, my friends, to have the least difficulty in understanding the great principles upon which the watches of other men go. I cannot look inside your breast, my reader, and see the machinery that is working there: I mean the machinery of thought and feeling. But I know exactly how it works, nevertheless: for I have long watched a machinery precisely like it.

There are a great many people in this world who feel that things are all wrong: that they have missed stays in life: that they are beaten: and yet who don't much mind. They are indurated by long use. They do not try to disguise from themselves the facts. There are some men who diligently try to disguise the facts: and who in some measure succeed in doing so. I have known a self-sufficient and disagreeable clergyman who had a church in a large city. Five-sixths of the seats in the church were quite empty: yet the clergyman often talked of what a good congregation he had, with a confidence which would have deceived any one who had not seen it. I have known a church where it was agony to any one with an ear to listen to the noise produced when the people were singing: yet the clergyman often talked of what splendid music he had. I have known an entirely briefless barrister, whose friends gave out that the sole reason why he had no briefs was that he did not want any. I have known students who did not get the prizes for which they competed: but who declared that the reason of their failure was, that though they competed for the prizes, they did not wish to get them. I have known a fast young woman, after many engagements made and broken, marry as the last resort a brainless and penniless blackguard: yet all her family talk in big terms of what a delightful connexion she was making. Now, where all that self-deception is genuine, let us be glad to see it: and let us not, like Mr. Snarling, take a spiteful pleasure in undeceiving those who are so happy to be deceived. In most cases, indeed, such trickery deceives nobody. But where it truly deceives those who practise it, even if it deceives nobody else, you see there is no true Resignation. A man who has made a mess of life, has no need to be resigned, if he fancies he has succeeded splendidly. But I look with great interest, and often with deep respect, at the man or woman who feels that life has been a failure: a failure, that is, as regards *this* world: and yet who is quite resigned. Yes: whether it be the unsoured old maid, sweet-tempered, sympathetic in others' joys, God's kind angel in the house of sorrow: or the unappreciated genius, quiet, subdued, pleased to meet even one who understands him amid a community which does not: or the kind-hearted clever man to whom eminent success has come too late, when those were gone whom it would have made happy: I reverence and love, more than I can express, the beautiful natures I have known thus subdued and resigned !

Yes: human beings get indurated. When you come to know well the history of a great many people, you will find that it is wonderful what they have passed through. Most people have suffered a very great deal, since they came into this world. Yet, in their appearance, there is no particular trace of it all. You would not guess, from looking at them, how hard and how various their lot has been. I once knew a woman, rather more than middle-aged. I knew her well, and saw her almost every day for several years, before I learned that the homely Scotchwoman had seen distant lands, and had passed through very strange ups and downs,

before she settled into the quiet orderly life in which
I knew her.   Yet when spoken to kindly, by one
who expressed surprise that all these trials had left
so little trace, the inward feeling, commonly sup-
pressed, burst bitterly out : and she exclaimed,
' It's a wonder that I'm living at all ! '   And it is a
wonder that a great many people are living, and
looking so cheerful and so well as they do : when
you think what fiery passion, what crushing sorrow,
what terrible losses, what bitter disappointments,
what hard and protracted work, they have gone
through.   Doubtless, great good comes of it.   All
wisdom, all experience, comes of suffering. I should
not care much for the counsel of the man whose
life had been one long sunshiny holiday.   There is
greater depth in the philosophy of Mr. Dickens,
than a considerable portion of his readers discern.
You are ready to smile at the singular way in
which Captain Cuttle commended his friend Jack
Bunsby as a man of extraordinary wisdom ; whose
advice on any point was of inestimable value.
' Here's a man,' said Captain Cuttle, ' who has been
more beaten about the head than any other living
man ! '   I hail the words as the recognition of a
great principle. To Mr. Bunsby, it befell in a literal
sense : but we have all been (in a moral sense) a
good deal beaten about both the head and the
heart before we grew good for much.   Out of the
travail of his nature : out of the sorrowful history

of his past life : the poet or the moralist draws the deep thought and feeling which find so straight a way to the hearts of other men. Do you think Mr. Tennyson would ever have been the great poet he is, if he had not passed through that season of great grief which has left its noble record in *In Memoriam?* And a youthful preacher, of vivid imagination and keen feeling, little fettered by anything in the nature of good taste, may by strong statements and a fiery manner draw a mob of unthinking hearers : but thoughtful men and women will not find anything in all *that*, that awakens the response of their inner nature in its truest depths : they must have religious instruction into which real experience has been transfused : and the worth of the instruction will be in direct proportion to the amount of real experience which is embodied in it. And after all, it is better to be wise and good, than to be gay and happy ; if we must choose between the two things : and it is worth while to be severely beaten about the head, if *that* is the condition on which alone we can gain true wisdom. True wisdom is cheap at almost any price. But it does not follow at all that you will be happy (in the vulgar sense) in direct proportion as you are wise. I suppose most middle-aged people, when they receive the ordinary kind wish at New Year's time of a Happy New Year, feel that *happy* is not quite the word : and feel *that*, too, though well aware that they have abundant reason for gratitude to a kind Providence. It is not *here* that we shall ever be happy : that is, completely and perfectly happy. Something will always be coming to worry and distress. And a hundred sad possibilities hang over us : some of them only too certainly and quickly drawing near. Yet people are content, in a kind of way. They have learnt the great lesson of Resignation.

There are many worthy people who would be quite fevered and flurried by good fortune, if it were to come to any very great degree. It would injure their heart. As for bad fortune, they can stand it nicely. They have been accustomed to it so long. I have known a very hard-wrought man, who had passed, rather early in life, through very heavy and protracted trials. I have heard him say that if any malicious enemy wished to kill him, the course would be to make sure that tidings of some signal piece of prosperity should arrive by post on each of six or seven successive days. It would quite unhinge and unsettle him, he said. His heart would go : his nervous system would break down. People to whom pieces of good luck come rare and small, have a great curiosity to know how a man feels when he is suddenly told that he has drawn one of the greatest prizes in the lottery of life. The kind of feeling, of course, will depend entirely on the kind of man. Yet very great prizes, in the way of dignity and duty, do for the most part fall to men who in some measure deserve them: or who at least are not conspicuously undeserving of them and unfit for them. So that it is almost impossible that the great news should elicit merely some unworthy explosion of gratified self-conceit. The feeling would in almost every case be deeper, and worthier. One would like to be sitting at breakfast with a truly good man, when the letter from the Prime Minister comes in, offering him the Archbishopric of Canterbury. One would like to see how he would take it. Quietly, I have no doubt. Long preparation has fitted the man who reaches that position for taking it quietly. A recent Chancellor publicly stated how *he* felt when offered the Great Seal. His first feeling, that good man said, was of gratification that he had fairly reached the highest reward of the profession to which he had given his life: but the feeling which speedily supplanted *that*, was an overwhelming sense of his responsibility and a grave doubt as to his qualifications. I have always believed, and sometimes said, that good-fortune; not so great or so sudden as to injure one's nerves or heart: but kindly and equable; has a most wholesome effect upon human character. I believe that the happier a man is, the better and kinder he will be. The greater part of unamiability, ill-temper, impatience, bitterness, and

M

uncharitableness, comes out of unhappiness. It is because a man is so miserable, that he is such a sour, suspicious, fractious, petted creature. I was amused, this morning, to read in the newspaper an account of a very small incident which befell the · new Primate of England on his journey back to London after being enthroned at Canterbury. The reporter of that small incident takes occasion to record that the Archbishop had quite charmed his travelling companions in the railway carriage by the geniality and kindliness of his manner. I have no doubt he did. I am sure he is a truly good Christian man. But think what a splendid training for producing geniality and kindliness he has been going through for a great number of years. Think of the moral influences which have been bearing on him for the last few weeks. We should all be kindly and genial if we had the same chance of being so. But if Dr. Longley had a living of a hundred pounds a year: a fretful ailing wife: a number of half-fed and half-educated little children: a dirty miserable house: a bleak country round: and a set of wrongheaded and insolent parishioners to keep straight: I venture to say he would have looked, and been, a very different man, in that railway carriage running up to London. Instead of the genial smiles that delighted his fellow-travellers (according to the newspaper story), his face would have been sour and his speech would have been snappish : he would have leant back in the corner of a second-class carriage, sadly calculating the cost of his journey; and how part of it might be saved by going without any dinner. Oh, if I found a four-leaved shamrock, I would undertake to make a mighty deal of certain people I know! I would put an end to their weary schemings to make the ends meet. I would cut off all those wretched cares which jar miserably on the shaken nerves. I know the burst of thankfulness and joy that would come, if some dismal load, never to be cast off, were taken away. And I would take it off. I would clear up the horrible muddle. I would make them happy : and in doing *that*, I know that I should make them good !

But I have sought the four-leaved shamrock for a long time, and never have found it : and so I am growing subdued to the conviction that I never will. Let us go back to the matter of Resignation ; and think a little longer about *that*.

Resignation, in any human being, means that things are not as you would wish; and yet that you are content. Who has all he wishes ? There are many houses in this world in which Resignation is the best thing that can be felt, any more. The bitter blow has fallen : the break has been made : the empty chair is left (perhaps a very little chair): and never more, while Time goes on, can things be as they were fondly wished and hoped. Resignation would need to be cultivated by human beings: for, all round us, there is a multitude of things very different from what we would wish. Not in your house, not in your family, not in your street, not in your parish, not in your country, and least of all in yourself; can you have things as you would wish. And you have your choice of two alternatives. You must either fret yourself into a nervous fever; or you must cultivate the habit of Resignation. And very often, Resignation does not mean that you are at all reconciled to a thing; but just that you feel you can do nothing to mend it. Some friend, to whom you are really attached, and whom you often see, vexes and worries you by some silly and disagreeable habit: some habit which it is impossible you should ever like, or ever even overlook: yet you try to make up your mind to it: because it cannot be helped; and you would rather submit to it than lose your friend. You hate the East wind: it withers and pinches you, in body and soul: yet you cannot live in a certain beautiful city without feeling the East wind many days in the year. And that city's advantages and attractions are so many and great, that no sane man, with sound lungs, would abandon the city merely to escape the East wind. Yet though resigned to the East wind, you are anything but reconciled to it.

Resignation is not always a good thing. Sometimes it is a very bad thing. You should never be resigned to things continuing wrong, when you may rise and set them right. I daresay, in the Romish Church, there were good men before Luther, who were keenly alive to the errors and evils that had crept into it: but who, in despair of making things better, tried sadly to fix their thoughts upon other subjects: who took to illuminating missals, or constructing systems of logic, or cultivating vegetables in the garden of the monastery, or improving the music in the chapel: quietly resigned to evils they judged irremediable. Great reformers have not been resigned men. Luther was not resigned: Howard was not resigned: Fowell Buxton was not resigned: George Stephenson was not resigned. And there is hardly a nobler sight, than that of a man who determines that he will NOT make up his mind to the continuance of some great evil: who determines that he will give his life to battling with that evil to the last: who determines that either that evil shall extinguish him, or he shall extinguish it! I reverence the strong, sanguine mind, that resolves to work a revolution to better things; and that is not afraid to hope it *can* work a revolution! And perhaps, my reader, we should both reverence it all the more that we find in ourselves very little like it. It is a curious thing, and a sad thing, to remark in how many people there is too much resignation. It kills out energy. It is a weak, fretful, unhappy thing. People are reconciled, in a sad sort of way, to the fashion in which things go on. You have seen a poor, slatternly mother, in a wayside cottage, who has observed her little children playing in the road before it, in the way of passing carriages; angrily ordering the little things to come away from their dangerous and dirty play: yet when the children disobey her, and remain where they were, just saying no more; making no farther effort. You have known a master tell his man-servant to do something about stable or garden: yet when the servant does not do it, taking no notice: seeing that he has been disobeyed, yet wearily resigned: feeling that there is no use in always fighting. And I do not speak of the not unfrequent cases in which the master, after giving his orders, comes to discover that it is best they should not be carried out, and is very glad to see them disregarded: I mean when he is dissatisfied that what he has directed is not done, and wishes that it were done, and feels worried by the whole affair: yet is so devoid of energy as to rest in a fretful resignation. Sometimes there is a sort of sense as if one had discharged his conscience by making a weak effort in the direction of doing a thing: an effort which had not the slightest chance of being successful. When I was a little boy, many years since, I used to think this: and I was led to thinking it by remarking a singular characteristic in the conduct of a school companion. In those days, if you were chasing some other boy who had

injured or offended you, with the design of retaliation; if you found you could not catch him, by
reason of his superior speed; you would have recourse to the following expedient. If your companion was within a little space of you, though a
space you felt you could not make less : you would
suddenly stick out one of your feet, which would
hook round his : and he stumbling over it, would
fall. I trust I am not suggesting a mischievous and
dangerous trick to any boy of the present generation. Indeed, I have the firmest belief that existing
boys know all we used to know, and possibly more.

All this is by way of rendering intelligible what
I have to say of my old companion. He was not a
good runner. And when another boy gave him a
sudden flick with a knotted handkerchief, or the
like; he had little chance of catching that other boy.
Yet, I have often seen him, when chasing another,
before finally abandoning the pursuit, stick out his
foot in the regular way, though the boy he was
chasing was yards beyond his reach. Often did the
present writer meditate on that phenomenon, in the
days of his boyhood. It appeared curious that it
should afford some comfort to the evaded pursuer,
to make an offer at upsetting the escaping youth,—
an offer which could not possibly be successful. But
very often, in after life, have I beheld in the conduct
of grown-up men and women, the moral likeness of
that futile sticking out of the foot. I have beheld

human beings who lived in houses always untidy and disorderly: or whose affairs were in a horrible confusion and entanglement: who now and then seemed roused to a feeling that this would not do : who querulously bemoaned their miserable lot ; and made some faint and futile attempt to set things right: attempts which never had a chance to succeed, and which ended in nothing.   Yet it seemed somehow to pacify the querulous heart.   I have known a clergyman in a parish with a bad population, seem suddenly to waken up to a conviction that he must do something to mend matters : and set agoing some weak little machinery, which could produce no appreciable result, and which came to a stop in a few weeks.   Yet that faint offer appeared to discharge the claims of conscience : and after it the clergyman remained long time in a comatose state of unhealthy Resignation.   But it is a miserable and a wrong kind of Resignation which dwells in that man, who sinks down, beaten and hopeless, in the presence of a recognised evil.   Such a man may be, in a sense, resigned : but he cannot possibly be content.

If you should ever, when you have reached middle age, turn over the diary or the letters you wrote in the hopeful though foolish days when you were eighteen or twenty, you will be aware how quietly and gradually the lesson of Resignation has been taught you.   You would have got into a terrible state of excitement if any one had told you then that you would have to forego your most cherished hopes and wishes of that time: and it would have tried you even more severely to be assured that, in not many years, you would not care a single straw for the things and the persons who were then uppermost in your mind and heart. What an entirely new set of friends and interests is that which now surrounds you: and how completely the old ones are gone! Gone, like the sunsets you remember in the summers of your childhood: gone, like the primroses that grew in the woods where you wandered as a boy. Said my friend Smith to me, a few days ago: 'You remember Emily Jones, and all about that? I met her yesterday, after ten years. She is a fat, middle-aged, ordinary-looking woman. What a terrific fool I was!' Smith spoke to me in the confidence of friendship: yet I think he was a little mortified at the heartiness with which I agreed with him on the subject of his former folly. He had got over it completely: and in seeing that he was (at a certain period) a fool, he had come to discern that of which his friends had always been aware. Of course, early interests do not always die out. You remember Dr. Chalmers: and the ridiculous exhibition about the wretched little likeness of an early sweetheart, not seen for forty years, and long since in her grave. You remember the singular way in which he signified his remembrance of her, in his

famous and honoured age. I don't mean the crying:
nor the walking up and down the garden walk
calling her by fine names. I mean the taking out his
card: not his *carte*; you could understand *that*: but
his visiting-card bearing his name; and sticking it
behind the portrait with two wafers. Probably it
pleased him to do so: and assuredly it did harm to
no one else. And we have all heard of the like
things. Early affections are sometimes, doubtless,
cherished in the memory of the old. But still, more
material interests come in: and the old affection
is crowded out of its old place in the heart. And
so, those comparatively fanciful disappointments sit
lightly. The romance is gone. The mid-day sun
beats down: and *there* lies the dusty way. When
the resolute and judicious mother of Christopher
North stopped his marriage with a person she
deemed unsuitable, we are told that the future professor nearly went mad; and that he never quite
got over it. But really, judging from his writings
and his biography, he bore up under it, after a little,
wonderfully well.

But looking back to the days which the old yellow
letters bring back, you will think to yourself, Where
are the hopes and anticipations of that time? You
expected to be a great man, no doubt. Well, you
know you are not. You are a small man: and never
will be anything else: yet you are quite resigned.
If there be an argument which stirs me to indigna-

tion at its futility; and to wonder that any mortal ever regarded it as of the slightest force : it is that which is set out in the famous soliloquy in *Cato*, as to the Immortality of the Soul. Will any sane man say, that if in this world you wish for a thing very much, and anticipate it very clearly and confidently, you are therefore sure to get it ? If that were so, many a little schoolboy would end by driving his carriage and four, who ends by driving no carriage at all. I have heard of a man whose private papers were found after his death all written over with his signature as he expected it would be when he became Lord Chancellor. Let us say his peerage was to be as Lord Smith. There it was, SMITH, C., SMITH, C., written in every conceivable fashion : so that the signature, when needed, might be easy and imposing. That man had very vividly anticipated the woolsack, the gold robe, and all the rest. It need hardly be said he attained none of these. The famous argument, you know of course, is that man has a great longing to be immortal; and that therefore he is sure to be immortal. Rubbish! It is not true that any longing after immortality exists in the heart of a hundredth portion of the race. And if it were true, it would prove immortality no more, than the manifold signatures of SMITH, C., proved that Smith was indeed to be Chancellor. No: we cling to the doctrine of a Future Life : we could not live without it : but we believe it, not because of undefined longings within ourselves, not because of reviving plants and flowers, not because of the chrysalis and the butterfly : but because 'our Saviour Jesus Christ hath abolished death, and brought light and immortality to light through the gospel.'

There is something very curious, and very touching, in thinking how clear and distinct, and how often recurring, were our early anticipations of things that were never to be. In this world, the fact is for the most part the opposite of what it should be to give force to Plato's (or Cato's) argument : the thing you vividly anticipate is the thing that is least likely to come. The thing you don't much care for : the thing you don't expect : is the likeliest. And even if the event prove what you anticipated; the circumstances, and the feeling of it, will be quite different from what you anticipated. A certain little girl three years old was told that in a little while she was to go with her parents to a certain city, a hundred miles off : a city which may be called Altenburg as well as anything else. It was a great delight to her to anticipate that journey, and to anticipate it very circumstantially. It was a delight to her to sit down at evening on her father's knee : and to tell him all about how it would be in going to Altenburg. It was always the same thing. Always, first, how sandwiches would be made : how they would all get into the carriage (which would come round to the door), and drive away to a certain railway station ! how they would get their tickets; and the train would come up ; and they would all get into a carriage together, and lean back in corners, and eat the sandwiches, and look out of the windows : and so on. But when the journey was actually made, every single circumstance in the little girl's anticipations proved wrong. Of course, they were not intentionally made wrong. Her parents would have carried out to the letter, if they could, what the little thing had so clearly pictured and so often repeated. But it proved to be needful to go by an entirely different way and in an entirely different fashion. All those little details, dwelt on so much, and with so much interest, were things never to be. It is even so with the anticipations of larger and older children. How distinctly, how fully, my friend, we have pictured out to our minds a mode of life, a home and the country round it, and the multitude of little things which make up the habitude of being : which we long since resigned ourselves to knowing could never prove realities ! No doubt, it is all right and well. Even St. Paul, with all his gift of prophecy, was not allowed to foresee what was to happen to himself. You know how he wrote that he would do a certain thing, 'as soon as I shall see how it will go with me !'

But our times are in the Best Hand. And the one thing about our lot, my reader, that we may think of with perfect contentment, is that they are so. I know nothing more admirable in spirit, and few things more charmingly expressed, than that little poem by Miss Waring which sets out that comfortable thought. You know it, of course. You should have it in your memory; and let it be one of the first things your children learn by heart. It may well come (if you live in Scotland) next after *O God of Bethel:* it breathes the self-same tone. And let me close these thoughts with one of its verses :

> There are briars besetting every path,
>   Which call for patient care :
> There is a cross in every lot,
>   And an earnest need for prayer :
> But a lowly heart that leans on Thee,
>   Is happy anywhere !

CHAPTER IX.

A REMINISCENCE OF THE OLD TIME :

BEING SOME THOUGHTS ON GOING AWAY.

OU know, I am sure, how as we advance in life, hours come in which we feel an impulse to sit down for a little, and try to revive an old feeling, before it dies away. And many of our old feelings are dying away; and will ultimately die out altogether. It is partly through use; and partly because our system, physical and psychical, is growing less sensitive as we go on. We do not feel things now as we used to do. We are getting stronger: the robuster nerves of middle age do not receive the vivid impressions of earlier years; and there are faintly-flavoured things which they cease to appreciate at all. We have come out from the green fields, and from the shady wood-lands: and we are plodding along the beaten high-way of life. It is the noon now; not perhaps without some tendency to decline towards evening:

and we look back to the dawn and to the morning, when the air was cool and fresh, and when the sky was clear. And we have grown hardened to the rougher work of the present time. We have all got lines, pretty deeply drawn, upon our faces: and a good many grey hairs. And if one could see a middle-aged soul, no doubt you would see about it something analogous to being wrinkled and grey. No doubt you would likewise discern something analogous to the thickening and toughening of the skin in the case of the middle-aged hand. Neither hand nor heart feels so keenly.

There is no help for it; but still one cannot help regretting it, the way in which things lose their first fresh relish by use. We ought to be getting more enjoyment out of things than we do. A host of very small matters, which we pass without ever noticing, would afford us real and sensible pleasure if we had not grown so accustomed to them. Prince Lee Boo, as we used to read, was moved to ecstatic wonder and delight by the upright walls and the flat ceiling of an ordinary room. They were new to him. There was a young Indian chief, many years ago, who came from the Far West to London, and was for a season a lion in fashionable society. He was a manly, clever young fellow: but in his English months he never got over his unsophisticated enjoyment of the furniture of English houses. And thoughtless folk despised him, when they ought rather to have envied him, as they witnessed his delight in the contemplation of a dinner-table where he had been accustomed to see a stretched bull's hide : and of plates, knives and forks, carpets, mirrors, window-curtains, and wash-hand stands. All these great luxuries, and a thousand more, *he* appreciated at their true value : while civilized men and women, through familiarity, had arrived at contempt of them. Which was right, the civilized folk or the savage man? Is it the human being who sees least in the things around him that ought to be proud : or is not the man rather to be envied who discerns in simple matters qualities and excellences which others do not discern? If you had so worn out your eyes by constant use, that you could no longer see, *that* would be nothing to plume yourself on ; you would have no right to think you had attained a position of superiority to the remainder of the human race, in whom the optic nerve still retained its sensitive-ness. Yet there are people who are quite proud that their mind has had its nerves of sensation partially paralyzed; and who would like you to think that those nerves are entirely paralyzed. 'I don't remark these things,' they will say with an air of disdain, when you point out to them some of the little material advantages which we enjoy in this country now-a-days. They convey that they think you must be a weak-minded person because you do remark these things : because you still feel it a curious thing to leave London in the morning, and after ten hours and a half of unfatiguing travelling to reach Edinburgh in the evening : or because you still are conscious of a simple-minded wonder when you send a message five hundred miles and get your answer back in a quarter of an hour. If there be a mortal whom I despise, it is the man who is anxious to impress you with the fact that he does not care in the least for anything. The human being who is proud because he has reached the *nil admirari* stage, is just a human being who is proud because a creeping paralysis has numbed his soul.

Yet without giving in to it, and without being proud of it, you are aware that the keen relish goes from that which you grow accustomed to. I have indeed heard it said concerning certain individuals whose supercilious and lofty air testified that some sudden rise in life had turned their head, that they lived in a state of constant surprise at finding themselves so respectable. But this statement was not true in its full extent. For after being for several years in a position for which nature never intended him, even Dr. Bumptious (before his elevation his name was Toady) must have grown to a certain measure accustomed to it. Even other people got accustomed to it. And though his incompetence for his place remained just as glaring as ever, they ceased to remark it; and came to accept it as something in the nature of things. You know, we do not perplex ourselves by inquiring every morning why there are such creatures as wasps, toads, and rattlesnakes. But if these beings were of a sudden introduced into this world for the first time, it would be different.

It is to be lamented, that the very fresh and sensible enjoyment which we derive from very little things when they are new to us, passes so completely away when they grow familiar. I remark that my fellow-creatures, who inhabit houses in this street, are very far from being duly thankful for the great privilege we possess, in having a post-office at the end of it. You write your letters in the forenoon after you have completed your more serious work; and upon each envelope you stick the representation of a face which is very familiar to us all, and very dear. If you are a wise man, you post your letters for yourself: and accordingly the first thing you do daily, when you go forth to your out-door business or duty, is to proceed to that little opening which receives the expression of so much care, so much kindness, so much worry, so much joy and sorrow, and to drop the documents in. Not many of the human beings who post letters and who receive them have any habitual sense of the supreme luxury they enjoy in that familiar institution of the post-office. Into that little opening goes your letter: a penny secures its admission, and obtains for it very distinguished consideration : and in a little while the most ingenious mechanism that has been devised by the most ingenious minds is hard at work conveying your letter, at tremendous speed, by land or sea : till next morning, unerring as the eagle upon its eyrie, it swoops down upon the precise dwelling at which you aimed it. When I say it swoops down upon a dwelling in the country, I mean to express poetically the fact that it comes jogging along in a cart drawn by a little white pony, which stops for the purposes of conversation whenever it meets anybody in the wooded lane I have in my mind. But in saying that the inhabitants of this street are not duly thankful for the post-office at the corner, I did not mean merely that they fail to understand what a blessing to Britain the system of postal communication is. Everybody, on ordinary days, fails to understand *that*. I was thinking of something else. I was thinking of the luxury of having a receiving-house so near. When I lived in the country, the post-office was five miles distant : and if you missed the chance of sending away your letters in the morning by the cart drawn by the white pony, you must wait till next day ; or you must send a special messenger to the old-fashioned town of red freestone dwellings, standing by a classic river's side. Let not that town be mentioned save in complimentary terms. Let me learn by the misfortune of another. An eminent native of the district which surrounds it, known in the world of letters, once upon a time published some remarks upon that town, disguising its pretty name in another of somewhat ludicrous sound. And when that eminent man shortly afterwards strove to persuade the inhabitants to send him to represent them in Parliament, the old offence was raked up, and it did him harm. This, however, is a digression. Let us return. When I came from the country, to live in this city, I felt it a great privilege, and something to be enjoyed freshly every time, to take my letters to the post-office two hundred yards off. It was delightful. Not once in the day, but (if need were) half a dozen times, could you write your letter, and in three minutes have it in the post-office. There was something very fresh and enjoyable in the reflection, as you stood by the receiving-house window, Now here in these minutes I am in the same position in which half an hour's smart driving, or an hour and a quarter's steady walking, would have placed one in departed days! Wonderful! But now, after several years of the enjoyment of this privilege, the fresh wonder has worn away. The edge of enjoyment is dulled. And though I try hard, in going to the post-office, to feel what a blessing it is, I cannot feel it as I would wish. Yes, the enjoyment of the post-office is gone in great measure: even as the unutterable greenness discerned by the stranger goes from the summer trees among which you have come to feel yourself at home: even as the sound of Niagara becomes inaudible to the waiters at the Niagara Hotel: even as the Bishop who was plucked at college gradually ceases to be astonished at finding himself a Bishop: even as Miss Smith, in a few weeks after she is married, no longer feels it strange to be called Mrs. Jones: even as the readers of what is with bitter irony called a *religious newspaper* lose their first bewilderment at finding a human animal writing an article filled with intentional misrepresentation, lying, and slandering, and ending the article by taking God to witness that in abusing the man he hates for his success and eminence, he is actuated by a simple regard to the Divine glory.

And thus it is, remembering how the old time and the old way fade out, that the writer has resolved to give a little space of comparative rest to reviving (as far as may be) something which used to have a strongly felt character of its own, in years which are gone, and which are melting into blue distance fast. Let me seek to bring up again the atmosphere of Going Away, as it used to be, and to be felt. No doubt, there is a certain fancifulness about moral atmospheres: not all men feel them alike; and there are robust natures which probably do not feel them at all. When a man comes to describe a house, a landscape, a mode of life, not as these are in literal fact, but as these impress himself: then we get into a realm of uncertainty and fancy. When a man ceases to say of a dwelling, that it is built of red brick, that it has so many windows in front, that it is so many stories high, that it has evergreens of such kinds round it, and the like : and when the man goes on to describe the house by quite other characteristics —saying that it is a sleepy-looking house, a dull house, a hospitable-looking house, an eerie strange-looking house, a house that makes you feel queer —then you feel that though the man may convey to another man, who is in sympathy with himself, a very true impression of the fact as it presents itself to him, still there are many people to whom such descriptions are really quite unintelligible; and that those who are most capable of understanding them are least likely to agree as to their truth. It is so with what I have called moral atmospheres : the pervading characteristic of a time, a scene, a way of life, a human being. Nor can it be admitted that there is anything of morbid sensitiveness in being keenly aware of these. Most people know the vague sort of sense that you have of being in a remote pastoral country, or of being in a busy town. You feel a difference in the morning whenever you awake; and before you have fully gathered up your consciousness: it pervades your very dreams. You remember periods of your life about

which there was a kind of flavour; strongly-felt,
but indescribable to others: not to be expressed in
any spoken words: Mendelssohn or Beethoven
might have come near expressing it in music: and
it comes back upon you in reading some passage *In Memoriam* which has nothing to do with
it, or in looking at the first yellow crocus in the
cold March sunshine, or in walking along a lane
with blossoming hawthorn on either hand, or in
smelling the blossoms of an apple-tree. And when
you look back, you feel the atmosphere surround
you again, with its fragrance a good deal gone,
and with its colours faded. It is a misty, ghost-
like image of a past life and its surroundings, that
steals vaguely before your mental sight: and possibly it cannot be more accurately or expressively
described, than by saying that the old time comes
over you.

Doubtless external scenery has a great deal to
do in the production of that general sense of a
character pervading one's whole mode of life, which
I mean by a moral atmosphere. It is especially
so if you lead a lonely life: or if you have not
many companions, and these not very energetic or
striking. How well many men in orders remember
the peculiar flavour of the time when they first
began their parochial duty! Years afterwards,
you go and walk up and down in the church where
you preached your first sermons; and you try to

awaken the feeling of that departed time. It comes
back, in a ghostly unsubstantial way : sometimes it
refuses to be wakened up at all. And the feeling,
whatever it may be, is (to many men) very mainly
flavoured by the outward scene in which that time
was spent. I can easily believe that there are
persons on whose mood and character no appreciable impression is produced by external scenery :
probably the reader knows one or two. They have
usually high cheek-bones, smoke-dried complexions,
and disagreeable voices : they think Mr. Tennyson
a fool, and tell you that *they* cannot understand
him, in a tone that conveys that in their judgment
nobody can. I have known men who declared
honestly that they did not think Westminster
Abbey in the least a more solemn place than a
red brick meeting-house with a flat ceiling, and
with its inner walls chastely whitewashed, or pa-
pered with a paper representing yellow marble.
My acquaintance with such individuals was slight :
and by mutual consent it speedily ceased. Give
us the man who frankly tells you how different a
man he is in this place from what he is in that :
how outward nature casts its light or its shadow
upon all his thinking and feeling. What would
you be, my friend, if you lived for months by a
misty Shetland sea ; or amid a wide Irish bogland ;
or in a wooden châlet at Meyringen ; or on a flat
French plain, with white ribbons of highway

stretching across it, bordered with weary poplars; or under the shadow of castle-crowned crags upon the Rhine; or amid the bustle of a great commercial town; or in the classic air of an ancient university city, with a feast of Gothic everywhere for the eyes, and with courts of velvety turf that has been velvety turf for ages? But here I get into the region of the fanciful; and though holding very strongly a certain theory about these things, I am not going to set it out here. Yet I cannot but believe, that when you read men's written thoughts, you may readily, if you be of a sensitive nature, *feel* the surroundings amid which they were written. Turn over the volume which was written in the country, by a man keenly alive to outward things and their influences; and you will be aware of a breeziness about the pages: a fresher air seems to breathe from them, the atmosphere of that simple life and its little cares. Turn over the Best of all books: read especially the accounts of patriarchal times in Genesis: and (inspiration apart) you will feel the presence of something indefinitely more than the bare facts recorded. You will feel the fresh breeze come to you over the ocean of intervening centuries: you will know that a whole life and its interests surround you again. And there seems to me no more marked difference between fictitious stories written by men of genius and written by commonplace people, than this: that the commonplace people make you aware

of just the incidents they record; while the man of
genius makes you aware of a vast deal more—of
the entire atmosphere of the surrounding circumstances and concerns and life. You will understand
what is meant when I remind you of the wonderful
way in which the battle of Waterloo is made to
surround and pervade a certain portion of the train
of events recorded in that thoroughly true history,
Mr. Thackeray's *Vanity Fair.*

Now all this is pleasant. I mean to the writer;
not necessarily to the reader. The writer has to
produce a multitude of pages, which to produce is
of the nature of grave work; and in them he must
hold right on, and discuss his subject under no
small sense of responsibility. But such pages as
this are his play; and he may without rebuke turn
hither and thither, and pluck the wild flowers on
either side of the path. Oh, how hard work it is to
write a sermon; and (when one is in the vein) how
easy it is to write an essay! And in saying that all
this is pleasant, the thing present to the author's
mind was the very devious course which his train
of thought has followed since the first sentence of
this dissertation was written. I have a great respect
for certain men, who write in a logical and scholarly
way. I admire and esteem such. When I read
their productions at all, I do so after breakfast,
when one's wits are fully awake. But in the evening,
by the fireside, when the day's work and worry are

over, and there remains the precious little breathing-space, I would rather not read them. Neither do I desire here to write like them.

Going Away is my subject. Going Away and its atmosphere, as it used to be, and as it is to many people now. Going Away from home. Not Going Away for ever; not Going Away for a long time; not Going Away under painful circumstances. Ordinary and commonplace Going Away.

And let me tell you, intrepid travellers, who think nothing of flying away to London, to Paris, to Chamouni, to Constantinople; that Going Away for a week or two, and to a distance not exceeding a hundred miles, is a very serious thing to a quiet, stay-at-home person. A multitude of contingencies suggest themselves in its prospect: there is the vague fear of the great, terrible outside world. It is as when a little boat, that has been lying safe in some sheltered cove, puts out to sea, to face the full might of winds and waves; when a lonely human being, who for months has plodded his little round of work and care, looking at the same scenes, and conversing with the same people, musters courage to go away for a little while. There is a considerable inertia to overcome; some effort of resolution is needed. When you have lived an unvaried life for many weeks in a quiet country place, your wish is to sit still. Yet there are great advantages which belong to people who have seen little or nothing.

They have so keen a sense of interest, and so lively an impression of the facts, in beholding something new. By-and-by they come to take it easily. You look out of the window of the railway carriage, and in reply to something said by a fellow traveller, you say, 'Ah, that's Berne, or that's Lausanne,' and you return to your *Times*, or your *Saturday Review*. You look forth on the left hand, as the train rounds a curve, and say, 'Strasburg spire; very fine. Four hundred and fifty feet high. It does not look nearly so much from this point.' Now once it was very different. It was a vivid sensation to see for the first time some town in England, or some lake or hill in Scotland. My friend Smith told me that once, for more than six years, beginning when he was eight and twenty, he never had stirred ten miles from his home and his parish, save when he went in the autumn for a few weeks to the seaside; and then he went always to the same place, a journey of four hours or so. It would have done him much good, had he been able sometimes through those years, which were very anxious and very trying ones, to have the benefit of a little change of scene. But he could not afford it; and in those days of depressed fortune, he had, literally, not a friend in this world, beyond the little circle of his own home. He had, indeed, some acquaintances; but they were able to understand him, or sympathise with him, about as much as a donkey could. But

better days came; as (let us trust) they will come,
through hard work and self-denial to most men, by
God's blessing; and Smith could venture on the
great enterprise of a journey to London. Ah! an
express train was a great thing to him; and a
journey of three hundred miles an endless pilgrimage. And he told me himself (he is in his grave
now, and no one who knew him will know him by
what has been said of him) that it was an extraordinary feeling to look out of the carriage-window,
and to think, Now Cambridge is only a few miles
off, over these flats! And farther on, when the
trains glided by the capital of the Fens, and the
noble mass of Peterborough Cathedral loomed
through the misty morning, it was a stranger object
to him than St. Sophia or even the Mosque of Omar
would be to you; and he thought how curious a
thing it would be to live on that wide plain, in that
quiet little city, under the shadow of that magnificent pile. Probably, my friend, you have been long
enough in many striking places to feel their first
interest and impression go: to feel their moral
atmosphere become inappreciable. You feel all *that*
keenly at first; but gradually the place becomes
just like anywhere else. After a while, the inner
atmosphere overpowers the outer: the world within
the breast gives its tone and colour to the scene
around you. I believe firmly, that if you want to
know a place vividly and really (I mean a town

of moderate extent), you ought to stay in it just a day and no more. By remaining longer, you may come to know all the churches and shops, and the like; but you will lose the pervading atmosphere and character of the whole. First impressions are always the most vivid; and I firmly believe they are in the vast majority of cases the most truthful. An observant and sensitive man, spending just a day in a town with twenty thousand inhabitants, knows what kind of place that town is, far better than an ordinarily observant person who has lived in it for twenty years.

The truth is, that a little of a thing is usually far more impressive than the whole of it, or than a great deal of it. Don't you remember how, when you were a child, lying in bed in the morning, you used to watch the day-light through the shutters? And you remember how bright it looked, through the narrow line where the shutters hardly met: it was like a glowing fire. At length, the shutters were thrown back, and they let in all the day; and it was nothing so bright. Even if the morning was sunshiny, there was a sad falling off: and perhaps the morning was dull and rainy. Even so is the glimpse of Peterborough from the passing express train, infinitely finer than the view of Peterborough to the man who lives in it all the year round. Even so has the quiet life of a cathedral city, a charm to the visitor for a day, who has come from a land where cathedrals are not, which fades away to such as spend all their days in the venerable place; and come to have associations not merely of glorious architecture and sublime music, but likewise of many petty ambitions, jealousies, diplomacies, and disappointments; and in short of Mr. Slope and Mrs. Proudie. Yes, a little of a thing is sometimes infinitely better than the whole: and it is the little which especially has power to convey that general estimate of a pervading characteristic which we understand by perceiving the moral atmosphere. And besides this, you may have a surfeit of even the things you like best. You heartily enjoy a little country Gothic church: you linger on every detail of it: it is a pure delight. But a great cathedral is almost too much: it wearies you: it overwhelms you. You may get, through one summer day, as much enjoyment out of Sonning Church, as out of York Minster. That perfection of an English parish church, with its perfect vicarage, by the beautiful Thames, is like a friend with whom you can cordially shake hands: the great minster is like a monarch to be approached on bended knee. Most people remember a case in which a thousandth part would have been far better than the whole: I mean the Great Exhibition in that fine shed which the nation declined to buy. You would have enjoyed the sight of a little of what was gathered there: but the whole was a fearful task to get through. I never beheld more wearied, dazed, stupified, disgusted, and miserable countenances, than among rich and poor under that roof. I wonder whether any mortal ever really enjoyed that glare and noise and hubbub; or felt his soul expanded under the influence of that huge educational institution. Too many magazines or books, too, coming together, convert into a toil what ought to be a pleasure. You look at the mass; and you cannot help thinking what a deal you have to get through. And that thought is in all cases fatal to enjoyment. Whenever it enters the heart of a little boy, contemplating his third plate of plum-pudding, the delight implied in plum-pudding has vanished. Whenever the hearer listens to the preacher describing what he is to do in the first and second place, and so on to the fifth or sixth, the enjoyment with which most sermons are heard is sensibly diminished. And even if you be very fond of books, there is a sense of desolation in being turned loose in a library of three hundred thousand volumes. That huge array is an incubus on your spirit. There is far more sensible pleasure when you go into a friend's snug little study, and diligently survey his thousand or twelve hundred books. And you know that if a man has a drawing-room a hundred feet long, he takes pains to convert that large room into a little one by enclosing a warm space round the fire with great screens for his evening retreat. Yes, a little is generally much better than a great deal.

A thing which precedes Going Away, is packing up. And this the wise man will do for himself: the more so, if he cannot afford to have any one to do it for him. There is a great pleasure in doing things for yourself. And here is one of the compensations of poverty. You open for yourself the parcel of new books you have bought; and with your own hand you cut the leaves. A great peer, of course, could not do this, I suppose. The volumes would be prepared for his reading, and laid before him with nothing to do but to read them. Now, it ought to be understood, that the reading of a book is by no means the only use you can put it to, or the only good you can get out of it. There is the enjoyment of stripping off the massive wrappings in which the volumes travelled from the bookseller's shop, through devious ways, to the country home. There is the enjoyment of cutting the leaves: which, if you have a large ivory paper knife, is a very sensible one. There is the enjoyment of laying the volumes, after their leaves are cut, upon your study table; and sitting down in an arm-chair by the fireside, and calmly and thoughtfully looking at them. There is the enjoyment of considering earnestly the place where they shall be put on your shelves, and then of placing them there, and of arranging the volumes which have been turned out to make room for them. All these pleasures you have, quite apart from the act of reading the books : and all these pleasures are denied to the rich and mighty man, who is too great to be allowed to do things for himself. He has only the end: we have both the end and the means which lead up to it. And the greater part of human enjoyment is the enjoyment of means, not of ends. There is as much solid satisfaction in going out and looking at your horse in his warm stable, as in riding or driving him. An eminent sportsman begins a book in which he gives an account of his exploits in hunting in a foreign country, by fondly telling how happy he was in petting up his old guns till they looked like new, and in preparing and packing ammunition in the prospect of setting off on his expedition. You can see that these tranquil and busy days of anticipation and preparation at home were at least as enjoyable as the more exciting days of actual sport which followed. Now, however much a duke might like to do all this, I suppose his nobility would oblige him to forego the satisfaction.

If you have a wife and children (and for the purposes of this essay I suppose you to have both,) the multitude of trunks and packing-cases in which their possessions are bestowed in the prospect of going away, are sought out and packed apart from any exertion or superintendence on your part. Your share consists in writing addresses for them; and in counting up the twenty-three things that are assembled in the lobby before they are loaded on cart, cab, or carriage. I have remarked it as a curious thing, that when a man with his wife and two or three children and three or four servants go to the seaside in autumn, the articles of luggage invariably amount to twenty-three. And it has ever been to me a strange and perplexing thought, how so many trunks and boxes are needed: and how, through various changes by land and sea, they get safely to their destination. There are few positions which awaken more gratitude and satisfaction in the average human being, than (having arrived at the sea-side place) to see the twenty-three things safe upon the little pier, after the roaring steamer which brought them has departed, and the little crowd has dispersed: when, amid the stillness, suddenly become audible, you tell the keeper of the pier to send your baggage to the dwelling which is to be your temporary home. A position even more gratifying is as follows: when, returning to town, your holiday over, you succeed, by the aid of two liberally-tipped porters, in recovering all your effects from the luggage-van of the railway train, amid an awful crowd and confusion on the platform, and accumulating them into a heap, for whose conveyance you would assuredly be called to pay extra but for the judicious largesse already alluded to: then in seeing them piled in and upon three cabs, in which you slowly wend your way to your door; and finally, in the lobby whence they originally started, counting up your twenty-three things once more. Yes, there is much pleasure attendant on the possession and conveyance of luggage: a pleasure mingled with pain, indeed, like most of our pleasures: a pleasure dashed with anxiety and clouded with confusion, yet ultimately passing into a sense of delightful rest and relief, as you count up the twenty-three things and find them all right, which you had hardly dared to hope they would ever be.

So much having been said concerning the general luggage of the family, let us return to the thought of your own personal packing. You pack your own portmanteau, arranging things in that order which long usage has led you to esteem as the best. And if you be a clergyman, you always introduce into that receptacle your sermon-case with two or three sermons. You do this, if you be a wise man, though there should not appear the faintest chance of your having to preach anywhere : having learned by experience how often and how unexpectedly such chances occur. And then, when your portmanteau is finally strapped up and ready to go, you look at it with a moralising glance, and think how little a thing it looks to hold such a great deal. It is like a general principle, including a host of individual cases. It is like a bold assertion, which you accept without thinking of all it implies. And in a short time that compendium of things immediately needful will be one among a score like it in the luggage-van. Thus, the philosopher may reflect, is every man's own concern the most interesting to himself, because every man knows best what is involved in his own concern.

There are many associations about the battered old leathern object : and it is sad to remark that it is wearing out. It is to many people a sensible trial to throw aside anything they have had for a long time. And this thing especially, which has faithfully kept so many things you intrusted to it, and which has gone with you to so many places, seems to cast a silent appealing look at you when you think it is getting so shabby that you must throw it aside. Some day you and I, my friend, will be like an old portmanteau ; and we shall be pushed out of the way to make room for something fresh. Probably it is worldly wisdom to treat trunks and men like that single-minded person Mr. Uppish, who steadfastly cuts his old friends as he gradually gets into a superior social stratum. Doubtless he has his reward.

It is invariably on Monday morning that certain human beings Go Away, in the grave and formal manner which has been spoken of. I mean with an entire family, and with the twenty-three trunks, many of them very large ones. Not unfrequently, a perambulator is present; also a nursery crib. And going at that especial period of the week, there is a certain thing inevitably associated with Going Away. That thing is the periodical called the *Saturday · Review*. It comes every Monday morning; and you cut the leaves after breakfast and glance over it: but you put off the reading of it till the evening. But on those travelling days, this paper is associated with the forenoon. Breakfast is a hasty meal that day. The heavy baggage, if you dwell in the country, has gone away early in a cart: the railway station is of course five miles off. And then, just a quarter of an hour after the period you had named to your man-servant, round comes the phaeton which can hold so much. It comes at the very moment you really desired to have it: for knowing that your servant will always be exactly a quarter of an hour too late, you always order it just a quarter of an hour before the time you really want it. Phaeton of chocolate hue, picked out with red and white: horse of the sixteen hands and an inch, jet black of colour, well-bred in blood, and gentle of nature; where are you both to-night? Through the purple moorlands, through the rich cornfields, along the shady lanes, up the High-street of the little town, we have gone together: but the day came at length when you had to go one way and I another: and we have each gone through a good deal of hard work doubtless since then. Pleasant it is driving home from the town in the winter afternoon, and reaching your door when it has grown pretty dark: pleasant is the flood of mellow light that issues forth when your door is opened : pleasant is it to witness the unloading of the vast amount and variety of things which, in various receptacles, that far from ponderous equipage could convey. Pleasant to witness the pile that accumulates on the topmost step before your door: pleasant to behold the bundle of books and magazines from the reading-club : pleasanter to see the less frequent parcel of those which you can call your own: pleasant to see the manifold brown-paper parcels enter the house, which seems to be such a devouring monster, craving ceaseless fresh supply. All this while the night is falling fast ; and the great trees look down ghost-like upon the little bustle underneath them. Then phaeton and horse depart: and in a little you go round to the stable-yard, and find your faithful steed, now dry and warm, in his snug stall, eagerly eating; yet bearing in a kindly way a few pats on the neck and a few pulls of the ears. And your faithful man-servant is quite sure to have some wonderful intelligence to convey to you, picked up in town that afternoon. In the country, you have not merely the enjoyment of rich summer scenery; of warm sunsets and green leaves shining golden : there is a peculiar pleasure known to the thorough country man, in the most wintry aspects of nature. The bleak trees and sky outside, the moan of the rising wind presaging a wild night, and the brawl of the swollen brook that runs hard by, all make one value the warmth and light and comfort within doors about forty times as much as you could value these simple blessings in a great city, where they seem quite natural, and matters of course. Of course, a great man would not care for these things; and would despise the small human being that does care for them. Let the great man take his own way; and let the small human being be allowed to follow his in peace.

This, however, is a deviation to an evening on which you come home : whereas our proper subject is a morning on which you go away from home. The phaeton has come to the door : many little things go in : finally the passengers take their seats, and the thick rugs are tucked in over their knees : then you take the reins (for you drive yourself), and you wind away outward till you enter the highway. The roads are smooth and firm : and for all the heavy load behind him, the black horse trots briskly away. Have I not beheld a human being, his wife, two children, a man-servant, and a woman-servant, steadily skimming along at a respectable nine miles an hour, with but one living creature for all the means of locomotion ? And the living creature was shining and plump, and unmistakably happy. The five miles are overcome, and you enter the court-yard of your little railway station. There, in a heap, cunningly placed on the platform where the luggage-van may be expected to rest when the train stops, is your luggage. The cart has been faithful: there are the twenty-three things. You have driven the last mile or two under a certain fear lest you might be too late; and that fear will quicken an unsophisticated country pulse. But you have ten minutes to spare. There are no people but your own party to divide the attention of the solitary porter. At length, a mile off, along the river bank, you discern the sinuous train: in a little, the tremendously energetic locomotive passes by you, and the train is at rest. You happily find a compartment which is empty; and there you swiftly bestow your living charge: and having done this you hasten to witness the safe embarkation of the twenty-three trunks and packages. All this must be done rapidly: and of course you take much more trouble than a more experienced traveller would. And when at length you hurriedly climb into your place, you sink down in your seat, and feel a delicious sense of quiet. The morning has been one of worry, after all. But now you are all right, for the next four hours. And that is a long look forward. You keenly appreciate this blink of entire rest. Your unaccustomed nerves have been stretched by that fear of being late:

then there was the hurry of getting the children into their carriage, and seeing after the twenty-three things: and now comes a reaction. For a few miles it is enough just to sit still, and look at the faces beside you and opposite you: and especially to watch the wonder imprinted on the two round little faces looking out of the window. First, looking out on either side, there is a deep gorge: great trees: rocks on one side, and on the other side a river. By-and-by the golden gleam of ripe corn-fields in the sunshine on either hand lightens up all faces. And now, forth from its bag comes the *Saturday Review*; and you read it luxuriously, with frequent pauses and lookings out between. Do the keen, sharp, brilliant men who write those trenchant paragraphs ever think of the calm enjoyment they are providing for simple minds? Although you do not care in the least about the subject discussed, there is a keen pleasure in remarking the skill and pith and felicity with which the writer discusses it. You feel a certain satisfaction in thinking that every Monday since that periodical started on its career, you have read it. It is a sort of intellectual thing to do. You reflect with pleasure on the statement made on oath by a witness in a famous trial. He described a certain person as ' a sensible and intelligent man who took in the *Times*.' What proof, then, of scholarly likings, and of power to appreciate what not everybody can appreciate, should be esteemed as furnished by the fact that a man pays for and reads the *Saturday Review?*

Now here, my reader, we have reached the very article of GOING AWAY. Many are the thoughts through which we approached it: here it is at last. Behold the human being, about the first day of August, seated in a corner of a railway carriage, whose cushions are luxurious, and whose general effect is of blue cloth within, and varnished teak without. Opposite the human being sits his wife. Pervading the carriage you may behold two children. And carefully tending them, and seeking vainly to keep them quiet, you may (in very many cases, for such excellent persons are happily not uncommon) discern a certain nurse, who is as a member of that little family circle: more than a trusted and valued servant; even a faithful friend. That is how human beings Go Away. That is the kind of picture which rises in the writer's mind, and in the mind of very many people in a like station in this life, when looking back over not many years.

There is a certain cumbrous enjoyment in all Going Away, bearing with you all these *impedimenta*: even when you are going merely for a Christmas week or the like. But the great Going Away is at the beginning of your autumn holidays. And thinking of this, I feel the prospect change from country to town : I think how the human being, wearied out by many months of hard work amid city bustle and pressure, leaves these behind; how the little children shut up their school-books, and their tired instructors are off for their turn of much-needed recreation : how the churches are emptied, and the streets deserted: how the congregation, assembled in one place on the last Sunday of July, is before the next one scattered far and wide, like the fragments of a bursting bombshell. But it is not now, in this mid-term of work, that one can recall the feelings of commencing holiday-time. Meanwhile, you are out of sympathy with it: and every good thing is beautiful in its time.

Was it worth while, thus to revive things so long past ? It has been pleasant for the writer; and a hundred things not recorded here have been awakened in the retrospect. And when these pages meet the right people's eye, they may serve to re-call simple modes of being and doing which are melting fast away. For the experience of ordinary mortals is remarkably uniform; and most of the people you know are in many respects extremely like yourself. Now let us cease, and sit down and think. There is indeed a temptation to go on. One would rather not stop in the middle of a page; I mean a manuscript page : and it is almost too much for human nature to know that we may add a few sentences more, and they will not be cut off. And there are positions too much for human nature. A sense of power and authority, as a general rule, is more than the average man can bear. Not long since I beheld, in the superhuman dignity of a policeman, something which deeply impressed this on my mind. The kitchen chimney of this dwelling caught fire. It is contrary to municipal law to let your kitchen chimney catch fire; and very properly so: so there was a fine to be paid. On a certain day, I was told there was a policeman in the kitchen, who desired an interview. I proceeded thither, and found him there. No language can convey an idea of the stern and unyielding severity of that eminent man's demeanour. He seemed to think I would probably plead with him to let Justice turn from her rigid course; and he sought, by his whole bearing, to convey that any such pleading would be futile; and that, whatever might be said, the half-crown must be paid, to be applied to public purposes. When I entered his presence, he sternly asked me what was my name. Of course, he knew my name just as well as I did myself: but there was something in the requirement fitted to make me feel my humble position before him. And having received the information, he made a note of it in a little book: and conveying that serious consequences would follow, he departed. A similar manifestation may be found in the case of magistrates in small authority. I have heard of such an individual, who dispensed justice from a seedy little bench with an awful state. He sat upon that bench, all alone: and no matter of the smallest importance ever came before him. Yet when expressing his opinion, he never failed to state that THE COURT thought so and so. A vague impression of dignity thus was made to surround the workings of the individual mind. It once befell, that certain youthful students, in a certain ancient university, had a strife with the police: and being captured by the strong arm of the law, were conveyed before such a magistrate. Sitting upon the judgment seat, he sternly upbraided the youths for their discreditable behaviour; adding, that it gave him special sorrow to witness such lawless violence in the case of individuals who were receiving a university eddication. He did not know, that unhappy magistrate, that there stood at his bar one whose audacious heart quailed not in his presence. 'Stop,' exclaimed that unutterably irreverent youth, interrupting the stern magistrate: 'let me entreat you to pronounce the word properly: it is not EDDICATION, it is EDUCATION.' And the magistrate's dignity suddenly collapsed, like a blown-up bladder when you insert a penknife. This incident is recorded to have happened at Timbuctoo, in the last century. I have no doubt the story is not true. Hardly any stories are true. Yet I have often heard it related. And like the legend of *The Ass and the Archbishop*, which is utterly without foundation, you feel that it ought to be true.

CHAPTER X.

CONCERNING OLD ENEMIES.

T may be assumed as certain, that most readers of this page have on some occasion climbed a high hill. It may be esteemed as probable, that when half-way up, they felt out of breath and tired. It is extremely likely that, having come to some inviting spot, they sat down and rested for a little, before passing on to the summit. Now, my reader, if you have done all that, I feel assured that you must have remarked as a fact that though when you sit down you cease to make progress, you do not go back. Yo do not lose the ground already gained. But if you ever think at all, even though it should be as little as possible, you must have discerned the vexatious truth that in respect of another and more important kind of progress, unless you keep going on, you begin to go back. You struggle, in a moral sense, up the steep slope: and you sit down at the top, thinking to yourself, Now *that* is overcome. But after resting for a while you look round : and lo ! insensibly you have been sliding down ; and you are back again at the foot of the eminence you climbed with so much pain and toil.

There are certain enemies with which every worthy human being has to fight, as regards which you will feel, as you go on, that this principle holds especially true : the principle that if you do not keep going forward, you will begin to lose ground and go backward. It is not enough to knock these enemies on the head for once. In your inexperienced days you will do this : and then, seeing that they look quite dead, you will fancy they will never trouble you any more. But you will find out, to your painful cost, that those enemies of yours and mine must be knocked on the head repeatedly. One knocking, though the severest, will not suffice. They keep always reviving : and struggling to their feet again : a little weak at first through the battering you gave them ; but in a very short time as vigorous and mischievous as ever. The Frenchman, imperfectly acquainted with the force of English words, and eager that extremest vengeance should be wreaked on certain human foes, cried aloud, ' KILL THEM VERY OFTEN !' And *that*, my friend, as regards the worst enemies we have got, is precisely what you and I must do.

If we are possessed of common sense to even a limited amount, we must know quite well who are our worst enemies. Not Miss Limejuice, who tells lies to make you appear a conceited, silly, and ignorant person. Nor Mr. Snarling, who diligently strives to prevent your reaching something you would like, because (as he says) the disappointment will do you good. Not the human curs that gnarl at your heels when you attain some conspicuous success or distinction; which probably you worked hard for, and waited long for. Not these. 'A man's foes,' by special eminence and distinction, are even nearer him than 'they of his own house:' a man's worst enemies are they of his own heart and soul. The enemies that do you most harm; and probably that cause you most suffering; are tendencies and feelings in yourself. If all within the citadel were right: if the troop of thoughts and affections *there* were orderly and well-disposed and well-guided: we should be very independent of the enemies outside. Outside temptation can never make a man do wrong, till something inside takes it by the hand, and fraternizes with it, and sides with it. The bad impulse within must walk up arm in arm with the bad impulse from without, and introduce it to the will, before the bad impulse from without, however powerful it may be, can make man or woman go astray from right. All this, however, may be taken for granted. What I wish to impress on the reader is this: that in fighting with these worst enemies, it is not enough for once

to cut them down, smash them, bray them in a
mortar. If you were fighting with a Chinese invader; and if you were to send a rifle bullet through
his head, or in any other way to extinguish his
life; you would feel that he was done with. You
would have no more trouble from *that* quarter.
But once shoot or slash the ugly beast which is
called Envy, or Self-Conceit, or Unworthy Ambition, or Hasty Speaking, or general Foolishness:
and you need not plume yourself that you will not
be troubled any more with him. Let us call the
beast by the general name of BESETTING SIN:
and let us recognise the fact that though you never
willingly give it a moment's quarter, though you
smash in its head (in a moral sense) with a big
stone, though you kick it (in a moral sense) till it
seems to be lying quite lifeless; in a little while it
will be up again, as strong as ever. And the only
way to keep it down, is to knock it on the skull
afresh every time it begins to lift up its ugly face.
Or, to go back to my first figure: you have climbed,
by a hard effort, up to a certain moral elevation.
You have reached a position, climbing up the great
ascent that leads towards God, at which you feel
resigned to God's will; and kindly disposed to all
your fellow-creatures, even to such as have done
you a bad turn already, and will not fail to do the
like again. You also feel as if your heart were not
set, as it once used to be, upon worldly aims and

ends : but as if you were really day by day working towards something quite different and a great deal higher. You feel humble : patient : charitable. You sit down there, on that moral elevation, satisfied with yourself; and thinking to yourself: Now, I am a humble, contented, kindly, Christian human being; and I am so for life. And let it be said thankfully, If you keep always on the alert, always watching against any retrogression, always with a stone ready to knock any old enemy on the head, always looking and seeking for a strength beyond your own,—you may remain all *that* for life. But if you grow lazy and careless, in a very little while you will have glided a long way down the hill again. You will be back at your old evil ways. You will be eager to get on, and as set on this world as if this world were all: you will find yourself hitting hard the man who has hit you : envying and detracting from the man who has surpassed you : and all the other bad things. Or if you do not retrograde so far as *that*: if you pull yourself up before the old bad impulse within you comes to actual bad deeds : still you will know that the old bad impulse within you is stirring; and that, by God's help, you must give it another stab.

Now this is disheartening. When, by making a great effort, very painful and very long, you have put such a bad impulse down, it is very natural to think that it will never vex you any more. The dragon has been trampled under the horse's feet: its head has been cut off: surely you are done with it. You have ruled your spirit into being right and good: into being magnanimous, kindly, humble. And then you fancied you might go a-head to something more advanced: you had got over the *Pons Asinorum* in the earnest moral work of life. You have extirpated the wolves from your England: and now you may go on to destroy the moles. The wolves are all lying dead, each stabbed to the heart. You honestly believe that you have got beyond them; and that whatever new enemies may assail you, the old ones, at least, are done with finally. But the wolves get up again. The old enemies revive.

I have sometimes wondered whether those men who have done much to help you and me in the putting down of our worst enemies, have truly and finally slain those enemies as far as concerns themselves. Is the man, in reading whose pages I feel I am subjected to a healthful influence, that puts down the unworthy parts of my nature, and that makes me feel more kindly, magnanimous, hopeful, and earnest than when left to myself: is that man, I wonder, always as good himself as for the time he makes me? Or can it be true that the man who seems not merely to have knocked on the head the lower impulses of his own nature; but to have done good to you and me, my friend, by helping to kill those impulses within us: has still to be fighting

away with beasts, like St. Paul at Ephesus: still
to be lamenting, on many days, that the ugly faces
of suspicion, jealousy, disposition to retaliate when
assailed, and the like, keep wakening up and flying
at him again? I fear it is so. I doubt whether
the human being lives in whom evil, however long
and patiently trodden down, does not sometimes
erect its crest, and hiss, and need to be trodden
down again. Vain thoughts and fancies, long extinguished, will waken up: unworthy tendencies
will give a push, now and then. And especially, I
believe it is a great delusion to fancy that a man
who writes in a healthy and kindly strain *is* what
he counsels. If he be an honest and earnest man,
I believe that he is striving after that which he
counsels; and that he is aiming at the spirit and
temper which he sets out. I think I can generally
make out what are a moral or religious writer's
besetting sins, by remarking what are the virtues
he chiefly magnifies. He is struggling after those
virtues: struggling to break away from the corresponding errors and failings. If you find a man who
in all he writes is scrupulously fair and temperate,
it is probable that he is a very excitable and pre-
judiced person : but that he knows it and honestly
strives against it. An author who always expresses
himself with remarkable calmness, is probably by
nature a ferocious and savage man. But you may
see in the way in which he restricts himself in the

matter of adjectives, and in which he excludes the superlative degree, that he is making a determined effort to put down his besetting sin. And probably he fancies, quite honestly, that he has finally knocked that enemy on the head. The truth no doubt is, that it is because the enemy is still alive, and occasionally barking and biting, that it is kept so well in check. There is just enough of the old beast surviving, to compel attention to it : the attention which consists in keeping a foot always on its head, and in occasionally giving it a vehement whack. The most eminent good qualities in human beings are generally formed by diligent putting down of the corresponding evil qualities. It was a stutterer who became the greatest ancient orator. It was a man who still bore on his satyr face the indications of his old satyr nature, who became the best of heathens. And as with Socrates and Demosthenes, it has been with many more. If a man writes always very judiciously, rely upon it he has a strong tendency to foolishness : but he is keeping it tight in check. If a man writes always very kindly and charitably, depend upon it he is fighting to the death a tendency to bitterness and uncharitableness.

A faithful and earnest preacher, resolved to say no more than he has known and felt; and remembering the wise words of Dean Alford, ' What thou hast not by suffering bought, presume thou not to teach ;'

would necessarily show to a sharp observer a great deal of himself and his inner being : even though rigidly avoiding the slightest suspicion of egotism in his preaching. And it need hardly be said that egotism is not to be tolerated in the pulpit.

After you have in an essay or a sermon described and condemned some evil tendency that is in human nature, you are ready to think that you have finally overcome it. And after you have described and commended some good disposition, you are ready to think that you have attained it; and that you will not lose it again. And for the time, if you be an honest man, you *have* smashed the foe ; you *have* gained the vantage ground. But, woe's me, the good disposition dies away ; and the foe gradually revives, and struggles to his legs again. Let us not fancy that because we have been (as we fancied) once right, we shall never go wrong. We must be always watchful. The enemy that seemed most thoroughly beaten, may (apart from God's grace) beat us yet. The publican, when he went up to the temple to pray, expressed himself in a fashion handed down to all ages with the *imprimatur* upon it. Yet, for all his speaking so fairly, the day might come when, having grown a reformed character and gained general approbation, he would stand in a conspicuous place and thank God that he was not as other men. Let us trust *that* day never came. Yet, if the publican had said to himself, as he went down to his house, Now, I have attained an excellent pitch of morality : I am all right : I am a model for future generations : that day would be very likely to come.

It is a humiliating and discouraging sight to behold a man plainly succumbing to an enemy which you fancied he had long got over. You may have seen an individual of more than middle age making a fool of himself by carrying on absurd flirtations with young girls, who were babies in long-clothes when he first was spoony. You would have said, looking at such a man's outward aspect, and knowing something of his history, that years had brought this compensation for what they had taken away, that he would not make a conspicuous ass of himself any more. But the old enemy is too much for him : and oh how long that man's ears would appear, if the inner ass could be represented outwardly! You may have seen such a one, after passing through a discipline which you would have expected to sober him, evincing a frantic exhilaration in the prospect of his third marriage. And you may have witnessed a person evincing a high degree of a folly he had unsparingly scourged in others. I have beheld, in old folk, manifestations of absurdity all very well in the very young, which suggested to me the vision of a stiff, spavined, lame, broken-down old hack, fit only for the knacker, trying to jauntily scamper about in a field with a set of spirited, fresh young colts. And looking at the spectacle, I have reflected on the true statement of the Venerable Bede, that there are no fools like old fools.

But here it may be said, that we are not to suppose that a thing is wrong, unless it can bear to be looked back on in cold blood. Many a word is spoken, and many a deed done, and fitly too, in the warmth of the moment, which will not bear the daylight of a time when the excitement is over. Mr. Caudle was indignant when his wife reminded him of his sayings before marriage. They sounded foolish now in Caudle's ears. This did not suffice to show that those sayings were not very fit at the time: nor does it prove that the tendency to say many things under strong feeling is an enemy to be put down. You have said, with a trembling voice, and with the tear in your eye, things which are no discredit to you: though you might not be disposed to say the like just after coming out of your bath in the morning. You needed to be warmed up to a certain pitch : and then the spark was struck off. And only a very malicious or a very stupid person would remind you of these things when you are not in a correspondent vein.

And now that we have had this general talk about these old enemies, let us go on to look at some of them individually. It may do us good to poke up a few of the beasts, and to make them arise and walk about in their full ugliness : and then to smite them on the head as with a hammer. Let this be a new slaying of the slain, who never can be slain too often.

Perhaps you may not agree with me when I say that one of these beasts is Ambition. I mean unscrupulous self-seeking. You resolved, long ago, to give no harbour to that: and so to exclude the manifold evils that came of it. You determined that you would resolutely refuse to scheme, or push, or puff, or hide your honest opinions, or dodge in any way, for the purpose of getting on. You know how eager some people are to let their light shine before men, to the end that men may think what clever fellows those people are. You know how anxious some men are to set themselves right in newspapers and the like : and to stand fair (as they call it) with the public. You know how some men, when they do any good work, have recourse to means highly analogous to the course adopted by a class of persons long ago, who sounded a trumpet before them in the streets to call attention to their charitable deeds. I know individuals who constantly sound their own trumpet, and that a very brazen one : sound it in conversation, in newspaper paragraphs, in advertisements, in speeches at public meetings. But you, an honest and modest person, were early disgusted by that kind of thing : and you determined that you would do your duty quietly and faithfully, spending all your strength upon your work, and not sparing a large percentage of it for the trumpet. You resolved that you would never admit the thought of setting yourself more favourably before your fellow-creatures. You learned to look your humble position in the face : and to discard the idea of getting any mortal to think you greater or better than you are. Yes : you hope that the petty self-seeking, which keeps some men ever on the strut and stretch, has been outgrown by you. Yet if you would be safe from one of the most contemptible foes of all moral manhood, you must keep your club in your hand ; and every now and then quiet the creature by giving it a heavy blow on the head. St. Paul tells us that he had ' *learned* to be content.' It cost him effort. It cost him time. It was not natural. He came down, we may be sure, with many a heavy stroke, on the innate disposition to repine when things did not go in the way he wanted them. And that is what we must do.

As you look back now, it is likely enough that you recall a time when self-seeking seemed thoroughly dead in you. You were not very old, perhaps : yet you fancied that (by God's help) you had outgrown ambition. You did your work as well as you could ; and in the evening you sat in your easy chair by the fireside : looking not without interest at the feverish race of worldly competition, yet free from the least thought of running in it. As for thinking of your own eminence, or imagining that any one would take the trouble of talking about you, *that* never entered

your mind.   And as you beheld the eager pushing
of other men, and their frantic endeavours to keep
themselves before the human race, you wondered
what worldly inducement would lead you to do the
like.   But did you always keep in that happy condition ?   Did you not, now and then, feel some little
waking up of the old thing : and become aware that
you were being drawn into the current ?   If so, let
us hope that you resolutely came out of it : and
that you found quiet in the peaceful backwater,
apart from that horrible feverish stream.

There is another old enemy, a two-headed monster, that is not done with when it has been killed
once.   It is a near relative of the last : it is the ugly
creature Self-Conceit and Envy.   I call it a two-
headed monster, rather than two monsters ; it is a
double manifestation of one evil principle : Self-
Conceit is the principle as it looks at yourself; Envy
is the same thing as it looks at other men.   I fear it
must be admitted that there is in human nature a
disposition to talk bitterly of people who are more
eminent and successful than yourself : and though
you expel it with a pitchfork, that old enemy will
come back again.   This disposition exists in many
walks of life.   A Lord Chancellor has left on record
his opinion, that nowhere is there so much envy and
jealousy as among the members of the English bar.
A great actor has declared that nowhere is there so

much as among actors and actresses. Several authors have maintained that no human beings are so bitter at seeing one of themselves get on a little, as literary folk. And a popular preacher has been heard to say that envy and detraction go their greatest length among preachers. Let us hope that the last statement is erroneous. But I fear that these testimonies, coming from quarters so various, lead to the conclusion that envy and detraction (which imply self-conceit) are too natural and common everywhere. You may have heard a number of men talking about one man in their own vocation who had got a good deal ahead of them : and who never had done them any harm except thus getting ahead of them : and you may have been amazed at the awful animosity evinced towards the successful man. But success, in others, is a thing which some mortals cannot forgive. You may have known people savagely abuse a man because he set up a carriage, or because he moved to a finer house, or because he bought an estate in the country. You remember the outburst which followed when Macaulay dated a letter from Windsor Castle. Of course, the true cause of the outburst was, that Macaulay should have been at Windsor Castle at all. Let us be thankful, my friend, that such an eminent distinction is not likely to happen either to you or me : we have each acquaintances who would never forgive us if it did. What a raking up of all the sore points in your history would follow, if the Queen were to ask you to dinner! And if you should ever succeed to a fortune, what unspeakable bitterness would be awakened in the hearts of Mr. Snarling and Miss Limejuice! If their malignant glances could lame your horses as you drive by them with that fine new pair, the horses would limp home with great difficulty. And if their eyes could set your grand house on fire, immediately on the new furniture going in, a heavy loss would fall either upon you or the Insurance Company.

But this will not do. As you read these lines, my friend, you picture yourself as the person who attains the eminence and succeeds to the fortune: and you picture Miss Limejuice and Mr. Snarling as two of your neighbours. But what I desire is, that you should change the case: imagine your friend Smith preferred before you: and consider whether there would not be something of the Snarling tendency in yourself. Of course, you would not suffer it to manifest itself: but it is there, and needs to be put down. And it needs to be put down more than once. You will now and then be vexed and mortified to find that, after fancying you had quite made up your mind to certain facts, you are far from really having done so. Well, you must just try again. You must look for help where it is always to be found. And in the long run you will succeed. It will be painful, after you fancied you had weeded out self-conceit and envy from your nature, to find yourself some day talking in a bitter and ill-set way about some man or some woman whose real offence is merely having been more prosperous than yourself. You thought you had got beyond that. But it is all for your good to be reminded that the old root of bitterness is there yet: that you are never done with it: that you must be always cutting it down. A gardener might as justly suppose that because he has mown down the grass of a lawn very closely to-day, the grass will never grow up and need mowing again, as we fancy that because we have unsparingly put down an evil tendency within us, we shall have no more trouble with it.

Did nature give you, my friend, or education develope in you, a power of saying or writing severe things, which might stick into people as the little darts stick into the bull at a Spanish bull-fight? I believe that there are few persons who might not, if their heart would let them, acquire the faculty of producing disagreeable things, expressed with more or less of neatness and felicity. And in the case of the rare man here and there, who says his ill-set saying with epigrammatic point, like the touch of a rapier, the ill-setness may be excused, because the thing is so gracefully said. We would not wish that tigers should be exterminated: but it is to be desired that they should be very few. Let there be spared a specimen, here and there, of the graceful, agile, ferocious savage. But you, my reader, were no great hand at epigrams, though you were ready enough with your ill-set remark: and after some experience, you concluded that there is something better in this world than to say things, however cleverly, that are intended to give pain. And so you determined to cut that off, and to go upon the kindly tack: to say a good and cheering word whenever you had the opportunity: to be ready with a charitable interpretation of what people do: and never to utter or to write a word that could vex a fellow-creature, who (you may be sure) has quite enough to vex him without your adding anything. Perhaps you did all this: rather overdoing the thing: ill-set people are apt to overdo the thing when they go in for kindliness and geniality. But some day, having met some little offence, the electricity that had been storing up during that season of repression, burst out in a flash of what may, by a strong figure, be called forked lightning: the old enemy had got the mastery again. And indeed a hasty temper, founding as it does mainly on irritability of the nervous system, is never quite got over. It may be much aggravated by yielding to it: and much abated by constant restraint: but unless the beast be perpetually seen to, it is sure to be bursting out now and then. Socrates, you remember, said that his temper was naturally hasty and bad: but that philosophy had cured him.   I believe it needs something much more efficacious than any human philosophy to work such a cure.   No doubt, you may diligently train yourself to see what is to be said in excuse of the offences given you by your fellow-creatures; and to look at the case as it appears from their point of view.   This will help. But though ill-temper, left to its natural growth, will grow always worse, there is a point at which it has been found to mend.   When the nervous system grows less sensitive through age, hastiness of temper sometimes goes.   The old enemy is weakened : the beast has been (so to speak) hamstrung. You will be told that the thing which mainly impressed persons who saw the great Duke of Wellington in the last months of his life, was what a mild gentle old man he was.   Of course, every one knows that he was not always so.   The days were, when his temper was hot and hasty enough.

And thus thinking of physical influence, let us remember that what is vulgarly called nervousness is an enemy which many men know to their cost is not to be got over.   The firmest assurance that you have done a thing many times, and so should be able to do it once more, may not suffice to enable you to look forward to doing it without a vague tremor and apprehension.   There are human beings, all whose work is done without any very great nervous strain : there are others in whose vocation there come many times that put their whole nature upon the stretch. And these times test a man. You know a horse may be quite lame, while yet it does not appear in walking. Trot the creature smartly: and the lameness becomes manifest. In like manner a man may be nervous, particular, crotchety, superstitious: while yet this may not appear till you trot him sharply: put him at some work that must be done with the full stretch of his powers. And then you will see that he has got little odd ways of his own. I do not know what is the sensation of going into battle, and finding one-self under fire: but short of that, I think the greatest strain to which a human being is usually subjected, is that of the preacher. A little while ago, I was talking with a distinguished clergyman: and being desirous of comparing his experience with that of his juniors, I asked him,

1. Whether, in walking to church on Sunday to preach, he did not always walk on the same side of the street? Whether he would not feel uncomfortable, and as if something were going wrong, if he made any change?

2. Whether when waiting in the vestry, the minute or two before the beadle should come to precede him into church, he did not always stand on the same spot? Whether it would not put him out of gear, to vary from that?

My eminent friend answered all these questions

in the affirmative. Of course there are a great
many men to whom I should no more have thought
of proposing such questions than I should think
of proposing them to a rhinoceros. Such men,
probably, have no little ways: and if they had,
they would not admit that they had. But my
friend is so very able a man, and so very sincere a
man, that he had no reason to be afraid of any one
thinking him little, though he acknowledged to
having his little fancies. And indeed, when you
come to know people well, you will find that they
have all ways that are quite analogous to Johnson's
touching the tops of all the posts as he walked
London streets. They would not exactly say, that
they are afraid of anything happening to them if
they deviated from the old track: but they think
it just as well to keep on the safe side, by not
deviating from it.

Possibly there was a period in your life, in which
you had no objection to get into controversies upon
political or religious subjects with other men:
which controversies gradually grew angry: and
probably ended in mutual abuse, but assuredly not
in conviction. But having remarked, in the case of
other controversialists, what fools they invariably
made of themselves: having remarked their ludicrous exaggeration of the importance of their
dispute, and the malice and disingenuousness with
which they carried on their debate (more especially

if they were clergymen) : having remarked, in brief, how very little a controversialist ever looks like a Christian : you turned, in loathing, from the whole thing, and resolved that you would never get into a controversy, public or private, with any mortal, upon any subject, any more. Stick to that resolution, my friend; it is a good one. But you will occasionally be tempted to break it. Whenever the old enemy assails you, just think what a demagogue or agitator, political or religious, looks like in the eyes of all sensible and honest men !

Perhaps you had a tendency to be suspicious; and you have broken yourself of it. Perhaps your temptation was to be easily worried by little cross-accidents, and to get needlessly excited. Perhaps your temptation was to laziness : to putting off duty till to-morrow : to untidiness : to moral cowardice. Whatever it was, my friend, never think yourself so cured of an evil habit, that you may cease to mow it down. If Demosthenes had left off attending to his speaking, he would have relapsed into his old evil ways. If St. Paul, after having learned to be content, had ceased to see to that, he would gradually have grown a grumbler.

I am going to close this little procession of old enemies which has passed before our eyes, by naming a large and general one. It is Folly. My friend, if you have attained to any measure of common sense now, you know what a tremendous fool you were once. If you do not know that, then you are a fool still. Ah, reader, wise and good, you know all the weakness, the silliness, the absurd fancies and dreams, that have been yours. I presume that you are ready to give up a great part of your earlier life: you have not a word to say for it. All your desire is that it should in charity be forgotten. But surely you will not now make a fool of yourself any more. There shall be no more now of the hasty talking, the vapouring about your own importance, the idiotic sayings and doings you wish you could bury in Lethe: and which you may be very sure certain of your kind friends carefully remember and occasionally recall. But now and then the logic of facts will convince you that the old enemy is not quite annihilated yet; and you say something you regret the moment it is uttered. You do something which indicates that you have lost your head for the time.

Let it be said, in conclusion, as the upshot of the whole matter, that the wise man will never think he is safe till he has reached a certain Place where no enemy can assail him more. I beg my friend Mr. Snarling to take notice, that I do not pretend to have pointed out in these pages the worst of those old enemies that get up again and run at us after they had been knocked on the head once, and more than once. If this had been a sermon, I should have given you a very different catalogue;

and one that would have awakened more serious thoughts. Not but that those which have been named are well worth thinking of. The day will never come, in this world, on which it will be safe for us to sit down in perfect security; and to say to ourselves, Now we need keep no watch; we may (in a moral sense) draw the charge from our revolver because it will not be needed; we may fall asleep and nothing will meddle with us the while. For all around us, my friend, are the old enemies of our souls and our salvation: some aiming at nothing more than to make us disagreeable and repulsive, petty and jealous; others aiming at nothing less than to make us unfit for the only Home where we can know perfect rest and peace: some stealing upon us more stealthily, silently, fatally, than ever the Indian crept through the darkness of night upon the traveller nodding over his watch-fire: some coming down upon us, strong and sudden as the tiger's agile spring. Well we know what to do: we must watch and pray. And the time will come at length, when the pack of wolves shall be lashed off for ever: when the evil within us shall be killed outright, and beyond all reviving: and when the evil around us shall be gone.

CHAPTER XI.

AT THE CASTLE:

WITH SOME THOUGHTS ON MICHAEL SCOTT'S FAMILIAR SPIRIT.

OT on a study table in a back parlour in a great city, shall these little blue pages be covered with written characters. Every word shall be written in the open air. The page shall be lighted by sunshine that comes through no glass; but which is tempered by coming through masses of green leaves. And this essay is not to be composed: not to be screwed out, to use the figure of Mr. Thackeray: not to be pumped out, to use the figure of *Festus.* It shall grow without an effort. When any thought occurs, the pencil shall note it down. No thought shall be hurried in its coming.

You know how after a good many months of constant work, with the neck always at the collar, you grow wearied, and easily worried. Little things become burdensome: and the best of work is felt as a task. You cannot reason yourself out of that : ten days' rest is the thing that will do it. Be thankful if then you can have such a season of quiet in as green and shady a nook of country as mortal eyes could wish to see : in a nook like this, amid green grass and green trees, and the wild flowers of the early summer. For this is little more than midway in the pleasant month of May.

It is a very warm, sunshiny morning. This is a little open glade of rich grass, lighted up with daisies and buttercups. The little glade is surrounded by large forest trees : under the trees there is a blaze of primroses and wild hyacinths. A soft west wind, laden with the fragrance of lilac and apple blossoms, wakes the gentlest of sounds (in a more expressive language than ours it would have been called *susurrus*) in the topmost branches, gently swaying to and fro. The swaying branches cast a flecked and dancing shadow on the grass below. Midway the little glade is beyond the shadow : and there the grass, in the sunbeams, has a tinge of gold. A river runs by, with a ceaseless murmur over the warm stones. Look to the right hand : and there, over the trees, two hundred yards off, you may see a gray and red tower motionless above the waving branches : and lower down, hardly surmounting the wood, a stretch of massive wall, with huge buttresses. Tower and wall crown a lofty knoll, which the river encircles, making it a peninsula. Wallflower grows in the crannies: a little wild apple-tree, covered with white blossoms, crowns a detached fragment of a ruined gateway: sweetbrier grows at the base of the ancient walls: ivy and honeysuckle climb up them: and where great fragments of fallen wall testify to the excellence of the mortar of the eleventh century, wild roses have rooted themselves in masses, which are now only green. That is THE CASTLE: all that can be seen of it from this point. There is more to be said of it hereafter. Hard by this spot, two little children are sitting on the grass, to whom some one is reading a story.

The wise man will never weary of looking at green grass and green trees. It is an unspeakable refreshment to the eye and the mind: and the daily pressure of occupation cannot touch one here. One wonders that human beings who always live amid such scenery do not look more like it. But some people are utterly unimpressionable by the influences of outward scenery. You may know men who have lived for many years where Nature has done her best with wood and rock and river: and even when you become well acquainted with them, you cannot discover the faintest trace in their talk or in their feeling of the mightily powerful touch (as it would be to many) which has been unceasingly laid upon them through all that time. Or you may have beheld a vacuous person at a pic-nic party, who amid traces of God's handiwork that should make men hold their breath, does but pass from the occupation of fatuously flirting with a young woman like himself, to furiously abusing the servants for not sufficiently cooling the wine. A great many of the highly respectable people, we all know, are entirely in the case of the hero of that exquisite poem of Wordsworth's, which Jeffrey never could bring himself to like.

> But Nature ne'er could find her way
> Into the heart of Peter Bell.
>
> In vain, through every changing year,
>   Did Nature lead him as before :
> A primrose by a river's brim,
> A yellow primrose was to him,
>   And it was nothing more.

A human being ought to be very thankful if his disposition be such that he heartily enjoys green grass and green trees. For there are clever men who do not : in a little while I shall tell you of an extraordinary and anomalous taste expressed on that subject by one of the cleverest men I know. If a man has a thousand a year, and his next neighbour five hundred : and if the man with five hundred makes his income go just as far as the larger one (and an approximation to doing so may be made by good management), it is plain that these two mortals are, in respect of income, on the same precise footing. The poorer man gets so much more enjoyment out of his yearly revenue, as makes up for the fact that the richer man's revenue is twice as great.

There is a like compensation provided for the lack of material advantages in the case of many men, through their intense appreciation of the beauty of natural scenery, and of very simple things. A rich man may possess the acres, with their yearly rental: a poor man, such as a poet, a professor, a schoolmaster, a clergyman or the like, may possess the landscape which these acres make up, to the utter exclusion of the landed proprietor. Perhaps, friendly reader, God has not given you the earthly possessions which it has pleased Him to give to some whom you know: but He may have given you abundant recompense, by giving you the power of getting more enjoyment out of little things than many other men. You live in a little cottage, and your neighbour in a grand castle: you have a small collection of books, and your neighbour a great one of fine editions in sumptuous bindings and in carved oak cases: yet you may have so great delight in your snug house, and your familiar volumes, that in regard of actual enjoyment, you may be the more enviable man. A green field with a large oak in the middle: a hedge of blossoming hawthorn: a thatched cottage under a great maple: twenty square yards of velvety turf: how really happy such things can make some simple folk!

Of course it occurs to one that the same people who get more enjoyment out of little pleasures, will get more suffering out of anything painful. Because your tongue is more sensitive than the palm of your hand, it is aware of the flavour of a pine-apple which your palm would ignore : but it is also liable to know the taste of assafœtida, of which your palm would be unconscious. The supersensitive nervous system is finely strung to discern pain as well as pleasure. No one knows, but the over-particular person, what a pure misery it is to go into an untidy room, if it be your own. There are people who suffer as much in having a tooth filed, as others in losing a limb. A Frenchman, some years since, committed suicide : leaving a written paper to say he had done so because life was rendered unendurable through his being so much bitten by fleas. This is not a thing to smile at. That poor man, before his reason was upset, had probably endured torments of which those around had not the faintest idea. I have heard a good man praised for the patience with which he bore daily for weeks the surgeon's dressing of a very severe wound. The good man was thought heroic. I knew him well enough to be sure that the fact was that his nature was dull and slow. He did not suffer as average men would have suffered under that infliction. There are human beings in touching whose moral nature you feel you are touching

the impenetrable skin of the hippopotamus. There
are human beings in touching whose moral nature
you feel you are touching the bare tip of a nerve.
Eager, anxious men are prone to envy imper-
turbable and slow-moving men. My friend Smith,
who is of an eager nature, tells me he looks with
a feeling a few degrees short of veneration on
a massive-minded and immovable being, who in
telling a story makes such long pauses at the end
of each sentence that you fancy the story done.
Then poor Smith breaks in hastily with something he wants to say: but the massive-minded
man, not noticing him, continues his parable till
he pauses again at the end of another sentence.
And Smith is made to feel as though he were very
young.

I have said that likings vary in regard to such
matters as the enjoyment of this scene. Oh this
green grass, rich, unutterably green, with the buttercups and daisies, with the yellow broom and the
wild bees, and the environment of bright leafy trees
that inclose you round: to think that there are people who do not care for you! It was but yesterday,
in a street of a famous and beautiful city, I met my
friend Mr. Keene. Keene is a warm-hearted, magnanimous, unselfish, brave, out-spoken human being:
as fine a fellow as is numbered among the clergy of
either side of the Tweed. Besides these things, he

is an admirable debater: fluent, ready, eloquent, hearty, fully persuaded that he is right and that his opponents are invariably wrong; and not without some measure of smartness and sharpness in expression. Keene approached me with a radiant face; the result partly of inherent good nature, and partly of a very hot summer day. He had come to the city to take part in the debates of the great ecclesiastical council of a northern country. I was coming to this place. He was entering the city, in fact, for many days of deliberation and debate: I was departing from it, for certain days of rest and recreation. I could not refrain from displaying some measure of exultation at the contrast between our respective circumstances. I shall be lying to-morrow (I said) on green grass under green trees: while you will be existing (the word used indeed was stewing) in that crowded building, with its feverish atmosphere highly charged with carbonic acid gas. To these words Keene replied, with simple earnestness: I shall be quite happy there: I don't care a straw for green grass and green leaves! Such was the sentiment of that eminent man. I pity him sincerely!

Here I paused: and thought for a little of the great ecclesiastical council, and of lesser ecclesiastical councils. And the following reflection suggested itself.

Our good principles are too often like Don Quixote's helmet. We arrive at them in leisure, in cool blood, with an unexcited brain, which is commonly called a clear head. Then in actual life, they too commonly fail at the first real trial. Don Quixote made up his helmet carefully with a vizor of pasteboard. Then to ascertain whether it was strong enough, he dealt it a blow with his sword. Thereupon it went to pieces.

In like manner, in our better and more thoughtful hours, we resolve to be patient, forgiving, charitable, kind-spoken, unsuspicious,—in short, Christian, for *that* includes all. And the first time we are irritated, we fail. We grow very angry at some small offence: we speak harshly, we act unfairly. I have heard a really good man preach. Afterwards I heard him speak in a lesser ecclesiastical council. He preached (so far as the sentiments expressed went) like an angel. He argued like just the reverse.

Ah, we make up our helmets with pasteboard. We resolve that henceforth we shall act on the most noble principles. And the helmets look very well so long as they are not put to the test. We fancy ourselves charitable, forgiving, Christian people, so long as we are not tried. A stroke with a sword, and the helmet goes to tatters. An attack on us: a reflection on us: a hint that we ever did wrong: and oh the wretched outburst of wrath, bitterness, unfairness, malignity!

Of course, the best of men, as it has been said, are but men at the best. Let us be humble. Let there be no vain self-confidence. And especially, let us, entering on every scene that can possibly try us (and when do we escape from such a scene?) earnestly ask the guidance of that Blessed Spirit of Whom is every good feeling and purpose in us; and without Whom our best resolutions will snap like reeds just when they are needed most to stand firm.

There is more to be said about the Castle. It is not a castle to which you go, that you may enjoy the society of dukes and other nobles, such as form the daily associates of the working clergy. By the payment of a moderate weekly stipend, this castle may become yours. The castle is in ruins: but a little corner, amid the great masses of crumbling stones which were placed here by strong hands dead for eight hundred years, has been patched up so as to make an unpretending little dwelling: and there you may find the wainscoted rooms, the quaint panelled ceilings of mingled timber and plaster, the winding turret stairs, the many secret doors, of past centuries. The castle stands on a lofty promontory of no great extent, which a little river encircles on two sides, and which a deep ravine cuts off from the surrounding country on the other two sides. You approach the castle over an arch

R

of seventy feet in height: which spans the ravine. In former days it was a drawbridge. The bridge runs out of the inner court of the castle: midway in its length it turns off at almost a right angle, till it joins the bank on the other side of the ravine. That little bridge makes a charming place to walk on: and it is a great deal longer than any quarter-deck. It is all grown over with masses of ancient ivy: the fragrance of a sweetbrier hedge in the castle court pervades it at present: you look down from it upon a deep glen, through which the little river flows. The tops of the tall trees are far beneath you: there are various plane-trees with their thick leaves. Wherever you look, it is one mass of rich foliage. Trees fill up the ravine: trees clothe the steep bank on the other side of the river: trees have rooted themselves in wonderful spots in the old walls: trees clothe the ascent that leads from the castle to that little summit near, crowned with one of the loveliest creations of the Gothic architect's skill. *That* is the chancel of a large church, of which only the chancel was ever built: and if you would behold a little chapel of inexpressible perfection and beauty; if you would discern the traces of the faithful and loving toil of men who have been for hundreds of years in their graves; if you would look upon ancient stones that seem as if they had grown and blossomed like a tree: then find out where that chapel is, and go and see it.

But you pass over the bridge; and under a ruined gateway, where part of a broken arch hangs over the passer-by, you enter the court. On the right hand, ruined walls of vast thickness. The like on the left hand: but midway, there is the little portion that is habitable. Enter: pass into a pretty large wainscoted parlour: look out of the windows on the further side. You are a hundred feet above the garden below. For on that side, there is below you story after story of low-browed chambers, arched in massive stone; and lower still, the castle wall rises from the top of a precipice of perpendicular rock. On the further side from the river, the chambers are hewn out of the living stone. What a view from the window of that parlour, first mentioned! Beneath, the garden, bright now with blossoming apple-trees: bounded by the river: and beyond the river, a bank of wood, three hundred feet in height. A little window in a corner looks down the course of the stream: there is a deep dell of wood, one thick luxuriance of foliage: with here and there the gleam of the flowing water.

This is our place of rest. Add to all that has been said an inexpressible sense of a pervading quiet.

Do you find, when you come to a place where you are to have a brief holiday, a tendency to look back on the work you have been doing; and to

estimate what it has come to after all? And have
you found, even after many months of grinding as
hard as you could, that it was mortifying to see
how little was the permanent result? Such seems to
be the effect of looking back on work. One thinks
of a case, parallel to the present feeling. There was
Jacob, looking back on a long life: on a hundred
and twenty years: and saying, sincerely, that his
days had been few and evil. Now, in a blink of
rest, my friend, look back on the results you have
accomplished in those months of hard work. You
thought them many and good at the time: now,
they seem to be no better than few and evil. It is
humiliating to think how little permanent result is
got by a working day. To bring things to book,
to actually count and weigh them, always makes
them look less. You may remember a calculation
made by the elder Disraeli, as to the amount of
matter a man could read in a lifetime. It is very
much less than you would have thought: perhaps
one-tenth of what an ordinary person would guess.
Thackeray, in his days of matured and practised
power, thought it a good day's work to write six of
the little pages of *Esmond*. A distinguished and
experienced author told me that he esteemed three
pages of the *Quarterly Review* a good day's work.
Some men judge a sermon, which can be given in
little more than half an hour, a sufficient result of
the almost constant thought of a week. Six little

pages, as the sole abiding result of a day on which
the sun rose and set, and the clock went the round
of the four-and-twenty hours: on which you took
your bath, and your breakfast, and read your newspaper, and in short went through the round of em-
ployments which make your habitude of being: six
pages: skimmed by the reader in five minutes!
The truth is, that a great part of our energy goes
just to bear the burden of the day, to do the work
of the time: and we have only the little surplus of
abiding possession. The way to keep ourselves
from getting mortified and disheartened, when we
look back on the remaining result of all our work,
is to remember that we are not here merely to
work: merely to produce that which shall be an
abiding memorial of us. It is well if all we do and
bear is forming our nature and character into something which we can willingly take with us when we
go away from this life.

This morning, after breakfast, I was sitting on
the parapet of the bridge already mentioned, looking
down upon the tops of two plane-trees, and feeling
a great deal the better for the sight. I believe it
does good to an ordinary mortal to look down on
the top of a large tree, and see the branches gently
waving about. Little outward phenomena have a
wonderful effect in soothing and refreshing the
mind. Some men say the sight and sound of the

sea calms and cheers them. You know how when a certain old prophet was beaten and despairing, the All-Wise thought it would be good for him to behold certain sublime manifestations of the power of the Almighty. We cannot explain the rationale of the process: but these things do us good. A wise and good and most laborious man told me that when he feels overworked and desponding, he flies away to Chamouni and looks at Mont Blanc: and in a few days he is set right. It was not a fanciful man who said that there is scenery in this world that would soothe even remorse. And for an ordinary person, not a great genius and not a great ruffian, give us a lofty bridge whence you may look down upon a great plane-tree.

All this, however, is a deviation. Sitting on the bridge and enjoying the scene, this thought arose. Greatly as one enjoys and delights in this, what would the feeling be if one were authoritatively commanded to remain in this beautiful place, doing nothing, for a month? And one could not but confess that the feeling would not be pleasant. The things you enjoy most intensely, you enjoy for but a short time: then you are satiated. When parched with thirst, what so delightful as the first draught of fair water? But if you were compelled to drink a fourth and fifth tumbler, the water would become positively nauseous. So is it with rest. You enjoy it keenly for a little while: but constrained idleness, being prolonged, would make you miserable. Ten days here are delightful: then back, with fresh appetite and vigour, to the dear work. But a month here, thus early in the year, would be a fearful infliction. You have not earned the Autumn holidays as yet.

It is in human nature, that when you feel the pressure of anything painfully, you fancy that the opposite thing would set you right. When you are extremely busy, and distracted by a host of things demanding thought, you think that pure idleness would be pleasant. So, in boyhood, on a burning summer day, you thought it would be delicious to feel cold. You went to bathe in the sea: and you found it a great deal too cold.

Charles Lamb, for a great part of his life, was kept very busy, at uncongenial work. Oftentimes, through those irksome hours, he thought how pleasant it would be to be set free from that work for ever. So he said that if he had a son, the son should be called NOTHING TO DO; and he should do nothing. Of course, Elia spoke only half-seriously. We know what he meant. But, in sober earnest, we can all see that NOTHING TO DO would have been a miserable as well as a wicked man. He would assuredly have grown a bad fellow. And he would just as surely have been a wretched being.

Every one knows the story of Michael Scott and

his Familiar Spirit. Of late I have begun to understand the meaning of that story.

Michael Scott, it is recorded, had a Familiar Spirit under his charge. We do not know how Michael Scott first got possession of that Spirit. Probably he raised it and then could not get rid of it: like the man who begged Dr. Log to propose a toast, and then Dr. Log spoke for three-quarters of an hour. . Michael Scott had to provide employment for that being, on pain of being torn in pieces. Michael gave the Spirit very difficult things to do. They were done with terrible ease and rapidity. The three peaks of the Eildon Hills were formed in a single night. A weir was built across the Tweed in a like time. Michael Scott was in a terrible state. In these days, he would probably have desired the Spirit to make and lay the Atlantic Telegraph Cable. But a happy thought struck him. He bade his Familiar make a rope of sea-sand. Of course, this provided unlimited occupation. The thing could never be finished. And the wizard was all right.

These things are an allegory. Michael Scott's Familiar Spirit is your own mind, my friend. Your own mind demands that you find it occupation: and if you do not, it will make you miserable. It is an awful thing to have nothing to do. The mill within you demands grist to grind: and if you give it none, it still grinds on, as Luther said: but it is itself it grinds and wears away. My friend Smith, having overworked his eyes at College, was once forbid to read or write for eighteen months. It was a horrible penance at first. But he devised ways of giving the machine work: and during that period of enforced idleness, he acquired the power of connected thinking without writing down each successive thought. Few people have that power. One of the rarest of all acquirements is the faculty of profitable meditation. Most human beings, when they fancy they are meditating, are in fact doing nothing at all; and thinking of nothing.

You will remember what was once said by a lively French writer: that we commonly think of idleness as one of the beatitudes of Heaven; while we ought rather to think of it as one of the miseries of Hell. It was an extreme way which that writer took of testifying to the tormenting power of Michael Scott's Familiar Spirit.

And one evil in this matter is, that it is just the men who lead the most active and useful lives, who are making Michael Scott's Spirit most insatiable. You give it abundance to do: and so when work is cut off from it, it becomes rampageous. You lose the power of sitting still and doing nothing. You find it inexpressibly irksome to travel by railway for even half an hour, with nothing to read. For the most handy way of pacifying the Spirit is to give it something to read. People tell you how disgusting it was when they had to wait for three-quarters of an hour for the train at some little country railway station. Michael Scott's Spirit was worrying and tormenting them, being kept without employment for that time. You know to what shifts people will have recourse, rather than have the Familiar Spirit coming and tormenting them. To give grist to the mill, to provide the Familiar Spirit with something to do, on a railway journey of twelve hours, they will read all the advertisements in their newspaper: they will go back a second and a third time over all the news: they will even diligently peruse the leading article of the *Little Pedlington Gazette.* They read the advertisements in *Bradshaw.* They try to make out, from that publication, how to reach, by many corresponding trains, some little cross-country place to which they never intend to go. Anything rather than be idle. Anything rather than lean back, quite devoid of occupation: and feel the Familiar Spirit worrying away within, as Prometheus felt the vulture at his liver. When I hear a young fellow say of some country place where he has been spending some time, that it is a horribly slow place, that it is the deadest place on earth, I am aware that he did not find occupation there for Michael Scott's Familiar Spirit.

One looks with interest at people in whose case that Spirit seems to have been lulled into torpidity :

has been brought to what a practical philosopher called *a dormouse state.* I read last night in a book how somebody 'leant his cheek on his hand and gazed abstractedly into the fire.' One who has trained the Familiar Spirit to an insatiable appetite for work, can hardly believe such a thing possible. You may remember a picture in a volume of the illustrated edition of the *Waverley Novels*, which represents a plump old abbot, sitting satisfied in a large chair, with the light of the fire on his face: doing nothing, thinking of nothing: and quite tranquil and content. One sometimes thinks, Would we could do the like! That fat stupid old abbot had led so idle a life, that the muscular power of the Familiar Spirit was abated: and its craving for work gone.

When you are wearied with long work, my reader, I wish you may have a place like this to which to come and rest. How good and pleasant it is for a little while! Your cares and burdens fall off from you. How insignificant many things look to one, sitting on this green grass, or looking over this bridge down into the green dell, that worried one in the midst of duty! If you were out in a hurricane at sea, and your boat got at last into a little sheltered cove, you would be glad and thankful. But only for a short time. In a little, you would be weary of staying there. We are so made that we cannot for any length of time remain quiescent and do nothing. And we cannot live on the past. The Familiar Spirit will not chew the cud, so to speak : you must give him fresh provender to grind. Perhaps there have been days in your life which were so busy with hard work, so alive with what to you were great interests, so happy with a bewildering bliss, that you fancied you would be able to look back on them and to live in them all your life, and they would be a possession for ever. Not so. It is the present on which we must live. You can no more satisfy Michael Scott's Spirit with the remembrance of former occupations and enjoyments, than you can allay your present hunger with the remembrance of beef-steaks brought you by the plump head-waiter at ' The Cock,' half-a-dozen years ago. Each day must bring its work : or the Spirit will be at you and stick pins into you.

A power of falling asleep, enables one to evade the Spirit. At night, going to bed, looking for a sleepless night, how many a man has said, Oh for forgetfulness ! When you have escaped into *that* realm, the Spirit can trouble you no more. You know the wish which Hood puts on the lips of Eugene Aram, tortured by an unendurable recollection : that he could shut his mind and clasp it with a clasp, as he could close his book and clasp it. Few men are more to be envied than those who have this power. Napoleon had it. So had the Duke of Wellington. At any moment either of these men could escape into a region where they were entirely free from the pressure of those anxieties which weighed them down while awake. Once the Duke with his aide-de-camp came galloping up to a point of the British lines whence an attack was to be made. He was told the guns would not be ready to open for two hours. 'Then,' said he, 'we had better have a sleep.' He sat down in a trench, leant his back against its side, and was fast asleep in a minute. That great man could at any time escape from Michael Scott's Spirit: could get into a country where the Spirit could not follow him. For in dreamless sleep you escape from yourself.

I have been told that there is another means of lulling that insatiable being into a state in which it ceases to be troublesome and importunate. It is tobacco. Some men say that the smoking of that fragrant weed soothes them into a perfect calm, in which they are pleasurably conscious of existing, but have no wish to do anything. Let me confess, notwithstanding, that I esteem smoking as one of the most offensive and selfish of the lesser sins. When I see smoke pouring out of the window of a railway carriage not specially allotted to smokers, I go no farther for evidence that that carriage is occupied by selfish snobs.

Young children have Michael Scott's Familiar Spirit to find employment for, just as much as their seniors. Who does not yet remember the horrible feeling which you expressed when a child by saying you had *nothing to do*? I have just heard a little thing say to his mother, ' Read me a story to make the time pass quick.' That was his way of saying 'to pacify the Familiar Spirit.' And we talk of *killing Time*, as though he were an enemy to be reduced to helplessness. There is an offensive phrase which sets all the idea more distinctly. There are silly fellows who ask you what o'clock it is by saying ' *How goes the enemy*?' This phrase indeed suggests thoughts too solemn and awful for this page. Let me ask, in a word, if Time be such, how about Eternity? But in every such case as those named, the enemy is not Time. It is Michael Scott's Familiar Spirit, demanding occupation. How fast Time goes, when the Spirit is pleasantly or laboriously employed! When people talk of killing Time, they mean knocking that strange being on the head, so to speak: stunning it for the hour. *That* may be done: but it is soon up again, importunate as ever.

I suppose, my reader, that you can remember times in which the face you loved best looked its sweetest; and tones, pleasanter than all the rest, of the voice that was always pleasantest to hear: thoughtful looks of the little child you seek in vain in the man in whom you lost it; and smiles of the little child that died.   Touched as with the light of eternity, these things stand forth amid the years of past time : they are as the mountain tops rising over the mists of oblivion : they are the possessions which will never pass your remembrance till you cease to remember at all.   And you know that Nature too has her moments of special transfiguration : times when she looks so fair and sweet that you are compelled to think that *she* would do well enough (for all the thorns and thistles of the Fall), if you could but get quit of the ever-intruding blight of Sin and Sorrow.   Such a season is this bright morning : with its sunshine that seems to us (in our ignorance) fair and joyous enough for that Place where there is no night : with its leaves green and living (would they but last) as we can picture of the Tree of Life : with its cheerful quiet that is a little foretaste of the perfect Rest which shall last for ever.   It is very nearly time to go back to work : but we shall cherish this remembrance of the place ; and so it will be green and sunshiny through winter days.

CHAPTER XII.

CONCERNING THE RIGHT TACK;

WITH SOME THOUGHTS ON THE WRONG TACK.

NOT many days since, I was walking along a certain street, in a certain city : and there I beheld two little boys of the better sort fighting furiously. There are people, claiming to be what is vulgarly called Muscular Christians, who think that a certain amount of fighting among boys is to be very much encouraged, as a thing tending to make the little fellows manly and courageous. For myself, I believe that God's law is wise as well as right : and I do not believe that angry passion (which God's law condemns), or that vindictive efforts to do mischief to a fellow-creature (which God's law also condemns), are things which deserve to be in any way encouraged; or are things likely to develop in either man or boy the kind of character which wise and good people would wish to see. Accordingly I interposed in the fight, and sought to make peace between the little men : supporting my endeavours by some general statement to the effect that good boys ought not to be fighting in that way. They stopped at once : no doubt both had had enough of that kind of thing. For one had a bloody nose ; and the other had a rudimentary black eye, which next morning would be manifest. But one of them defended himself against the charge of having done anything wrong, by saying, with the energy of one who was quite assured that he had the principles of eternal justice on his side, ' I have a right to hit him, because he hit me first !'

Of course, these were suggestive words. And I could not but think to myself, walking away from the little fellows after having composed their strife, Now *there* is the principle upon which this world goes on. There is not a deeper-rooted tendency in human nature, than that which is exhibited in that saying of that fine little boy. For he *was* a fine little boy ; and so was the other. The great principle on which most human beings go, in all the relations and all the doings of life, is just that which is compendiously expressed in the words, ' I have a right to hit you, if you hit me first.' You may trace the manifestations of that great principle in all possible walks of life, and among all sorts and conditions of men. One man or woman says something unkind of another : the other feels quite entitled to retaliate by saying something unkind of the first. And this tendency appears early. I once heard a little boy of four years old say, with some indignation of manner : ' Miss Smith said I was a troublesome monkey : if she ever says *that* again, I'll say that she is an ugly old maid !' One man says, in print, something depreciatory of another; finds fault with something the other man has said, or written, or done. Then the other man retorts in kind : pays off the first man by publishing something depreciatory of *him*. A great many of the political essays which we read in the newspapers; and a great many of the reviews of books we meet; are manifestly dictated and inspired by the purpose to revenge some personal offence : to clear off scores by hitting the man who has hit you. A sharp, clever person reads the book written by an enemy, with the determination to pick holes in it : not that the book is bad, or that he thinks it bad : but its author has given him some offence, and *that* is to be retaliated. You remember, of course, that very clever and very bitter article on Mr. Croker's edition of Boswell's *Life of Johnson*, which is contained in Lord Macaulay's selection of essays from the *Edinburgh Review*. Was there any mortal who supposed that when Macaulay's own *History of England* appeared, Mr. Croker would review it otherwise than with a determination to find faults in it ? Was there any mortal surprised to find that Mr. Croker, having been hit by Macaulay, endeavoured to hit Macaulay again ? And if Macaulay's *History* had been absolutely immaculate, had been a thousand times better than it is, do you suppose *that* would appreciably have affected the tone of Mr. Croker's review of it? I am far from saying that Mr. Croker deliberately made up his mind to do injustice to Lord Macaulay. It is likely enough he thought Macaulay richly deserved all the ill he said of him. A great law of mind governs even human beings who never came to a formal resolution of obeying it : as a stream never pauses to consider whether, at a certain point, it shall run downhill or up. When Sir Bulwer Lytton, in his poem of *The New Timon*, alluded to Mr. Tennyson in disparaging terms as *Miss Alfred*, no one was surprised to read, in a few days, that terribly trenchant copy of verses in which Mr. Tennyson called Sir Bulwer a Bandbox, and showed that the true Timon was quite a different man from the Bandbox with his mane in curl-papers. For such is the incongruous imagery which the reader will carry away from that poem. And if you happen, my reader, to be acquainted with three or four men who have opportunity to carry on their quarrels in print, or by speeches in deliberative assemblies ; and if you refuse to take part in the quarrels which divide them, and keep resolutely on friendly terms with all : you will be struck by the fact that the system of mutual hitting and retaliation, carried on for

a while, quite incapacitates these men for doing each
other anything like justice : each will occasionally
caution you against his adversary as a very wicked
and horrible person : while you, knowing both, are
well aware that each is in the main an able and
good-hearted human being, not without some salient
faults, of course : and that the image of each which
is present to the mind of the other is a frightful caricature : is about as like the being represented as the
most awful photograph ever taken by an ingenious
youthful amateur is like you, my good-looking friend.
I have named deliberative assemblies.   Everybody
knows in how striking a fashion you will find the
great principle of retaliation exhibited in such : and
nowhere, I lament to say, more decidedly than in
presbyteries, synods, and general assemblies, where
you might naturally expect better things.   I have
heard a revered friend say, that only the imperative
sense of duty would ever lead him to such places :
and that the effect of their entire tone upon his moral
and spiritual nature was the very reverse of healthful.   One man, in a speech, says something sharp of
another : of course, when the first man sits down,
the second gets up, and says something unkind of
his brother.   And you will sometimes find men,
with a calculating rancour; and with what Mr.
Croker, speaking of Earl Russell, called 'a spiteful
slyness;' wait their opportunity, that they may deal
the return blow at the time and place where it will

be most keenly felt.   Now all this, which is bad in
anybody, is more evidently bad in men who on the
previous Sunday were, not improbably, preaching on
the duty of forgiving injuries.   All clergymen have
frequent occasion to repeat certain words which run
to the effect, ' And forgive us our trespasses, as we
forgive them that trespass against us.' Yet you may
find a clergyman, here and there, whose reputation
is high as a very hard hitter ; and as one who never
suffers any breath of assault to pass without keenly
retaliating.   If you touch such a man, however dis-
tantly : if, in the midst of a general panegyric, you
venture to hint that anything he has done is wrong :
he will flare up, and you will have a savage reply.
You know the consequence of touching *him*, just as
you know the consequence of giving a kick to a ferocious bulldog.   Now, is that a fine thing? Is it anything to boast of? I have heard a middle-aged man
(not a clergyman) state in an ostentatious manner,
that he never forgot an offence: that whoever touched
him would some day (as schoolboys say) *catch it.*
All this struck me as tremendously small.   In the
case of most people who talk in that way, it is not
true.   They are not nearly so bad as they would
like you to think them.   They don't cherish resentments in that vindictive way.   But if it were true,
it would be nothing to be proud of.   I have heard
a man boast that he had never thanked anybody for
anything all his life.   I thought him very silly.   He

expected me to think him very great. I well remember how, in a certain senate, after two older members, each a wise and good man when you got him in his right mind, had spent some time in mutual recrimination, a younger member took occasion to point out that all this was very far from being right or pleasing. To which one of the good men replied, in a ferocious voice, and with a very red face, as if *that* answer settled the matter, ' *But who began it ?*' No doubt, the other *had* begun it : and that good man took refuge in the angry schoolboy's principle, ' I have a right to hit him, because he hit me !'

I have been speaking, you see, of those little offences, and those little retaliations, which we have occasion to observe daily, in the comparative trimness and restraint of modern life : and in a state of society where a certain Christian tone of feeling, and the strong hand of the law, limit the offences which can be commonly given, and the vengeance which can be commonly taken. My good friend A, who has been several times attacked in print by B, would probably kick B, if various social restraints did not prevent him. But, however open the way might be, I really don't believe that A would cut B's throat, or burn his house and children and other possessions. No : I don't think he would. Still, there is nothing I less like to do, than to talk in a dogmatic and confident fashion. If Mr. C applies to the university of D for the honorary degree of Doctor of Music, and is refused that distinction, mainly (as C believes) through the opposition of Professor E ; although C may retort upon E by a malicious article in a newspaper, containing several gross falsehoods, I really believe, and I may say I hope, and even surmise, that C, even if he had the chance, would not exactly poison E with strychnine. And I may say that I firmly believe, from the little I have seen of C's writings (by which alone I know him), that nothing would induce C to poison E, if C were entirely assured that if he poisoned E, he (C) would infallibly be detected and hanged. But we are cautious now : and, through various circumstances, our claws have been cut short. It was different long ago. Of course we all know how, in the old days, insult or injury was often wiped out in blood : how it was a step in advance, even to establish the stern principle of 'an eye for an eye, and a tooth for a tooth: hand for hand, foot for foot, burning for burning, wound for wound, stripe for stripe.' For *that* principle made sure that the retaliation should at least not exceed the first offence : while formerly, and even afterwards where that principle was not recognised, very fanciful offences, and very small injuries, sometimes resulted in the quenching of many lives : in the carrying fire and sword over great tracts of country : and in the perpetuating of bloody feuds between whole tribes for age after age. You know that there have been countries and times in which Revenge was organised into a scientific art; in which the terrible *vendetta*, proclaimed between families, was maintained through successive centuries till one or the other was utterly extinguished: and a regularly kept record preserved the story how this and the other member of the proscribed race had been ruined, or imprisoned in a hopeless dungeon, or by false testimony brought within the grasp of cruel laws, or directly murdered outright, by some one of the race to which was committed the task of vengeance. You know how the dying father has, with his latest breath, charged his son to devote himself to the destruction of the clan that lived beyond the hill or across the river, because of some old offence whose history was almost forgot: you know how the Campbell and the Macgregor, the Maxwell and the Johnstone, the Chattan and the Quhele—in Scotland—were hereditary foes; and how, in many other instances, the very infant was born into his ancestors' quarrel. You have heard how a dying man, told by the minister of religion that now he must forgive every enemy as he himself hoped to be forgiven, has said to his surviving child, ' Well, *I* must forgive such a one ; but my curse be upon you if *you* do !' I am not going to give you a historical view, or anything like a historical view, of a miserable subject : but every reader knows well that there is not a blacker nor more deplorable page in the history of human kind, than that which tells us how faithfully, how unsparingly, how bloodily, the great principle of returning evil for evil has been carried out by human beings : the great rule, not of doing to others as you would that they should do to you, but of doing to others as they have done to you, or perhaps as you think they would do to you if they had the chance : in short, the great fundamental principle, of universal application, set out in the words of my little friend with the inchoate black eye, 'I have a right to hit him, because he hit me first !'

Now, all this kind of thing is what I mean by THE WRONG TACK.

My friendly reader, there is another way of meeting injury and unkindness : and a better way. The natural thing, unquestionably, is, to return evil for evil. The Christian thing, and the better way, is to 'overcome evil with good.' There was a certain Great Teacher, who was infinitely more than a Great Teacher, who taught all who should be His followers till the end of time, that the right thing would always be to meet unkindness with kindness : to forgive men their trespasses, as we hope our Heavenly Father will forgive ours : to love our enemies, bless them that curse us, do good to them that hate us, and pray for them which despitefully use us and persecute us,—if such people be.

And an eminent Philosopher, whom some people would probably appreciate more highly if he had not been also an inspired Apostle, spoke not unworthily of his Divine Master when he said, ' Recompense to no man evil for evil : dearly beloved, avenge not yourselves : If thine enemy hunger, feed him ; if he thirst, give him drink.   Be not overcome of evil, but overcome evil with good.'

Now, all this kind of thing is what I mean by THE RIGHT TACK.

There is no need at all to try formally to define what is intended by the Right Tack.   Everyone knows all about it: and its meaning will become plainer as we go on. Of course, the general idea is, that we should try to meet unkindness with kindness : unfairness with fairness : a bad word with a good one. The general idea is this : Such a neighbour or acquaintance has spoken of you unhandsomely: has treated you unjustly.   Well, you determine that *you* will not go and make yourself as bad as he is ; and carry on the quarrel, and increase the bad feeling that already exists ; by trying to retort in kind: by saying a bad word about *him*, or by doing *him* an unfriendly turn. No : you resolve to go upon another tack entirely. You will treat the person with scrupulous fairness. You try to think kindly of him, and to discover some excuse for his conduct towards you : and if an opportunity occurs of doing him a kind turn, you do it, frankly and heartily. Let me say, that if you try, in a fair spirit, and in a kind spirit, to discover some excuse for the bad way in which that person has treated you, or spoken of you, you will seldom have much difficulty in doing so. You will easily think of some little provocation you gave him, very likely without in the least intending it; you will easily see that your neighbour was speaking or acting under some misconception or mistake: you will easily enough think of many little things in his condition—painful, mortifying, anxious things —which may well be taken as some excuse for worse words and doings than ever proceeded from him concerning you. Ah, my brother, most people in these days, if you did but know all their condition, all about their families and their circumstances, have so many causes of disquiet, and anxiety, and irritation, to fever the weary heart, and to shake the shaken nerves, that a wise and good man will never make them offenders for a hasty word; or even for an uncharitable suspicion or an unkind deed, very likely hardly said or done till it was bitterly repented. My friend Smith, who is one of the best of men, was one day startled, attending a meeting of a certain senatorial body, to hear Mr. Jones get up and make a speech in the nature of a most vicious attack upon Smith. Smith listened attentively to a few paragraphs: and then, turning to the man next to him, put the following question : ' I say, Brown, is not that poor fellow's stomach often very much out of order?' ' He suffers from it horribly,' was the true reply. ' Ah that's it, poor fellow,' said Smith ; ' I see what it is that is exacerbating his temper, and making him talk in that way.' And when Jones sat down, Smith got up, with a kindly face : I don't mean with a provokingly benevolent and forgiving look : and in a simple, earnest way, justified the conduct which had been attacked, in a manner which conveyed that he was really anxious that Jones should think well of him : all this without the slightest complaint of Jones's bitterness, or the least reference to it. Smith had only done Jones justice in all this. He had done no more than allow for something which ought to be allowed for. And Jones was fairly beaten. After the meeting, he went to Smith and asked his pardon : saying that he really had been feeling so ill that he did not know very well what he was saying. Smith shook hands with poor Jones in a way that warmed Jones's heart : and they were better friends than ever from that day forward. But in the lot of many a man, there are worse things than little physical uneasinesses, for which a wise man will always allow in estimating an offence given. Yes : there are people with so much to embitter them : poor fellows so sadly disappointed : clever, sensitive men so terribly misplaced, so grievously tried : with their keenly sensitive nature so daily rasped, so horribly blistered, by coarse, uncongenial natures and by unhappy circumstances : that I am not afraid to say that a truly good man, if such a poor fellow pitched into him ever so bitterly, or did anything short of hitting him over the head with a more than commonly thick stick, would do no more than beg the poor fellow's pardon.

But mind, too, my friend, that all this kindly way of judging your fellow-creatures — all this returning of good for evil,—must be a real thing, and not a pretence. It must not be a hypocritical varnishing over of a deep angry and bitter feeling within us. It must not be something done with the purpose of putting our neighbour still further and still more conspicuously in the wrong. And far less must it consist in mere words with no real meaning. Neither must it consist, as it sometimes in fact does, in saying of an offending neighbour, ' I bear him no malice : I forgive him heartily : I make no evil return for his infamous conduct towards me :' when in truth, in the very words of forgiveness, you have said of your offending neighbour just the very worst you could say. You may remember certain lines which appeared in a London newspaper several years since, which purported to be a free translation into rhyme of a speech made in the House of Peers by an eminent bishop. In that speech the blameless prelate spoke of a certain order of men whose tastes were very offensive to him.   He said they

> Were the vilest race
> That ever in earth or hell had place :
> He would not prejudge them—no, not he,
> For his soul o'erflowed with charity.
> Incarnate fiends, he would not condemn ;
> No, God forbid he should slander them :
> Foul swine, their lordships must confess
> He used them with Christian gentleness.
> He hated all show of persecution,—
> But why weren't they sent to execution ?

I have no doubt whatever that these lines (which form part of a considerable poem) are an extreme exaggeration of what the bishop did actually say : yet I have just as little doubt that in his speech the bishop did exhibit something of that tone.   For I have known human beings, not a few, who diligently endeavoured to combine the forgiving of a man with the pitching into him just as hard as they conveniently could.   Now, that will not do.   You must make your choice.   You cannot at the same time have the satisfaction of wreaking your vengeance upon one who has injured you, and likewise the magnanimous pleasure of thinking that you have Christianly forgiven him.   Your returning of good for evil must be a real thing.   It must be done heartily, and without reservation in your own mind : or it is nothing at all.   Uriah Heep, in Mr. Dickens's beautiful story, forgave David Copperfield for striking him a blow. But Uriah Heep never did anything more vicious, more thoroughly malignant, than that hypocritical act. But it was vicious and malignant, just because it was hypocritical. In matters like this, sincerity is the touchstone.

I suppose most readers will agree with me when I say, that I know no Christian duty which is so grievously neglected by people claiming to be extremely good. There is no mistake whatever as to what is the Christian way of meeting an unkindness or an unfriendly act : it is very desirable that professing Christians had more faith in its efficiency. It would be well if we could all heartily believe, and act upon the belief, that our Maker knows and advises the right and happy way of meeting a bad turn when it may be done to us, however naturally our own hearts may suggest a very different way. But I fear that our experience of life has convinced most of us, that this duty of returning good for evil is one that is very commonly and very thoroughly shelved. A great many people set it aside, as something all very good and proper : very fit for the Bible to recommend, setting up (as the Bible of course ought to do) a perfect ideal : but as something that *will not work.* We have all a little of that feeling latent in us. And here and there you may find a human being, perhaps a person of an exceedingly loud and ostentatious religious profession, who is so touchy, so ready to take offence, and then so vindictive and unsparing in following up the man that gave it, and in retaliating by word and deed,—by abusive speeches, and malicious writings, and ill-set demeanour generally,—that it is extremely plain, that though that man might sympathetically shake his head if he were told to 'overcome evil with good,' and accept *that* as a noble precept, still his real motto ought rather to be that simple and compendious rule of life, 'I will hit you, if you hit me!'

I am going to point out certain reasons which make me call the rule of meeting evil with good *the Right Tack*; and the rule of meeting evil with evil *the Wrong Tack*. For one thing, the Right Tack is the effectual way. What the second thing is, I don't choose to tell you till you arrive at it in the regular course of diligently reading these pages. Let there be no skipping. So, for one thing at a time, the Right Tack is the effectual thing.

Of course, the natural impulse is, to return a blow, and to resent an injury or insult. *That* is the first thing that we are ready to do. We do that almost instinctively: certainly with little previous reflection. And a brute does *that*, just as naturally as a man. It is nothing to boast of, that you stand on the same level as a vicious horse, or a savage bulldog, or an angry hornet. But, then, *that* does not *overcome* the evil. No: it perpetuates and increases it. It provokes a rejoinder in kind; *that* provokes another: and thus the mischief grows, till from a small offence at the beginning, vast and comprehensive sin and misery have arisen. But go on the other tack: and you will soon see, from the little child at play, up to the worn man with his long experience of this world, how the soft answer turns away wrath, and the kind and good deed beats the evil! There is a beautiful little tract, called *The Man that killed his Neighbours*: which sets forth how a good man, coming to a cantankerous district, by pure force of persevering and hearty kindness, fairly killed various unfriendly neighbours, who met him with many unfriendly acts. He killed the enemy, that is: he did not kill the individual man: but the enemy was altogether annihilated: and the individual man continued to exist as a fast friend. There is something left in average human nature even yet, which makes it very hard indeed to go on doing ill to a man who goes on showing kindness to you. You may get that tract for twopence: go and pay your twopence, and (after finishing this essay) read that tract. No doubt, there is so much that is mean and unworthy in some hearts, and people so naturally judge others by themselves, that there may be found those who cannot understand this returning of good for evil: who will suspect there is something wrong lurking under it: and who will not believe that it

is all sincere and hearty. And many an honest and
forgiving heart has felt it as a trial to have its good
intentions so misconceived. My friend Green once
wrote an article in a magazine. In a certain
brilliant weekly periodical there appeared a notice
of that article, finding fault with it. And a week or
two after, in another article in the magazine,
Green, in a good-natured way, replied to the notice
in the weekly periodical; and while defending
himself in so far, admitted candidly that there was
a good deal of truth in the strictures of the weekly
periodical. Green did all that, just as bears and
lions growl and fight, because it was 'his nature
to:' it cost him no effort; and assuredly there was
no hypocritical affectation in what he did: he felt
no bitterness, and so he showed none: he was
amused by the clever attack upon him, and showed
that he was amused. Some time after this, I read
an ill-natured notice of Green in a newspaper, in
which, among his other misdoings, there was
reckoned up this rejoinder to the brilliant weekly
periodical. He was likened to Uriah Heep, already
mentioned: he was accused of hypocrisy, of arrogant
humility, and the like. Of course, it was manifest
to all who knew Green, that his assailant knew as
much about Green's character as he does about the
unexplored tracts of Central Africa. But a mean-
spirited man cannot even understand a generous
one: and the assailant could not find it in himself

to believe that Green was a frank, honest man, writing out of the frankness of an unsuspecting heart. So, X and Y were once attacked in print by Z: X thereafter cut Z.   Y remained on friendly terms with Z, as previously.   Y pointed out to X that it is foolish to quarrel with a man for attacking you, even severely, upon properly critical grounds.   Y further said, that he would never quarrel with a man who attacked him even in the most unfair way : that he would treat the attacking party with kindness, and try to show him that his unfavourable estimate was a mistaken one.   ' Ah,' replied X, ' you are scheming to get Z to puff you !' To meet evil with good, X plainly thought, is a thing that could not be done in good faith, and just because it is the right thing to do.   There must be some underhand, unworthy motive.   And the greatest obstacle that you are likely to find, in habitually meeting evil with good, will be the misconstruction of your conduct by some of the people that know you.   No doubt, Uriah Heep himself, and all his relatives, will be ready to represent that you are a humbug and a sneak. Well, it is a great pity. But you cannot help *that*.   Go on still on *the Right Tack* : and by-and-by it will come to be understood that you go upon it in all honesty and truth, and with no sinister nor underhand purpose. And when this comes to be understood, then the evil in almost every case will be overcome, and that effectually.

No human being, unless some quite exceptionally hardened reprobate, will long go on doing ill to another who only and habitually returns good for it.

This is not an essay for Sunday reading : it is meant to be quietly read over upon the evening of any day from Monday till Saturday inclusive. But that is no reason why I should not say to you, my friend, that you and I ought to bring the whole force of our Christian life and principle to bear upon this point.   Let us determine that, by the help of God's Holy Spirit, without whom we can do nothing as we ought, we shall faithfully go upon the right tack through all the little ruffles and offences of daily life.   If the sharp retort comes to your lips, remember that it touches the momentous question whether you are a Christian at all, or not, that you hold that sharp word back, and say a kind one.   If Mr. A., or Miss B. (a poor old maid, soured a good deal by a tolerably bitter life), speak unkindly of you, or do you some little injustice, say a good word or do a good deed to either of them in return. Pray for God's grace to help you habitually to do all *that*.   It will not be easy to do all *that* at the first; but it will always grow easier the longer you try it.   It will grow easier, because the resolution to go on the right tack will gain strength by habit. And it will grow easier too, because when those around you know that you honestly take Christ's own way of returning an injury, not many will have the heart to injure you: very few will injure you twice. I have the firmest belief, that the true system of Mental Philosophy is that which is implied in the New Testament: and that there never was any one who knew so well the kind of thing that would suit the whole constitution of man, and the whole system of this universe, as He who made them both.

One case is worth many reasonings. Let me relate a true story. Not many years since there was in Mesopotamia a Christian merchant; of great wealth, and with the Right Spirit in him. A neighbouring trader, who did not know much about the Christian merchant, published a calumnious pamphlet about him. The Christian merchant read it: it was very abusive and wicked and malicious. In point of style it was something like the little document which contains the articles about *Good Words* which appeared in a newspaper called *Christian Charity*. The Christian merchant, I repeat, read the pamphlet: all he said was, that the man who wrote it would be sorry for it some day. This was told the libellous trader: who replied that he would take care that the Christian merchant should never have the chance of hurting him. But men in trade cannot always decide who their creditors shall be: and in a few months the trader became a bankrupt, and the Christian merchant was his chief creditor.

The poor man sought to make some arrangement that would let him work for his children again. But every one told him that this was impossible without the consent of Mr. Grant. *That* was the Christian merchant's honoured name. 'I need not go to *him*,' the poor bankrupt said: 'I can expect no favour from *him*.' 'Try him,' said somebody who knew the good man better. So the bankrupt went to Mr. Grant; and told his sad story, of heavy losses, and of heartless work and sore anxiety and privation: and asked Mr. Grant's signature to a paper already signed by the others to whom he was indebted. 'Give me the paper,' said Mr. Grant, sitting down at his desk. It was given: and the good man, as he glanced over it, said, 'You wrote a pamphlet about me once:' and without waiting a reply, handed back the paper, having written something upon it. The poor bankrupt expected to find *libeller*, or *slanderer*, or something like that written. But no: there it was, fair and plain, the signature that was needed to give him another chance in life. 'I said, you would be sorry for writing that pamphlet,' the good man went on. 'I did not mean it as a threat. I meant that some day you would know me better, and see that I did not deserve to be attacked in that way. And now,' said the good man, 'tell me all about your prospects: and especially tell me how your wife and children are faring.' The poor trader told him, that to partly meet his debts he had given up everything he had in the world; and that for many days they had hardly had bread to eat. 'That will never do,' said the Christian merchant, putting in the poor man's hand money enough to support the pinched wife and children for many weeks. 'This will last for a little, and you shall have more when it is gone: and I shall find some way to help you, and by God's blessing you will do beautifully yet. Don't lose heart: I'll stand by you!' I suppose I need not tell you that the poor man's full heart fairly overflowed, and he went away crying like a child. Yes, the Right Tack is the effectual thing! To meet evil with good, fairly beats the evil, and puts it down. The poor debtor was set on his feet again: the hungry little children were fed. And the trader never published an attack upon that good man again as long as he lived. And among the good man's multitude of friends, as he grew old among all the things that should accompany old age, there was not a truer or heartier one than the old enemy thus fairly beaten! Yes, my reader: let us go upon the Right Tack!

And now for the other reason I promised to give you why I call all this the Right Tack. It is not merely the most effectual thing: it is the happiest thing. You will feel jolly (to use a powerful and classical expression) when, in spite of strong temptation to take the other way, you resolutely go on the Right Tack. I suppose that when the poor trader, already named, went away with his full heart, feeling himself a different man from what he had been when he entered the merchant's room, and hastening home to tell his wife and children that he had found God's kind angel in the shape of a white-haired old gentleman in a snuff-coloured suit, and wearing gaiters,— I suppose there would not be many happier men in this world than that truly Christian merchant prince. He was very much accustomed, indeed, to the peculiar feeling of a man who has returned good for evil : but this feeling is one which no familiarity can bring into contempt. But suppose Mr. Grant had gone on the other tack : said, 'You libelled me once : it is my turn now : you shall smart for it :' I don't think any of us would envy him his malignant satisfaction. And when he went home that night to his grand house, and enjoyed all the advantages which came of his great wealth, I don't think he would relish them more for thinking of the bare home where the poor debtor had gone, with his last hopes crushed, and for thinking of the little hungry children ;—of little Tom sobbing himself to sleep without any supper,— of little Mary, somewhat older, saying, with her thin white face, that she did not want any. At least, if he *had* found happiness in all this, most human beings, with human hearts, would class him with devils, rather than with men. Give me Lucifer at once, with horns and hoofs, rather than the rancorous old villain in the snuff-coloured suit!

It causes suffering to ordinary human beings, to be involved in strife. It is a dull, rankling pain. It has a cross-influence on all you do. And reading your Bible, and praying to God, it will often come across you with a sad sense of self-accusing. You will not be able to entirely acquit yourself of blame. You will feel that all this is not very consistent with your Christian profession : with your seasons at the communion-table : with your prayers for forgiveness as you hope to be forgiven : with the remembrance that in a little while you must lay down your weary head, and die. The man who has dealt another a stinging blow, in return for some injury : the man who has made an exceedingly clever and bitter retort, in speech or in writing : may feel a certain complacency, thinking how well he has done it, and what vexation he has probably caused to a fellow-sinner and fellow-sufferer. But he cannot be happy. He *cannot!* He cannot know the real glow of heart that you will feel, my reader, when God's blessed Spirit has helped you, with all your heart, to do something kind and good to an offending brother. Yes, it is the greatest luxury in which a human being can indulge himself, the luxury of going upon the Right Tack when you are strongly tempted to go upon the Wrong!

I must speak seriously. I cannot help it. All
this is unutterably important; and I cannot leave
you, my friend, with any show of lightness in speaking about it. All this is of the very essence of our
religion: it goes to the great question, whether or
not we are Christian people at all: it touches the
very ground of our acceptance with God, and the
pardon of our manifold sins. There are certain
words never to be forgotten: 'If ye forgive men
their trespasses, your Heavenly Father will also
forgive you: But if ye forgive not men their trespasses, neither will your Father forgive your trespasses.' Yes: the taint of rankling malice in our
hearts, when we go to God and ask for pardoning
mercy, will turn our prayers into an imprecation
for wrath. 'Forgive us our debts, as we forgive
our debtors:' Forgive us our sins against Thee, just
as much as we forgive other men their offences
against us: that is, not at all! Think of the un-
forgiving man or woman who returns evil for evil,
going to God with *that* prayer! I cannot say how
glad and thankful I should be, if I thought that all
this I have been writing would really influence some
of those who may read this page, to resolve, by
God's grace, that when they are daily tempted to
little resentments by little offences,—and it is only
by these that most Christians in actual life are
tried,—they will habitually go on the Right Tack!
But remember, my friend, that nothing you have

read is more real and practical,—nothing bears
more directly upon the interests of the life we are
daily leading, with all its little worries, trials, and
cares,—than what I say now: that it is only by the
help and grace of the Holy Spirit of God that you
can ever thoroughly and effectually do what I mean
by going upon the Right Tack. A calm and kindly
temperament is good: a disposition to see what
may be said in defence of such as offend you, is
good: and doubtless these are helps: but something
far more and higher is needed. There must be a loftier and more excellent inspiration than that of the
calm head and the kind heart. You will never do
anything rightly, never anything steadfastly, that
goes against the grain of human nature, except by
the grace of that Blessed One who makes us new
creatures in Christ. There will be something that
will not *ring sound* about all that meeting evil with
good, which does not proceed from the new heart,
and the right spirit sanctified of God.

Now, let there be no misunderstanding of all
this: and no pushing it into an extreme opposed to
common sense. All this that has been said, has
been said concerning the little offences of daily life.
As regards these, I believe that what I have called
the Right Tack is the effectual thing and the happy
thing. But I am no advocate of the principle of
non-resistance. I am no member of the Peace
Society. I have no wish to see Britain disband her

armies, and dismantle her navy, and lie as a helpless prey at the mercy of any tyrant or invader. No: I should wish our country's claws to be sharp and strong: *that* is the way to prevent the need for their use from arising. I should, with regret, but without conscientious scruple, shoot a burglar who intended to murder me. I heartily approve the blowing of a rebel sepoy away from a cannon. And though the punishment of death, as inflicted in this country, is a miserable necessity, still I believe it is a necessity, and a thing morally right, in almost every case in which it is inflicted. All that has been said about the returning of good for evil is to be read in the light of common sense. There are bad people whom you cannot tame or put down, except by the severe hand of Justice. And in taming them in the only possible way, you are doing nothing inconsistent with the views set forth in these pages. It would take too much time to argue the matter fully out: and it is really needless. A wrongheaded man, a member of the Peace Society, has published a pamphlet in which he frankly tells us that if he, and his wife and children, were about to be murdered by a burglar, and if there was no possibility of preventing this murdering except by killing the burglar; then it would be the duty of a Christian to die as a martyr to his principles, and peaceably allow the burglar to murder him and his family. Really there is nothing to be said in reply to such a puzzle-head, except that I would just as soon believe that black is white, as that *that* is a Christian duty. There are exceptional human beings who are really wild beasts : and who must be treated precisely as a savage wild beast should be treated. And even in the matter of injuries of a less decided character than the murdering of yourself, your wife and children, it is as plain as need be that a wise and good man may very fitly defend himself against the aggression of a ruffian. When Mr. Macpherson threatened to thrash Dr. Johnson for expressing doubts as to the genuineness of Ossian, Dr. Johnson was quite right to provide a stick of great size and weight, and to carry it about with him for the purpose of self-defence. And while desirous to obey the spirit of the Saviour's command, there are few things of which I feel more certain, than that if a blackguard struck my good friend Dr. A. on the right cheek, the blameless divine would not turn the other also. Nor need we make the least objection to the motto of a certain Northern country, which conveys that people had better be careful how they do that country any wrong, inasmuch as that country won't stand it. There is nothing amiss in the *Nemo me impune lacesset.* Don't meddle with us : we have not the least wish to meddle with you.

CHAPTER XIII.

CONCERNING NEEDLESS FEARS.

T the present moment, I feel very uncomfortable. Not physically, but mentally and morally. And I do not know why. What I mean is, that a little ago some disagreeable thought was presented to my mind, which put me quite out of sorts. And though I have forgotten what the disagreeable thought was, its effect remains: and I still feel out of sorts. I am aware of a certain moral aching, which I cannot refer to its cause. I suppose, my reader, you have often felt the like. You have been conscious of a certain gloom, depression, bewilderment: not remembering what it was that started it. But after a little time it suddenly flashes on you; and you remember the whole thing.

I can imagine a man going to be hanged, waking up on the fatal morning with a dull aching sense of something wrong, he does not know what: till all

at once the dreadful reality glares upon him. Some
of us have had the experience, as little boys, when
coming back to consciousness on the morning of the
day we had to return to school, far away from home.
In certain cases, returning to school is to a boy not
many degrees less unendurable than being hanged
is to a man. Of course there is no remorse in the
case of the little schoolboy: and here is a discrepance
between the cases suggested. But indeed it is vain
to estimate the relative crushing powers of two great
trials. Each at the time is just as much as one can
bear.

But (to go back a little), just as a strong hand,
seven hundred years since, set a large stone in its
place in a cathedral wall, and the stone remains
there to-day, though the hand that placed it is gone
and forgot : in like manner some painful reflection
jars the human mind, and puts it out of joint ; and
it remains jarred and out of joint after the painful
reflection has passed away. A cloud passes between
us and the sun ; and a sudden gloom and chill fall
upon all things. But, strange to say, in the moral
world, after the cloud that brought the gloom and
chill has passed, the gloom and chill remain. And
thus, a human being may feel very uncomfortable,
and know that he has good reason for being uncomfortable ; yet not know what the reason is. If
you receive ten letters before breakfast, you open
them all and read them hastily. It is very likely

that one of the ten contains some rather disagreeable communication. You forget, in a minute, as you skim the newspaper and take your breakfast, what that disagreeable communication was. Yet still you take your breakfast with a certain weight upon your spirits : with a certain vague sense of something amiss.

What is it that is wrong this Saturday evening, 9.10 P.M. ? Nothing is wrong physically. Too thankful would this writer be, if he could but be assured that on all the Saturday evenings of his life he would be as happily placed as he is now. To-morrow he is to preach at his own church : and during the week all but gone, he hath prepared two new discourses to be preached on that day. Indurated must be that man's conscience, or very lightly must that man take his work, who does not feel a certain glow of satisfaction on the Saturday evening of a week wherein he has prepared two new discourses. You remark, I don't say two new sermons. No sensible mortal can prepare, or would try to prepare, two new sermons in one week. But he may prepare one sermon, and one lecture : which (being added one to the other) will be found to amount to two discourses. But any one who knows the long and hard work which goes to the production of a sermon which people may be expected to listen to, will feel, as he sews up his manuscript, the peculiar satisfaction which attends the contemplation of 'something attempted, something done.'

Yes, I remember now. Something I thought of this morning has come with me all the day, making me feel gloomy even while forgetting what it was. You know how a severe sting from a nettle leaves behind it a certain starting pain, hours after the first heat of the sting is gone. So it was here. And in this, too, is a point of difference between the material and moral world. In the material world, if a table stands on three legs, and you in succession saw off the three legs, the table goes down. But in the moral world (especially in the case of old women), if a belief, or a feeling, founds upon three reasons (or legs), though you in succession take away those reasons, the table often still stands as before. The physical table cannot do without legs. The moral table often stands firmest when it has no legs whatever. The beliefs which men often hold most resolutely, are those for which not merely they can give no reason, but for which no reason could be given by anybody.

I was thinking of the fears which eat the heart out of so many lives. And this was my reflection.

When I was a boy, there was exhibited in London what was called a Centrifugal Railway. Let

me request you earnestly to attend to the subjoined
diagram.

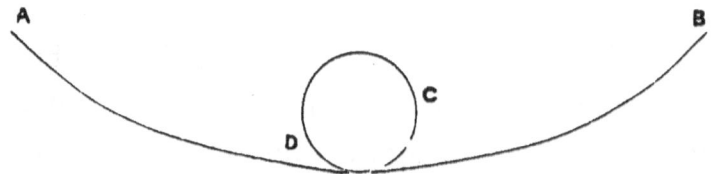

The line A D C B represents the Centrifugal
Railway.   You started from the point A in a little
carriage.   It acquired a very great velocity in running down the descent from A to D : a velocity so
great that it ran right round the circle C, turning
the passenger with his head downwards ; and finally,
got safely to B.   At the point B the passenger got
out : and if he were a person of sense (which, under
the circumstances, was by no means probable), he
resolved never to travel by the Centrifugal Railway
any more.

Now, you observe that in turning the circle C the
passenger was in a very critical position.   He had
good reason to be thankful when the circle was
fairly turned ; and he had, with unbroken bones,
reached B.   And it struck me, that all our life here
is like the circle C on the Centrifugal Railway.   I
shall be able to think differently in a day or two :
more hopefully and cheerfully : but it was borne in
upon me that after all, my friends, we are doing no
more in this life than getting round the circle C :
and that there are so many risks in the way, that

we may be very glad and thankful when it is done. He was a wise man in former days who said (let me translate his words into my peculiar idiom) ' I call no man happy before he has got round the circle C.' And desponding times will come to all, in which they will think of the innumerable sad possibilities which hang over them, and the sorrowful certainties which are daily drawing nearer, and the dangers of getting off the line altogether and going to destruction. I look ahead, many a one will sometimes be disposed to say: and there are many, many things which I know may go wrong. Oh I would be thankful if I and those dear to me were safely round the circle C; and had got safely to the point B: even though some people shrink from that latter point as long as they possibly can.

Of course, this is a gloomy kind of view: but such views will sometimes push themselves upon one, and will not be put off. I hope it will go away shortly. It will go away all the sooner for my having made you partaker of it. I have in my mind an abstract eidolon, an image of the reader of this page; who is my confidential friend. To him I have told very many things which I have hardly ever told to any one else. And I want him to take his share of this vexatious view about the circle C, that so it may lie lighter on myself. All this life, of push, struggle, privation, trickery, getting on, failure: all this life, in which one man becomes Chancellor, and another

Prime Minister, and another a weary careworn
drudge, and another a self-satisfied blockhead, and
another a poor needlewoman labouring eighteen
hours a day for a few pence: all this life, of kings
and priests and statesmen, of cripples and beggars,
of joyful hearts and sorrowful hearts: of scheming
and working, as if there were no other world —
is no more than our getting round the circle C.
We are cast on that incline that begins from A, at
our birth; and our business is, to get safely to B.

Every day that dawns upon many people is a little
circle C. In the morning they are aware that various
things may go wrong in it; and of course they do
not know what the day may bring forth. We are
environed by many unknown dangers; and any
day we may say the hasty word, or do the foolish
thing, which may involve us in great trouble. Even
the most sagacious and prudent man may some
day be taken off his guard. And the accidents
which may befall us are quite innumerable. It is a
wonder we have got on so far in life as we have,
so little battered by the chances of the way. You
know some one who went out from his own home
on a frosty day, and in three minutes came back
pale and fainting, having fallen and fractured his
wrist. The pain was great; and the seclusion from
work was absolute for awhile. What could we do
if the like happened to us? Some one else thought
but one step of a stair remained for him to descend,

while in fact there were two : and the consequences of that misapprehension remained with him painfully to the end of his life. And thus, looking back on last year, one feels it was a most protracted and perilous circle C. It was made up of days, each of which might have brought we know not what with it. We have got safely round that circle, indeed : but at the beginning we were not sure that we should. If we could have had such an assurance, it would have spared us many fears. These fears are for the most part forgot, when we look back ; and feel how needless they were. But they were very real things at the time they were felt; and they were a terrible drawback from the pleasures of anticipation and of actual fact. When you look back on a few weeks or months of foreign travel, the whole thing has a fixed and certain look : the thing that has been is a thing for ever. But what a shifting tract of shadows it was, when you were looking forward to it ; and a tract not without several alarming spectres, vaguely stalking about over it. Now we know that we got safely back : but when we started, we did not know that we should. It was like leaving the point A, and flying round the circle C : whereas now we have reached the point B, and we have forgot our emotions in actually flying round the circle.

Two or three days ago, three friends of the writer sailed from Southampton, on their way to Egypt

and the Holy Land. They are to be away three
months. They are experienced travellers, and have
seen very many cities and men : and doubtless they
started with no feelings but those of pleasurable
anticipation. When I heard of their going my first
feeling was one of envy. How delightful to cast
aside all this perpetual toil, that overtasks one's
strength, and keeps one ever on the stretch : and
have three months for the mind to regain its elasticity, much diminished by its being kept always
bent ! And then, what strange, unfelt moods of
thought and feeling one would experience, when
surrounded by the scenes and associations of those
tracts of this world ! You would accumulate store
of new ideas and remembrances ; and in the first
sermons and essays you would write after returning, you would be (in a moral sense) curveting about
like a young colt in a pasture, and not plodding
like an old steady hack along the highway ! But
when I tried to put myself (in fancy) in the place
of my friends : when I thought of the long, unknown
way, and of the unsettled tribes of men : when I
thought of Mr. Buckle at Damascus : when I thought
of possible fevers and of most certain bugs : when I
thought how when human beings go to the East for
three months, they may chance never to come back
at all : then to a quiet stay-at-home person, who
has seen hardly anything, the circle C appeared
invested with many grounds of alarm ; and I was

reconciled to the fact that I was not stepping on
board the *Ellora* amid a great roar of escaping
steam, nor going down to the choky little berth,
and surveying my belongings there. Thus did I
repress the rising envy in my breast. But when
my friends come back again, portentous images
with huge beards: when they have made the Nile,
and Olivet, and Gethsemane, and the Dead Sea, a
possession for as long as memory serves them: when
they have got fairly and triumphantly round the
circle C, and happily reached the point of safety
B; then, I fear, the envious feeling will recur.

Oh, if we could but get quit of our needless
fears! Of those fears (that is) which take so much
from the enjoyment of life, and which the result
proves to have been quite groundless!

Some folk, with very robust nervous systems, probably know but little of these. But from large experience of my fellow-creatures, rich and poor ; and
from careful investigation of their features; I begin
to conclude that such fears are very common things.
Most middle-aged faces have an anxious look. You
can see, even when they bear a cheerful expression,
that they are capable in a moment of taking that
painful aspect of anxiety and apprehension. I do
not mean by fear the indulgence of physical cowardice : happily few of the race that inhabits Britain
will; on emergency, prove deficient in physical pluck.

But I mean that most middle-aged people, who have children, are somewhat cowed by the unknown Future : and that the too ready imagination can picture out a hundred things that may go wrong. *Anxius vixi,* wrote the man in the middle ages. And anxious we live yet ; and probably always will live, in this world.

If you go out in the dark expecting to see a ghost, you will very likely take a white sheet hung on a hedge for one. And even so, people in their feverish state of apprehension sometimes are dreadfully frightened by things which in a calmer mood they would discern had nothing alarming about them. Every one is sharp enough to see this, in the case of other people. You will find a man who will say to you, ' What a goose Smith is to worry himself about that table-cloth on the holly, and declare it is an apparition, and that it has bad news for him :' and in a few minutes you will be aware that the man who says all this, is furtively looking over his shoulder at a white donkey feeding under a thick hedge, and dreading that it is a polar bear about to devour him.

It is curious to think how often these needless fears, which cause so much unnecessary anxiety and misery, are the result of pure miscalculation : and this miscalculation not made in a hurry, but deliberately. I have a friend who told me this. When he was married, he had exactly 500*l.* a year, 'and no means of adding to that income. So as he could not increase his income, his business was to keep down his expenditure below it. But neither he nor his wife knew much about household management; and (as he afterwards found) he was a good deal victimised by his servants. After doing all he could to economise, he found, at the end of the third month of his financial year, that he had spent exactly 125*l.* Four times 125*l.*, he calculated, made 600*l.* a year, which was just 100*l.* more than he had got: so the debtor's prison appeared to loom in view; or some total change in his mode of life, which it seemed almost impossible for him to make, without very painful circumstances. And for weeks, the thought almost drove him distracted. Day and night it never was absent. At length, one day, brooding over his prospects, he suddenly discovered that four times 125 make just 500, and not 600: so that all his fears were groundless. He was relieved, he told me: but somehow his heart had been so burdened and sunk by those anxious weeks, that though the cause of anxiety was removed, it was a long time before it seemed to recover its spring.

Now my friend had all his wits about him. There was nothing whatever of that causeless delusion which shades off into insanity. But somehow he thought that $125 \times 4 = 600$: and his conclusion was that ruin stared him in the face.

I have heard of a more touching case. A certain man brought to a friend a sum of money, rather less than a hundred pounds; and asked the friend to keep it for him. He said it was all he had in the world, and that he did not know what he was to do when it was gone. He had been a quite rich man; but one of those swindling institutions whose directors ought to be hung, and are not, had involved him in great money responsibilities by its downfall. In a few days after leaving the money with his friend, the poor man committed suicide. Then his affairs were examined by competent persons; and it was found that after meeting all possible liabilities, he had been worth several hundreds a year. But the poor fellow had miscalculated: and here was the tragic consequence.

No doubt, he had been so terribly apprehensive, that he had been afraid to make a thorough examination as to how his affairs stood. Human beings often undergo much needless fear, because they are afraid to search out all the facts. For fear of finding the fact worse than they fear, they often fear what is much worse than the fact. They go on through life thinking they have seen a ghost, and miserable in the thought: whereas, if they had but screwed their courage to the point of examining, they would have found it was no more than a table-cloth drying upon a line between two poles. Oh that we could all, for ever, get rid of this moral cowardice! If you think there is something the matter with your heart, go to the doctor and let him examine. Probably there is nothing earthly wrong. And even if there be, it is better to know the worst than live on week after week in a vague wretched fear. Let us do the like with our affairs. Let us do the like with our religious difficulties: with our theological perplexities. The very worst thing you can do is to lock the closet door when you think probably there is a skeleton within. Fling it wide open: search with a paraffin lamp into every corner. A hundred to one, there is no skeleton there at all. But from youth to age, we must be battling with the dastardly tendency to walk away from the white donkey in the shadow, which we ought to walk up to. I have seen a little child, who had cut her finger, entreat that it might just be tied up, without ever being looked at: she was afraid to look at it. But when it *was* looked at, and washed and sorted, she saw how little a thing it was for all the blood that came from it: and about nine-tenths of her fear fled away.

You have heard of Mr. Elwes, the wealthy miser, frightening a guest by walking into his bedroom during the night, and saying, ' Sir, I have just been robbed of seven guineas and a half, which was all I had in the world!' Here, of course, we enter the domain of proper insanity. For the fears which a man of vast fortune has lest he may die in the

workhouse, belong essentially to the same class
with those of the man who thinks he is glass, and
that if he falls he will break: or who thinks he is
butter, and if he goes near the fire he will melt.
And though all needless fears are morbid things,
which the healthy mind would shake off, yet there
is a vast distance between the morbid apprehensions
and the morbid depressions of the practically sane
man; and the phenomena of the mind which is
truly insane.

The truth seems to be, that some people must
have a certain amount of misery; and it will attach
itself to any peg. If not to this, then to another:
but the misery is *due*. And I defy you by any
means to lift such people above the slough of their
apprehensions. As you remove each cause of alarm,
they will fix upon another. First, they fear that
their means will not carry them from year's end to
year's end. *That* fear proves groundless. Next,
they fear that though their present income is ample,
somehow it will fall off. *That* fear proves groundless. Next, they are in dread as to the provision
for their children: and here, doubtless, most men
can find a cause of anxiety that will last them
through all their life. But it is their nature to be
always imagining something horrible. They live
in dread that they may quarrel with some friend;
or that some general crash will come some day,

they don't know how. And if all other causes of apprehension were absolutely removed, they would make themselves wretched to a suitable degree by fearing lest an earthquake should swallow up Great Britain; or that Dr. Cumming's calculations as to the end of the world may prove true. In short, if a human being be of a nervous, anxious temperament, it is as certain that such a human being will find some peg to hang his fears upon; as it is that a man who is the possessor of a hat will find something, wherever he goes, to hang it or lay it upon.

All this seems to be especially true in the case of people who have been heavily tried in youth. Human beings may be subjected to a treatment in their early years that seems to take the hopeful spring out of them. Unless where there is very unusual stamina of mind and body, they never quite get over it. You may damage a man so, that he will never quite get over it: you may give the youthful mind a wrench, whose evil effect will cling to it through all life. There are things in the moral world, which are like an injury to the spine, never recovered from; but that grows and strengthens with the man's growth and strength. And no good fortune, no happiness, coming afterwards, can ever make amends. The evil has been done; and it cannot be undone.

You have beheld a horse, no more than six years of age: but which is dull and spiritless, and its forelegs somewhat bent and shaky. Why are these things so? It has easy work now: good feeding: kind usage. Yes, but it was driven when too young. It was set to hard work then. And the creature never has got over it and never will. It is too late for any kindness now to make up for the mischief done at three years old.

I am firmly persuaded it is so with many human beings. They had an unhappy home as little boys. The love of the beautiful in nature and art was starved out in them. They were committed to the care of a self-conceited person, utterly devoid of common sense. All mirth was forbidden, as something sinful: life was made hard and savourless. They grew up under a bitter sense of injustice and oppression; and with the conviction that they were hopelessly misunderstood. Or, later, the weight of care came down upon them very heavily. There are many people who, for most of the years between twenty and thirty, never know what a light heart is. And by such things as these the spring of the spirit is broken. A dogged stedfastness of purpose may remain: but the elasticity is gone. The writer has no knowledge of Mr. Thackeray's character and career, except from the accounts of these which have been published since his death by some who knew him well. But it is strongly impressed on one, in reading these, that amid all the success and fame and love of his latter years, a certain tone of melancholy remained, testifying that former days, of unappreciated toil, of care and anxiety, had left a trace that never could go. It is only of a limited and exceptional order of troubles, that the memorable words can be spoken with any shade of truth: *Forsan et hæc olim meminisse juvabit.* I do not believe that the memory of pure misery can ever be other than a miserable thing.

If this were a sermon, I should now go on to set forth, at full length, what I esteem to be the best and worthiest means of getting free from those needless fears of which we have been thinking. But in this essay, I pass these briefly by for the present; and proceed to suggest a lesser cure for needless anxiety, which is not without its wholesome effect on some minds.

I believe that when you are worrying yourself by imagining all kinds of evils as likely to befall you, it will do you a great deal of good to be allowed to see something of other people who are always expecting something awful to happen, and with a morbid ingenuity devising ways of making themselves miserable. You will discern how ridiculous such people look: how irritating they are : how so far from exciting sympathy, they excite indignation. The Spartans were right to make their slaves drunk; and thus to cure their children of the least tendency to the vice of drunkenness, by letting them see how ugly it looks in another.   I request Mr. Snarling to take notice, that when I say the Spartans were right in doing this, I don't mean to say that they did an act which is in a moral sense to be commended or justified.   All I mean is, that they took a very effectual means to compass the end they had in view.   You never feel the badness of your own faults so keenly, as when you see them, carried a little farther, in somebody else. And so a human being, naturally very nervous and evil-foreboding, is corrected, when he sees how absurd it looks in another.   My friend Jones told me, that after several months of extremely hard head-work, which had lowered his nervous system, he found himself getting into a way of vaguely dreading what might come next ; and of receiving his letters in the morning with many anticipations of evil.   But happily a friend came to visit him, who carried all this about a hundred degrees farther : who had come through all his life ex-pecting at least an earthquake daily, if not the end of the world.   And Jones was set right.   In the words of Wordsworth, ' He looked upon him, and was calmed and cheered.'   Jones saw how like a fool his friend seemed ; and there came a healthy reaction ; and he opened his letter-box bravely every morning, and was all right again.   Yes, let us see the Helot drunk ; and it will teach us to keep sober.   My friend Gray told me that for some little space he felt a growing tendency to scrubbiness in money matters. But having witnessed pinching and paring (without the least need for them) carried to a transcendent degree by some one else, the very name of economy was made to stink in his nostrils; and he felt a mad desire to pitch half-crowns about the streets wherever he went. In this case, the reaction went too far: but in a week or two Gray came back to the middle course, which is the safest and best.

But, after all, the right and true way of escaping from what Dr. Newman has so happily called 'care's unthankful gloom,' and of casting off needless fears, lies in a different direction altogether. It was wise advice of Sydney Smith, when he said that those who desire to go hopefully and cheerfully through their work in this life, should 'take short views:' not plan too far ahead: take the present blessing and be thankful for it. It was indeed the best of all possible advice: for it was but a repetition, in another form, of the counsel of the Kindest and Wisest: 'Take therefore no thought for the morrow: for the morrow shall take thought for the things of itself: Sufficient unto the day is the evil thereof.' There is no doubt whatever, that the true origin of all these forebodings of evil, is our lack of trust in God. We all bear a far greater burden of anxiety than we need bear: just because we *will* try to bear our burden for ourselves, instead of casting it on a stronger arm. We try to provide for our children and ourselves: forgetting the sure promise to all humble Christian people, that 'the Lord will provide.' And when we seek to cast off our load of care, by the help of those comfortable words of Holy Scripture which invite us to trust everything to God, we try too much to reason ourselves into the assurance that we need not be so care-laden as we are: we forget that the only way in which it is possible for us to believe these words in our heart, and to take the comfort of them, is by heartily asking God that they may be carried home to us with the irresistible demonstration of the Holy Spirit. How the circle C would lose its fears, if we did but feel, by His gracious teaching, that it is the way which God designed for us: and that He will 'keep us in all our ways!' Whenever I see man or woman, early old with anxiety, and with a face deeply lined with care, I think of certain words which deserve infinitely better than to be printed in letters of gold: and I wish that such a one, and that all I care for, were numbered among the people who have a right to take these words for their own:

'Be careful for nothing: but in everything, by prayer and supplication with thanksgiving, let your requests be made known to God. And the peace of God, which passeth all understanding, shall keep your hearts and minds through Christ Jesus.'

CHAPTER XIV.

BEATEN.

DO you know this peculiar feeling? I speak to men in middle age.

To be bearing up as manfully as you can : putting a good face on things : trying to persuade yourself that you have done very fairly in life after all : and all of a sudden to feel that merciful self-deception fail you, and just to break down : to own how bitterly beaten and disappointed you are, and what a sad and wretched failure you have made of life?

There is no one in the world we all try so hard to cheat and delude, as ourself. How we hoodwink that individual, and try to make him look at things through rose-coloured spectacles! Like the poor little girl in Mr. Dickens's touching story, we *make believe very much.* But sometimes we are not able to make believe. The illusion goes. The bare, unvarnished truth forces itself upon us : and we see what miserable little wretches we are : how poor and petty are our ends in life: and what a dull weary round it all is. You remember the poor old half-pay officer, of whom Charles Lamb tells us. *He* was not to be disillusioned. He asked you to hand him the silver sugar-tongs in so confident a tone, that though your eyes testified that it was but a teaspoon, and that of Britannia metal, a certain spell was cast over your mind. But rely on it, though that half-starved veteran kept up in this way before people, he would often break down when he was alone. It would suddenly rush upon him what a wretched old humbug he was.

Is it sometimes so with all of us? We are none of us half-satisfied with ourselves. We know we are poor creatures, though we try to persuade ourselves that we are tolerably good. At least, if we have any sense, this is so. Yet I greatly envied a man whom I passed in the street yesterday; a stranger, a middle-aged person. His nose was elevated in the air: he had a supercilious demeanour, expressive of superiority to his fellow-creatures, and contempt for them. Perhaps he was a prince, and so entitled to look down on ordinary folk. Perhaps he was a bagman. The few princes I have ever seen, had nothing of his uplifted aspect. But what a fine thing it would be, to be able always to delude yourself with the belief that you are a great and important person: to be always quite satisfied with yourself, and your position. There are people who, while repeating certain words in the litany, feel as if it was a mere form signifying nothing, to call themselves *miserable sinners.* There are some who say these words sorrowfully from their very heart; feeling that they express God's truth. They know what weak, silly, sinful beings they are: they know what a poor thing they have made of life, with all their hard work, and all their planning and scheming. In fact, they feel beaten, disappointed, down. The high hopes with which they started, are blighted: were blighted long ago. They think, with a bitter laugh, of their early dreams of eminence, of success, of happiness. And sometimes, after holding up for a while as well as they could, they feel they can do it no longer. Their heart fails them. They sit down and give up altogether. Great men and good men have done it. It is a comfort to many a poor fellow to think of Elijah, beaten and sick at heart, sitting down under a scrubby bush at evening far in the bare desert, and feeling there was no more left, and that he could bear no more. Thank God that the verse is in the Bible.

'But he himself went a day's journey into the wilderness, and came and sat down under a juniper tree: and he requested for himself that he might die: and said, It is enough: now, O Lord, take away my life; for I am not better than my fathers.'

I thought of Elijah in the wilderness the other night. I saw the great prophet again. For human nature is the same in a great prophet as in a poor little hungry boy.

At nine o'clock on Saturday evening, I heard pitiful, subdued sobs and crying outside. I know the kind of thing that means some one fairly beaten. Not angry, not bitter: smashed. I opened the front-door: and found a little boy, ten years old, sitting on the steps, crying. I asked him what was the matter. I see the thin, white, hungry, dirty little face. He would have slunk away, if he could: he plainly thought his case beyond all mending. But I brought him in, and set him on a chair in the lobby: and he told his story. He had a large bundle of sticks in a ragged sack: firewood. At three o'clock that afternoon, he had come out to sell them. His mother was a poor washerwoman, in the most wretched part of the town: his father was killed a fortnight ago by falling from a scaffold. He had walked a long way through the streets: about three miles. He had tried all the afternoon to sell his sticks: but had sold only a halfpenny-worth. He was lame, poor little man, from a sore leg, but managed to carry his heavy load. But at last, going down some poor area stair in the dark, he fell down a whole flight of steps, and hurt his sore leg so that he could not walk, and also got a great cut on the forehead. He had got just the halfpenny for his poor mother: he had been going about with his burden for six hours, with nothing to eat. But he turned his face homewards, carrying his sticks: and struggled on about a quarter of a mile: and then he broke down. He could go no further. In the dark cold night, he sat down and cried. It was not the crying of one who hoped to attract attention: it was the crying of flat despair.

The first thing I did (which did not take a moment) was to thank God that my door-steps had been his juniper tree. Then I remembered that the first thing God did when Elijah broke down, was to give him something to eat. Yes, it is a great thing, to keep up physical nature. And the little man had had no food since three o'clock till nine. So there came, brought by kind hands (not mine) several great slices of bread and butter (jam even was added), and a cup of warm tea. The spirit began to come a little into the child. And he thought he could manage to get home if we would let him leave his sticks till Monday. We asked him what he would have got for his sticks if he had sold them all: ninepence. Under the circumstances, it appeared that a profit of a hundred per cent. was not exorbitant: so he received eighteen pence, which he stowed away somewhere in his rags: and the sack went away, and returned, with all the sticks emptied out. Finally, an old gray coat of rough tweed came, and was put upon the little boy, and carefully buttoned: forming a capital great coat. And forasmuch as his trowsers were most unusually ragged, a pair of such appeared, and being wrapped up, were placed in the sack, along with a good deal of bread and butter. How the heart of the child had by this time revived! He thought he could go home nicely. And having very briefly asked the Father of the fatherless to care for him, I beheld him limp away in the dark. All this is supremely little to talk about. But it was quite a different thing to see. To look at the poor starved little face: and the dirty hand like a claw: to think of ten years old: to think of one's own children in their warm beds: to think what all this would have been to one's self as a little child. Oh, if I had a four-leaved shamrock, what a turn-over there should be in this world!

When the little man went away, I came back to my work. I took up my pen, and tried to write; but I could not. I thought I saw many human beings besides Elijah in the case of that child. I tried to enter into the feeling (it was only too easy) of that poor little thing in his utter despair. It was sad enough, to carry about the heavy bundle hour after hour, and to sell only the half-penny worth. But it was dreadful, after tumbling down the stair, to find he was not able to walk; and still to be struggling to carry back his load to his bare home, which was two miles distant from this spot. And at last to sit down in misery on the step in the dark night, stunned. He would have been quite happy if he had got ninepence, God help him. When I was a boy, I remember how a certain person who embittered my life in those days was wont to say, as though it summed up all the virtues, that such a person was a man who looked at both sides of a shilling before spending it. It is such a sight as the little boy on the step that makes one do the like : that helps one to understand the power there is in a shilling. But many human beings, who can give a shilling rather than take it, are as really beaten as the little boy. They too have got their bags, filled with no matter what. Perhaps poetry, perhaps metaphysics, perhaps magazine articles, perhaps sermons. They thought they would find a market, and sell these at a great profit : but they found none. They have fallen down a stair ; and broken their leg and bruised their head. And now, in a moral sense, they have sat down in the dark on a step : and though not crying, are gazing about them blankly.

Perhaps you are one of them.

CHAPTER XV.

GOSSIP.

WHO invents the current lies? I suppose a multitude of people give each their little contribution, till the piece of malignant tattle is formed into shape.

There are many people, claiming to be very religious people, who are very willing to repeat a story to the prejudice of some one they know: though they have very little reason to think it true, and have strong suspicions that it is false. There is a lesser number of respectable people, who will positively invent and retail a story to the prejudice of some one they know, being well aware that it is false. In short, most people who repeat ill-natured stories may be arranged in these two classes:

1. People who lie:
2. People who lie, and know they lie.

The intelligent reader is requested to look upon the words which follow: and then he will be informed about a malicious, vulgar, and horribly stupid piece of gossip.

MR. AND MRS. GREEN
ALWAYS
DRESS FOR DINNER.

My friend Mr. Green lately told me, that quite by accident, he found that in the little country town where he lives, and of which indeed he is the Vicar, it had come to be generally reported that in every bedroom in his house, a framed and glazed placard was hung above the mantelpiece, bearing the above inscription. Miss Tarte and Mr. Fatuous had eagerly disseminated the rumour, though it was impossible to say who had originated it. Probably Miss Tarte had one day said to Mr. Fatuous that Mr. Green ought to have such a placard so exhibited; and that some day Mr. Green probably would come to have such a placard so exhibited. A few days afterwards Mr. Fatuous said to Miss Tarte that he supposed Mr. Green must have his placards up by this time. And next day, on the strength of that statement, Miss Tarte told a good many people that the placards were actually up. And the statement was willingly received and eagerly repeated by those persons in that town who are always delighted to have something to tell which shows that anyone they know has done something silly or bad. At last, a friend

of Mr. Green's thought it right he should know
what Mr. Fatuous and Miss Tarte were saying.
And Mr. Green, who is a resolute person, took
means to cut these individuals short. My friend
has exactly one spare bedroom in his house: and
no one who is not an idiot need be told that no
such inscription was ever displayed or ever dreamt
of in his establishment. Next Sunday Mr. Green
preached a sermon from the text, *Thou shalt not
bear false witness against thy neighbour.* And
after pointing out that it was unnecessary that the
commandment should forbid false witness to the
advantage of one's neighbour, inasmuch as nobody
was likely ever to bear *that*: he went on to point out,
with great force of argument, that if man or woman
habitually told lies to the prejudice of their neighbours, their Christian character might justly be held
as an imperfect one, even though they should attend
all the week-day services and missionary society
meetings within several miles. Mr. Fatuous and
Miss Tarte complained that this was very unsound
doctrine. And Miss Tarte wrote a letter to the
Record, in which she stated that the vicar habitually
preached the doctrines of Bishop Colenso.

One is most unwilling to believe it; yet I am
compelled by the logic of facts to think that malice
towards all their fellow-creatures is an essential
part of the constitution of many people. All the
particles of matter, we know, exert on each other

a mutual repulsion. Is it so with the atoms that make up human society? Many people dislike a man, just because they know nothing about him. And when they come to know something about him, they are sure to dislike him even more. In a simple state of society, if you disliked a man, you would knock him on the head. If an Irishman, you would shoot him from behind a hedge. The modern civilised means of wreaking your wrath on the man you dislike, is different. You repeat tattle to his prejudice. You tell lies about him. This is the weapon of warfare in Christian countries. Two things there are the wise man will not trust, if said by various persons we all know:

1. Anything to their own advantage:
2. Anything to their neighbour's prejudice.

It is a bad sign of human nature, that many men should have so much to say to the prejudice of anyone they know. But it is a much worse sign of human nature, that many men should hear with delight, and speak with exaggeration, anything to the prejudice of people whom they know nothing about. The man you know may have given you offence. The man of whom you know nothing cannot possibly have done so. And if you hate him, and wish to do him harm, it can only be because you are prepared to hate the average specimen of your race. We all know those who, if they met a fellow-creature out in the lonely desert, would see in him not a friend but an enemy; and would prepare to shoot him, or hamstring him unobserved. For the people I mean prefer to deal their blow unseen. There are those who, as boys at school, would never have a fair fight with a companion : but would secretly give him a malicious poke, when unobserved. And such men, I have remarked, carry out the system when they have reached maturity. They will not boldly face the being they hate; but they secretly disseminate falsehoods to his disadvantage.

But it is sad to think that the hasty judgments men form of one another are almost invariably unfavourable ones. It is sad to think that people come to have such malignant feeling towards other people who are quite unknown to them. A short time ago, at a public meeting, Mr. Jones was proposed as a suitable person to be the town Beadle. Jones did not want the Beadleship, being already in possession of a preferable situation of the same character. When his name was proposed, an old individual rose to oppose him. That was all natural. But this individual was not content to oppose Jones's claims to the Beadleship. He positively gnashed his teeth in fury at Jones. He had no command of language, and could but imperfectly express his hatred; but he foamed at the mouth, the veins of his head swelled up, and he trembled in every limb with eager wrath, as he declared that he would

never consent to Jones being Beadle: that if Jones
was appointed Beadle, he himself (his name was
Mr. Curre) would forthwith quit the town and never
again enter it. Curre had never exchanged a word
with Jones in all his life. Yet he hated Jones: and
the mention of Jones's name thus infuriated him,
even as a scarlet rag a bull. Poor Curre was not a
bad-hearted fellow, after all: and at a subsequent
period Jones made his acquaintance. Now one
great principle which Jones holds by is this: that
if any man hate you, it must be in some measure
your own fault: you must in some way have given
offence to the man. So Jones, who is a very genial
and straightforward person, asked Curre to tell him
honestly why he had so keenly opposed his appointment to the Beadleship: adding that he feared he
had given Curre offence in some way or other,
though he had never intended it. And Curre, after
some hesitation, and with a good deal of shame,
replied, ' Well, the fact is, I could not bear to see
you riding such a fine horse: and Mr. Sneakyman
told me you paid a hundred and twenty pounds for
it.' ' My friend Curre,' was the reply, ' I gave just
forty for that horse: and how could you believe
anything said by Sneakyman ?' Curre assured Jones
that the reason why he had disliked him was just
that he knew so little of him: and that when he
came to know him, his dislike immediately passed
into a real warm and penitent regard. And when

Curre died soon after, he left Jones ten thousand pounds. Curre had no relations: so it was all right. And Jones had nineteen children: so it was all right for him too.

Reader, take a large sheet of paper: foolscap paper.

Take a pen. Sit down at a table where there is ink.

Write out a list of all the persons you dislike: adding a brief statement of the reason or reasons why you dislike each of them.

Having written accordingly, ask yourself this question: Am I doing well to be angry with these persons? Have they given me offence to justify this dislike?

And now, listen to this prophecy. You will be obliged to confess that they have not. You will feel ashamed of your dislike for them. You will resolve to cease disliking them.

Believe one who has tried. Here, on this table, is a large foolscap page. Three names did I write down of people I disliked. Then I wrote down the cause why I disliked the first. And it looked, being written down, so despicably small, that I felt heartily ashamed. And now, you large page, go into the fire: and with you, these dislikes shall perish. At this moment, I don't dislike any human being: and if anybody dislikes me, I hope he will cease doing so. If ever I gave him offence, I am sorry for it.

Yet I cannot quite agree with Jones in thinking that in every case where dislike is felt, it is at least in part the fault of the disliked person. In many cases it is: not in all. A retired oilman of large wealth, bought a tract of land, and went to reside on it. He found that his parish clergyman drove a handsome carriage, and had a couple of men-servants. The old oilman was infuriated. The clergyman's wife erected a conservatory: the oilman had an epileptic fit. Now all this was entirely the oilman's own fault. A retired officer went to live in a certain rural district. He dined at six o'clock. Several people round, who dined at five, took mortal offence. Oh for the abolition of white slavery! When will human beings be suffered to do as they please?

I have remarked, too, that most stupid people hate all clever people. I have witnessed a very weak and silly man repeat, with a fatuous and feeble malignity, like a dog without teeth trying to bite, some story to the prejudice of an eminent man in the same profession. And even worse: you may find such a man repeat a story not at all to the disadvantage of the eminent man, under the manifest impression that it *is* to his disadvantage. I have rarely heard Mr. Snarling say anything with more manifest malignity, than when he said that my friend Smith had bought a fire-proof safe in which to keep his sermons. Well, was there any harm in that ?   'Bedwell said he would take nothing under the chancellorship,' said Mr. Dunup.   Perhaps Bedwell should not have said so: but the fact proved to be that he got the chancellorship.

Clergymen of little piety or ability, and with empty churches, dislike those clergymen whose churches are very full.   You may discern this unworthy feeling exhibited in a hundred pitiful spiteful little ways.   I have remarked, too, that the emptier a man's church grows, the higher becomes his doctrine.   And flagrant practical neglect of duty is in some cases compensated by violent orthodoxy: the orthodoxy being shown mainly by accusing other people of heterodoxy.

Unworthy people hate those who do a thing better than themselves.   An inefficient rector empties his church.   He gets a popular curate who fills it.   The parishioners present the curate with a piece of plate.   Forthwith the rector dismisses the curate.   Or perhaps the rector dare not venture on that.   He waits till the curate gets a parish of his own: and then he diligently excludes him from the pulpit whence his sermons were so attractive.   His old friends shall never see or hear him again, if the rector can prevent it.   And further, the rector and his wife disseminate wretched little bits of scandal as to the extravagant sayings and doings of the curate, all exaggerated and mostly invented.

The heroic way of taking gossip, is that in which

the old Earl Marischals took it, when it was a
more serious thing than now. Above the door of
each of their castles, there were written on the stone
these words:

> THEY HAIF SAYD:
> QHAT SAYD THEY?
> LAT THEM SAY!

CHAPTER XVI.

CONCERNING CUTTING AND CARVING :

WITH SOME THOUGHTS ON TAMPERING WITH THE COIN OF THE REALM.

I BEHELD, as in a Vision, the following remarkable circumstances :

There was a large picture, by that great artist Mr. Q. R. Smith, hung up in a certain public place. It appeared to me that the locality partook of the nature of a market-place in a populous city : and numbers of human beings beheld the picture. A little vulgar boy passed, and looked at it : his words were these : ' My eye ! Ain't it spicy ? Rather !' A blooming maiden gazed upon it : and her remark was as follows : ' Sweetly pretty !' But a man who had long painted wagons for agricultural purposes, and who had recently painted a signboard, after looking at the picture for a little, began to improve it with a large brush, heavily loaded with coarse red and blue, such as are used for painting wagons. Another man came, a house-painter : and he touched the picture in several parts, with a brush filled with that white material which is employed for finishing the ceiling of rooms which are not very carefully finished. These persons, though horribly spoiling the picture, did honestly intend to improve it; and they fancied they had much improved it. Finally there came a malicious person, who was himself an artist ; and who envied and hated the first artist for painting so well. As for this man, he busied himself upon the principal figure in the picture. He made its eyes horribly to squint. He put a great excrescence on its nose. He painted its hair a lively scarlet. And having hideously disfigured the picture, he wrote beneath it, *Q. R. Smith pinxit.* And he pointed out the canvas to all his friends, saying, ' That's Smith's picture : isn't it beautiful ? '

Into this Vision I fell, sitting by the evening fire. The immediate occasion of this Vision was, that I had been reading a little volume, prettily printed and nicely bound, purporting to be *The Children's Garland from the Best Poets, selected and arranged by Coventry Patmore.* There I had been pleasantly reviving my recollection of many of the pieces, which I had been taught to read and repeat as a boy at school. And as I read, a sense of wonder grew, gradually changing to a feeling of indignation. I said to myself (speaking hastily and unjustly, as people do), Surely Mr. Coventry Patmore's

modesty has led him to take credit on his title-page
for much less than he deserves.   He has not merely
selected and arranged these pieces from the Best
Poets : he has also (according to his own ideas)
improved them.   We have (I thought) in this volume, the picture of Q. R. Smith, touched up with
red and whitewash, and having the eyes and nose
altered by the painter of signboards.   Or to speak
more accurately, in reading this volume, we are
requested to walk through a gallery of paintings by
great masters, almost all improved, in many places,
by the same painter of wagon-wheels, with the
same large brush filled with coarse red.   As we go
on with the book, we come upon some poem which
we have known all our lives : and every word of
which is treasured and sacred in our memory.   But
we are made to feel that this is indeed our old
friend : but his nose is cut off, and one of his eyes
is put out.   Such was my first hasty and unjust
impression.   Every poem of those I remembered
from childhood, had a host of verbal variations from
the version in which I knew it.   In Southey's
well-known verses about *The Bell on the Inchcape
Rock*, I counted thirty-seven.   There were a good
many in Campbell's two poems; one called *The
Parrot*, and the other about Napoleon and the
British sailor.   So with Cowper's *Royal George :* so
with Macaulay's *Armada*.   So with Scott's *Young
Lochinvar :* so with Byron's *Destruction of Sen-*

nacherib : so with Wordsworth's poem as to the dog that watched many weeks by his dead master on Helvellyn : so with Goldsmith's *Good people all, of every sort :* so with Mrs. Hemans' *Graves of a Household.* Mr. Patmore tells us in his Preface, that 'in a very few instances he has ventured to substitute a word or phrase, where that of the author has made the piece in which it occurs unfit for children's reading.' But on my first reading of his book, it appeared that he had made alterations by scores, most of them so trivial as to be very irritating. But I proceeded to investigate. I compared Mr. Patmore's version of each poem, with the version of each poem contained in the last edition of its author's works. And though I found a few variations, made apparently through careless transcribing : and though I was annoyed by considerable disregard of the author's punctuation and capitals ; still it appeared that in the main Mr. Patmore gives us the pieces as their authors left them : while the versions of them, given in those books which are put into the hands of children, have in almost every case been touched up by nobody knows whom. So that when Mr. Patmore's book falls into the hands of men who made their first acquaintance with many of the pieces it contains, in their schoolboy days ; and who naturally prefer the version of them which is surrounded by the associations of that season : Mr. Patmore will be unjustly accused of having cut and carved upon the dear old words. Whereas, in truth, the present generation has reason to complain of having been introduced to the wrong things in youth: so that now we cannot rightly appreciate the right things. And for myself, my first unjust suspicion of Mr. Patmore, speedily dispelled by investigation, led me to many thoughts upon the whole subject of literary honesty and dishonesty in this matter.

It seems to me quite essential that a plain principle of common faithfulness should be driven into those persons who edit and publish the writings of other men. If you pretend to show us Raphael's picture, let it be exactly as Raphael left it. But if your purpose be to exhibit the picture as touched up by yourself, do not mendaciously call the picture a Raphael. Call it what it is: to wit, Raphael altered and improved by Snooks. If you take a sovereign, and drill several holes in it, and fill them up with lead, you will be made to feel, should you endeavour to convey that coin into circulation, that though you may sell it for what it is worth as a sovereign plugged with lead, you had better not try to pass it off upon people as a genuine sovereign. All this is as plain as may be. But there are many collectors and editors of little poems, who take a golden piece by Goldsmith, Wordsworth, Campbell, or Moore: and punch out a word here and there, and stick in their own miserable little plug of pinchbeck. And then, having thus debased the coin, they have the impudence to palm it off upon the world with the superscription of Gold-smith, Wordsworth, Campbell, or Moore. It is needful, I think, that some plain principles of literary honesty should be instilled into cutting and carving editors. Even Mr. Palgrave, in his *Golden Treasury*, is not free from some measure of blame; though his sins are as nothing compared with those of the editors of school collections and volumes of sacred poetry. Mr. Palgrave has not punched out gold to stick in pinchbeck: but in one or two glaring instances, he has punched out gold and left the vacant space. Every one knows that exquisite little poem of Hood's, *The Death Bed*. That poem consists of four stanzas. Mr. Palgrave gives us in his book a poem which he calls *The Death Bed*; and puts at the end of it the honoured name of Hood. But it is not Hood's *Death Bed;* any more than a sovereign with one half of it cut off would be a true sovereign. Mr. Palgrave gives us just two stanzas: Hood's first and last; leaving out the two intermediate ones. In a note, whose tone is much too confident for my taste, Mr. Pal-grave attempts to justify this tampering with the coin of the realm. He says that the omitted stanzas are very ingenious, but that ingenuity is not in accordance with pathos. But what we want is Hood with his own peculiar characteristics: not

Hood with the corners rubbed off to please even so
competent a critic as Mr. Palgrave. In my judgment, the two omitted stanzas are eminently characteristic of Hood. I do not think they are very
ingenious: they express simple and natural feelings: and they are expressed with a most touching
and pathetic beauty. And on the whole, if you
are to give the poem to the world as Hood's, they
seem to have an especial right to stand in it. If
you give a picture of a bison, surely you should
give the hump: even though you may think the
animal would be more graceful without it. We
want to have the creature as God made it: with
the peculiarities God gave it.

The poems which are cut and carved to the
extremest degree, are hymns. There is indeed
some pretext of reason here: for it is necessary
that hymns should be made, in respect of the doctrines they set forth, to fit the views of the people
who are to sing them. Not that I think that this
justifies the practice of adulterating the text. But
in the few cases where a hymn has been altered so
completely as to become virtually a new composition; and a much better composition than it was
originally: and where the authorship is a matter
really never thought of by the people who devoutly
use the hymn; something is to be said for this
tampering. For the hymn is not set forth as a
poem written by this man or that: but merely as a

piece which many hands may have brought into its present shape; and which in its present shape suits a specific purpose. You don't daub Raphael's picture with wagon paint; and still exhibit it as a Raphael. You touch it up according to your peculiar views: and then exhibit it saying merely, Is not that a nice picture? It is nobody's in particular. It is the joint doing of many men, and perhaps of many years. But where hymns are presented in a literary shape, and as the productions of the men who wrote them, the same law of honesty applies as in the case of all other literary work. I observe, with very great satisfaction, that in the admirable *Book of Praise* lately published by Sir Roundell Palmer, that eminent lawyer has made it his rule 'to adhere strictly in all cases in which it could be ascertained, to the genuine uncorrupted text of the authors themselves.' And Sir Roundell Palmer speaks with just severity of the censurable, but almost universal practice of tampering with the text.

I confess that till I examined Mr. Patmore's volume, I had no idea to what an extent this literary clipping of the coin had gone, even in the matter of poetry for clipping and altering which there is no pretext of reason. It appears to me a duty, in the interest of truth, to protest against this discreditable cutting and carving. There are various editors of school-books, and other collections of poetry for the young, who seem incapable of giving the shortest poem by the greatest poet, without improving it here and there with their red brush. No statue is presented to us without first having its nose knocked off. And of course there is no necessity here for squaring the poems to some doctrinal standard. It is a pure matter of the editor's thinking that he can improve the compositions of Campbell, Wordsworth, Moore, Goldsmith, Southey, Scott, Byron, Macaulay, or Poe. So that in the case of every one of these manifold alterations the question is just this simple one: Whether Wordsworth or some pushing Teacher of Elocution is the best judge of what Wordsworth should say: whether we are to hold by these great poets, believing that they most carefully considered their most careful pieces; or to hold by anybody who chooses to alter them. There is something intensely irritating in the idea of Mr. Smith, with his pencil in his hand, sitting down with a volume of Wordsworth, every word in every line of which was carefully considered by the great poet, and stands there because the great poet thought it the right word; and jauntily altering a word here and there. The vision still returns to me of the sign-painter touching up Raphael. But I have no doubt whatsoever that Mr. Smith or Mr. Brown thinks himself quite equal to improving Wordsworth. The self-sufficiency of human beings is wonderful. I have heard of a man who thought he could improve things better than anything of Wordsworth's. Probably you never heard of the youthful Scotch divine who lived in days when stupid bigotry forbade the use of the Lord's Prayer in the pulpits of the Scotch Church. That young divine went to preach for an aged clergyman who was somewhat wiser than his generation: and who accordingly told the young divine in the vestry before service that the Lord's Prayer was habitually used in that church. 'Is it necessary,' said the young divine, 'that I should use the Lord's Prayer?' 'Not at all,' replied the aged clergyman, 'if you can use anything better.' But the young divine was true to his party: and he used certain petitions of his own, which he esteemed as improvements on the Lord's Prayer.

You may be quite sure that in the compositions of any careful writer, you could not alter many words without injury to the writer's style. You could make few alterations which the writer would approve. In a careful style, rely on it there was some appreciable reason present to the author's mind for the employment of almost every word; and for each word's coming in just where it does. This is true even of prose. And I should fancy that few men would long continue to write for any periodical the editor of which was wont to cut and carve upon their articles. You remember how bitterly Southey used to complain of the way in which

Lockhart altered his. But all this holds good with infinitely greater force in the case of poetry: especially in the case of such short gems as many of those in Mr. Patmore's volume. The prose writer, however accurate, covers his pages a day: each sentence is carefully weighed; but weighed rapidly. But the poet has lingered long over every word in his happiest verse. How carefully each phrase has been considered: how each phrase is fitted to all the rest! I declare it seems to me, there is something sacred in the best stanzas of a great poet. It is profanation to alter a word. And you know, how, to the sensitively strung mind and ear of the author a single wrong note makes discord of the whole: the alteration of a word here and there, may turn the sublime to the ridiculous. And such alterations may be made in all good faith, by people whose discernment is not sharpened to this particular use. There was a pretty song, popular some years ago, which was called *What are the wild waves saying?* The writer had many times heard that song: but he hardly recognised its name when he heard it once asked for by the title of *What are the mad waves roaring?* Let us have the poet's work as he left it. You do not know how painfully the least verbal alteration may jar upon a sensitive ear. I hold that so sacred is the genuine text of a great poet, that even to the punctuation; and the capital letters, however eccentric their use may be;

it should be esteemed as sacrilege to touch it. Let me say here that no man who does not know the effect upon poetry of little typographical features is fit to edit any poet. It seems to me, that Mr. Coventry Patmore fails here. It is plain that he does not perceive, with the sensitiveness proper to the editor of another man's poetry, what an effect upon the *expression* of a stanza or a line is produced by typographical details. Mr. Patmore not unfrequently alters the punctuation which the authors (we may suppose) adopted after consideration; and which has grown, to every true reader of poetry, as much a part of the stanza as its words are. Every one knows how much importance Wordsworth attached to the use of capital letters. Now, in the poem entitled *Fidelity* (*Children's Garland*, p. 248) Mr. Patmore has at *nine* different places substituted a small letter for Wordsworth's capital: considerably to the destruction of the expression of the piece: and at any rate, to the clipping of the coin Wordsworth left us. In the last verse of Poe's grand poem, *The Raven*, Mr. Patmore has, in six lines, made *five* alterations: one quite uncalled for; *four* for the worse. Poe wrote *demon:* Mr. Patmore chooses to make it *dæmon:* Poe wrote 'the shadow that *lies* floating on the floor:' Mr. Patmore substitutes *is* for *lies:* to the detriment of the sense. And Poe ends the stanza thus:

And my soul from out that shadow that lies floating on the
   floor
   Shall be lifted—nevermore!

It is extraordinary how many variations for the
worse Mr. Patmore introduces into the last line.
He makes it,

   Shall be lifted ' Nevermore.'

1st. The dash before the *nevermore* is omitted :
a loss.

2nd. The *Nevermore* is made to begin with a
capital : which though very right in preceding
stanzas, is here absurd.

3rd. The *Nevermore* is marked as a quotation :
which it is not.   It is one in the preceding stanzas,
and is properly marked as one : but here the mark
of quotation is wrong.

4th. Poe puts, most fitly, a mark of exclamation
after the *nevermore!*   If ever there was a stanza
which should end with that point, it is here.   But
Mr. Patmore, for no earthly reason, leaves it out.

Now, some folk may say these are small matters.
I beg to say that they are *not* small matters to any
accurate reader : and above all, to any reader with
an eye for the *expression* of poetry.   And no man,
who has not an eye for these minute points, and
who does not feel their force, is fit for an editor of
poetry.   I am quite sure that no mortal, with an
eye for such niceties, will deny, that each of Mr.
Patmore's *four* alterations of one line of Poe, is an

alteration for the worse. I have taken as the proper representation of Poe, the best American edition
of his whole works, in four volumes. But if you look
at the beautiful little edition of his poems, edited by
Mr. Hannay, you will find that the accurate scholar
has given that stanza exactly as the American
edition gives it : and of course, exactly right. If
Mr. Patmore does not understand how indescribably
irritating these little cuttings and carvings are to a
careful reader or writer, he is not the man to edit
the *Children's Garland,* or any other collection of
poetry. Every one can imagine the indignation
with which Wordsworth the scrupulous and Poe the
minutely accurate would have learned that their
best poems were, either through carelessness, or
with the design of making them better, altered by
Mr. Patmore, even in the matter of capital letters
and points : and that finally the result was to be
exhibited to the world, not as Raphael touched up
by Smith the sign-painter, but as Raphael pure and
genuine.

And while thus fault-finding at any rate, I am
obliged to say that though acquitting Mr. Patmore
of any vain-glorious purpose of improving those
Best Poets from whom he has selected his *Garland,*
I cannot acquit him of culpable carelessness in a
good many instances. Though he may not have
smeared the great master's picture with red paint,
he has not been sufficiently careful to present the

picture to us unsmeared by anybody else.   Except
in those 'very few instances' in which he has
changed a word or phrase ' unfit for children's reading,' we have a right to expect an accurate version
of the text.   But it is quite easy to point out instances in which Mr. Patmore's reading could not
have been derived from any edition of the poet,
however bad : nor can any one say that Mr. Patmore's reading is an improvement upon the *textus
receptus*.   The third and fourth lines of Macaulay's
poem, *The Armada*, run as follows :

> When that great fleet invincible against her bore in vain
> The richest spoils of Mexico, the stoutest hearts of Spain.

Mr. Patmore makes two alterations in these lines.
For *that great fleet* he reads *the great fleet*, to the
detriment alike of rhythm and meaning.   And for
the richest spoils of Mexico, he reads *the richest
stores*.   It is extremely plain that *spoils* is a much
better word than *stores*.   It was not the *stores* of
Mexico ; that is, the wealth stored up in Mexico ;
that the Armada bore.   It was the *spoils* of
Mexico ; that is, the wealth which the Spaniards
had taken away from Mexico ; that the Armada
bore.   It is possible that the Spaniards may have
taken away *all* the wealth of Mexico : in which
case the *spoils* and the *stores* would coincide in fact.
But they would still be totally different in con-

ception; and so exact a writer as Macaulay would never confound the two things.

Next, let us turn to Campbell's touching verses entitled *The Parrot.* Campbell put at the top of his verses the words, *The Parrot : a domestic Anecdote.* Mr. Patmore puts the words, *The Parrot : a true Story.* The poem tells us, very simply and beautifully, how a certain parrot, which in its early days had been accustomed to hear the Spanish language spoken, was brought to the island of Mull: where, we may well suppose, it heard no Spanish. It lived in Mull for many years, till its green and gold changed to grey : till it grew blind and apparently dumb. But let the story be told in the poet's words :

> At last, when blind and seeming dumb,
>   He scolded, laugh'd, and spoke no more,
> A Spanish stranger chanced to come
>   To Mulla's shore
> He hail'd the bird in Spanish speech,
>   The bird in Spanish speech replied,
> Flapp'd round his cage with joyous screech,
>   Dropt down, and died.

In glancing over Mr. Patmore's reading of this little piece, I am annoyed by observing several alterations in Campbell's punctuation : every alteration manifestly for the worse. But there is a more serious tampering with the text. The moral of the poem, of course, is that parrots have hearts and memories as well as we. And the poem sets out by stating that great principle. The first verse is:

> The deep affections of the breast,
>   That Heaven to living things imparts,
> Are not exclusively possess'd
>   By human hearts.

Mr. Patmore has the bad taste, not to say more, to leave that verse out. I cannot see any good reason why. The principle it states is one which a word or two would render quite intelligible to any child. Indeed, to any child who could not take in that principle, the entire story would be quite unintelligible. And I cannot recognise Mr. Patmore's treatment of this poem as other than an unjustifiable tampering with the coin of the realm.

There is another poem of Campbell's which fares as badly. Campbell calls it *Napoleon and the British Sailor.* Mr. Patmore, in his zeal for cutting and carving, calls it *Napoleon and the Sailor: a true Story.* This poem, like the last, sets out with a principle or sentiment; and then goes on with the facts. Mr. Patmore takes it upon himself to leave out that first verse: and then to daub the second verse in order to make it intelligible in the absence of the first. I hold this to be utterly unpardonable. It is emphatically Raphael improved by the sign-painter. And the pretext of anything 'unfit for children's reading' will not hold here. Any child that could understand the story, would understand this first verse:

> I love contemplating—apart
> From all his homicidal glory,
> The traits that soften to our heart
> Napoleon's story!

Then Campbell's second verse runs thus:

> 'T was while his banners at Boulogne
> Armed in our island every freeman,
> His navy chanced to capture one
> Poor British seaman.

Thus simply and naturally does the story which follows, rise out of the sentiment which the poet has expressed. But as Mr. Patmore has cut out the sentiment, he finds it necessary to tamper with the second verse: and accordingly he starts in this abrupt, awkward, and ugly fashion; which no true reader of Campbell will behold without much indignation: and which would have roused the sensitive poet himself to still greater wrath:—

> Napoleon's banners at Boulogne
> Armed in our island every freeman,
> His navy chanced

And so on. Here, you see, in the verse as improved by Mr. Patmore, we have two distinct propositions; separated by a comma. Mr. Patmore not merely has no eye for punctuation; but is plainly ignorant of its first principles. If any schoolboy, after having had the use of the colon and

semicolon explained to him, were to use a comma
in such fashion in an English theme, he would
richly deserve a black mark for stupidity; and he
would doubtless receive one. But apart from this
lesser matter, which will not seem small to any one
with a sense of grammatical accuracy, I ask whether
it be not too bad that Campbell's natural and
beautiful verse should be adulterated into this irritating caricature of it.

Let us next test Mr. Patmore's accuracy in
exhibiting Sir Walter Scott. Everybody knows
Lady Heron's Song which Sir Walter himself called
Lochinvar: but which Mr. Patmore, eager for
change, calls *Young Lochinvar.* Sir Walter's first
two lines are these:

> O, young Lochinvar is come out of the west,
> Through all the wide Border his steed was the best.

Mr. Patmore cannot render these simple lines
accurately. He begins *West* with a capital letter:
which, right or wrong, Sir Walter did not. Then
he puts a point of exclamation after *West*, where
Sir Walter has a comma. Sir Walter tells us that
Lochinvar's *steed was the best*: Mr. Patmore improves the statement into *his steed is the best.* The
very pettiness of these changes makes them the
more irritating. Granting that Mr. Patmore's reading is neither better nor worse than the original,
why not leave us the poem as the great man gave

it us? Through all that well-known song, one is
worried by Mr. Patmore's wretched little smears of
red paint. The punctuation throughout is no longer
matter for an imposition: it is matter for a flogging.
Sir Walter says,

> So *boldly* he entered the Netherby Hall:

Mr. Patmore with his brush makes it *so bravely.*
And, eager for change at any price, Mr. Patmore
gives us a new spelling of the name of the river
Esk. Sir Walter, like everybody else, spells that
word *Esk.* Mr. Patmore is not content with this,
but develops the word into *Eske.* Sir Walter
describes a certain locality as *Cannobie Lee*: Mr.
Patmore improves the name into *Cannobie* LEA.
And finally, the song ending with a question, Sir
Walter ends it with a point of interrogation. But
Mr. Patmore, impatient of the restraints of grammar,
concludes with a point of exclamation.

All this is really too bad. Byron fares no better:
and Mr. Patmore's alterations are of the same irritating and contemptible kind. Byron wrote

> And there lay the steed with his nostril all wide,
> But through it there rolled not the breath of his pride;

Mr. Patmore cannot leave this alone. In the first
line he reads *nostrils* for *nostril*: in the second, *them*
for *it.* Now, not only are Byron's words the best,
just because Byron chose them: but Byron's de-
scription is strikingly true to fact. Every one who

has ever seen a horse fallen, or a horse dead, knows how remarkably *flat* the creature lies upon the ground. It is startling to find the sixteen hands of height when the animal was upon his legs, turned to something that hardly surpasses your knee when the creature is lying upon his side. And the head of a dead horse, lying upon the ground, would show *one* nostril and not *two*. You would see only the upper one: and remark that the warm breath of the creature was no longer rolling through *that*. These little matters make just the difference between being accurate and being inaccurate: between being right and being wrong.

I do not know whether it be from a desire to improve Mr. Keble's name, that Mr. Patmore, in his *Index of Writers*, alters it to *Keeble*. I object likewise to Mr. Patmore's improving Barnfield's couplet

> She, poor bird, as all forlorn,
> Leaned her breast up till a thorn:

by substituting *against* for *up till*. The very stupidest child would know, after one telling, the meaning of *up till*: and Mr. Patmore's alteration is a destruction of the antique flavour of the piece.

The thoughtful reader, who has had some experience of life, must have arrived at this conviction: that if two or three slices of a leg of mutton are extremely bad, all the rest of the leg is probably bad too. I have not examined the whole of Mr.

Patmore's volume: but I am obliged to conclude, from the absence of minute accuracy in the pieces which I have examined, that the entire volume is deficient in minute accuracy. Now, in a book like this, accuracy is the first thing. If any scholar were to take up a play of Æschylus or Aristophanes, and find it as carelessly edited as several of the poems which we have considered, I think the scholar would be disposed to throw that play into the fire. And I cannot for my life see why perfect accuracy should be less sought after by an editor of English poems than by an editor of Greek plays.

But on the general question of cutting and carving I would almost go so far as to say, that after a poem has been current for years, and has found a place in many memories, not even its author has a right to alter it. Nothing, at least, but an improvement the most extraordinary, can justify such a breaking in upon a host of old associations. It is a mortifying thing, when a man looks, in later life, into the volumes of his favourite author, to find that the things he best remembers are no longer there. Even manifest improvement cannot reconcile us to the change. When the present writer was a youth at college, he cherished an enthusiastic admiration for John Foster's *Essays.* Let it be said, his admiration is hardly less now. I read and re-read them in a large octavo volume: one of the earlier editions, which had not received the author's latest corrections. Yet I valued every phrase: and I well remember how aggrieved I felt when I got an edition with Foster's final emendations: and found that Foster had cut out, and toned down, and varied, just the things of which my memory kept the firmest hold. One feels as though one had a vested interest in what had been so prized and lingered over. You know how Wordsworth and Moore kept touching up their verses: generally for the worse. I do not think the last edition which Wordsworth himself corrected, is the best edition of his poetry. In that poem of his which has already been named, concerning the faithful dog on Helvellyn, he made, late in life, various little changes: which not being decidedly for the better, must be held as for the worse. For any change from the dear old way is for the worse, unless it be very markedly for the better. And surely, after describing the finding of the poor tourist's body, the old way, which was this:

> Sad sight! the shepherd, with a sigh,
> Looks round, to learn the history:

is quite as good as the new way, which is this:

> The appalled Discoverer with a sigh,
> Looks round, to learn the history.

No rule, indeed, can be laid down here. No great poet cuts and carves upon his own produc-

tions so much as Mr. Tennyson. You remember
how

> Revered Victoria, you that hold—

has changed into

> Revered, beloved, oh you that hold.

You remember how in the story of the schoolboys who stole a litter of pigs, the passage,

> We paid in person, scored upon that part
> Which cherubs want:

has now dropped all reference to the scoring. And
Locksley Hall bristles with verbal alterations, which
every careful reader of Tennyson knows. One
bows, of course, in the presence of Mr. Tennyson;
and does not venture to set up one's own taste as
against his. Yet, let me confess it, I miss and I
regret some of the old things. Doubtless there are
passages which at the first were open to hostile
criticism, and which met it: which now have been
raised above all cavil. There is that passage in
the *Dream of Fair Women*, which describes the
death of Iphigenia. She tells of it herself. Here
is the verse as it stands even in the seventh edition :

> The tall masts quivered as they lay afloat,
>   The temples and the people and the shore;
> *One drew a sharp knife thro' my tender throat*
>   *Slowly,—and nothing more.*

Every one feels how unpleasant is the picture conveyed by the last two lines. It passes the limits of

tragedy, and approaches the physically revolting. It is, likewise, suggestive rather of the killing of a sheep or pig, than of the solemn sacrifice of a human being. I confess, I incomparably prefer the simplicity of the inspired statement : ' And Abraham stretched forth his hand, and took the knife to slay his son.' We don't want any details as to how the knife was to be used ; or as to the precise point at which it was to let out life. It would jar, were we to read, ' Abraham stretched forth his hand, and was just going to cut Isaac's throat.' Now Mr. Tennyson is worse than that : for he gives us, doubtless with painful accuracy, the account of the actual cutting of the throat. Then, besides this, Mr. Tennyson's verse, as it used to stand, was susceptible of a wrong interpretation. I do not mean that any candid reader would be likely to mistake the poet's sense : but I mean that an ill-set critic would have occasion for misrepresenting it. You may remember that a severe critic *did* misrepresent it. In an ancient Review, you may see the verse printed as I have given it above : and then the critic goes on to say something like this : ' What an unreasonable person Iphigenia must have been ! " He cut my throat : nothing more :" what more could the woman possibly want ? ' Of course, *we* know what the poet meant : but, in strictness, what he meant he did not say. But look to the latest edition of Mr. Tennyson's poems; and you

will be content. Here is the verse now. You will
see that it has been most severely cut and carved;
but to a most admirable result:

> The high masts trembled as they lay afloat;
> The towers, the temples wavered, and the shore ;
> The bright death quivered at the victim's throat,
> Touched, and I knew no more.

I should fancy, my friend, that you have nothing
to say against such tampering with the coin. This
is as though a piece of baser metal were touched
with the philosopher's stone, and turned to gold.
And there have been cases in which a very felici-
tous change has been made by one man upon the
writing of another. A single touch has sometimes
done it. I wonder whether Mr. Palgrave was aware
that in giving in his book those well-known verses
To Althea from Prison, which he rather absurdly
describes as by *Colonel* Lovelace (why does he not
tell us that his extracts from a greater poet are by
William Shakespeare, *Esquire*?), there is one verse
which he has not given as Lovelace wrote it:

> When I lie tangled in her hair
> And fetter'd to her eye,
> The birds, that wanton in the air,
> Know no such liberty.

Lovelace wrote ' the *gods* that wanton in the air:'
and *birds* was substituted by Bishop Percy. It is
a simple and obvious substitution : and the change
is so greatly and so unquestionably for the better,

that it may well be accepted : as indeed it has universally been.

The mention of a happy substitution naturally suggests the most unhappy substitutions on record. You may remember how the great scholar, Bentley, puffed up by his success in making emendations on Horace and Terence, unluckily took it upon himself to edit Milton. And here indeed, we have, with a vengeance, Raphael improved by the painter of wagons. Milton wrote, as everybody knows :

> No light, but rather darkness visible :

but Bentley, eager to improve the line, turns it to

> No light, but rather *a transpicuous gloom.*

There is another passage in which the contrast between the master and the wagon-painter is hardly less marked. Where Milton wrote,

> Our torments also may in length of time
> Become our elements :

Bentley, as an improvement, substituted the following remarkable passage,

> Then, *as 'twas well observed,* our torments may,
> Become our elements.

It is to be admitted that the stupidity of Bentley's reading, is even surpassed by its impudence. Of course, the principle taken for granted at the beginning of such a work is, that Bentley's taste and judgment were better than Milton's. For, you observe, there was no pretext here of restoring a more accurate reading, lost through time : there was no pretext of giving more exactly what Milton wrote. There was no question as to Milton's precise words : but Bentley thought to make them better. And there is something insufferable in the picture of the self-satisfied old Don, sitting down in his easy chair with *Paradise Lost*: and, pencil in hand, proceeding to improve it. Doubtless he was a very great classical scholar : but unless his wits had mainly forsaken him when he set himself to edit Milton, it is very plain that he never could have been more than an acute verbal critic. Thinking of Bentley's *Milton*, one imagines the Apollo Belvedere put in a hair-dresser's window, with a magnificent wig : and dressed in a suit of clothes of the very latest fashion. I think likewise of an incident in the life of Mr. N. P. Willis, the American author. When he was at college in his youth, the head of his college kept a white horse, which he was accustomed to drive in a vehicle of some kind or other. Mr. N. P. Willis and his companions surreptitiously obtained temporary possession of the horse; and painted it crimson, with a blue mane and tail. I confess that I like Mr. N. P. Willis better for that deed, than for anything else I ever heard of his doing : and I may mention, for the satisfaction of my younger readers, that the colours used in painting the horse were of such a nature, that they adhered to the animal for a lengthened period, notwithstanding all endeavours to remove them. Now Dr. Bentley, in editing Milton, did as it were paint the white horse crimson and blue; and then exhibit it to the world, saying, 'That is Smith's fine horse!' Nor should it be accepted as any apology for like conduct on the part of any editor, that the editor in good faith has such a liking for these colours, that he thinks a horse looks best when it looks blue and crimson. And though the change made by an editor be not of such a comprehensive nature as the painting of an entire horse anew, but rather consists of a multitude of little touches here and there;—as points changed, capitals left out, and *whiches* for *thats*; still the result is very irritating. You know that a very small infusion of a foreign substance can vitiate a thing. Two drops of prussic acid in a cup of water: two smears of red paint across the Raphael: affect the whole. I know hardly any offence, short of great crime, which seems to me deserving of so severe punishment, as this of clipping the coin of the realm of literature.

There is something, too, which irritates one, in the self-sufficient attitude which is naturally assumed by a man who is cutting and carving the composition of another. It is an evil which attends all reviewing, and which a modest and conscientious reviewer must feel keenly, that in reviewing ano-

ther man's book, you seem to assume a certain
superiority to him. For in every case in which
you find fault with him, you are aware that the
question comes just to *this* : whether your opinion
or his is worth most. To which may be added the
further question : whether you or he have devoted
most time and thought to forming a just opinion
on this particular point. But when a man sits
down not merely to point out an author's faults,
but to correct them ; the assumption of superiority
is more marked still. And everybody knows that
the writings of great geniuses have been unsparingly cut and carved by very inferior men.
You know how Byron sent *The Siege of Corinth* to
Mr. Gifford, giving him full power to alter it to
any extent he pleased. And you know how Mr.
Gifford did alter it; by cutting out all the good
passages and leaving all the bad. The present
writer has seen a man in the very act of cutting
and carving. Once upon a time, I entered a
steamer which was wont to ply upon the waters of
a certain noble river, that winds between Highland
hills. And entering that bark, I beheld a certain
friend, seated on the quarter-deck, with a little
volume in his hand. I never saw a man look
more entirely satisfied with himself than did my
friend; as he turned over the leaves of the little
volume in a hasty, skipping fashion; and jauntily
scribbled here and there with a pencil. I beheld

him in silence for a time, and then asked what on
earth he was doing. 'Oh,' said he, 'I am a member
of the committee appointed by the Great Council
to prepare a new book of hymns to be sung
throughout the churches of this country. And
this little volume is a proof copy of the hymns
suggested : and a copy of it is sent to each member
of the committee to receive his emendations. And,
as you see, I am beguiling my time in sailing down
the river by improving these hymns.' In this easy
manner did my friend scribble whatever alterations
might casually suggest themselves, upon the best
compositions of the best hymn writers. Slowly
and laboriously had the authors written these
hymns, carefully weighing each word : and weighing each word perhaps for a very long time. But
in the pauses of conversation, with no serious
thought whatsoever, but willing to testify how
much better he knew what a hymn should be than
the best authors of that kind of literature, did my
friend set down his random thoughts. 'Give me
that volume,' said I, with no small indignation. He
gave it to me, and I proceeded to examine his
improvements. And I can honestly say that not
merely was every alteration for the worse; but that
many of the alterations testified my friend's utter
ignorance of the very first principles of metrical
composition ; and that all of them testified the
extreme narrowness of his acquaintance with that

species of literature. Some of the verses, as altered by him, were astounding specimens of rhythm. The only thing I ever saw which equalled them was a stanza by a local poet, very zealous for the observance of the Lord's day. Here is the stanza :—

Ye that keep horses, read psalm 50 :
To win money on the Sabbath day, see that ye never be so
    thrifty !

In Scotland, we have a psalter and a hymnal imposed by ecclesiastical authority; so that in all parish churches there is entire uniformity in the words of praise. But it worries one to enter a church in England, and to find, as one finds so often, that the incumbent has published a hymnal, the sale of which he ensures by using it in his church : and all the hymns in which are cut and carved to suit his peculiar doctrinal and æsthetical views. The execrable taste and the remarkable ignorance evinced in some of these compilations, have on myself, I confess, the very reverse of a devotional effect. And the inexpressible badness of certain of the hymns I have seen in such volumes, leads me to the belief that they must be the original compositions of the editor himself. There is an excellent little volume of Psalms and Hymns, collected by Mr. Henry Herbert Wyatt, of Trinity Chapel, Brighton : but even in it, one is annoyed by occasional needless changes. In Bishop Heber's beautiful hymn, which begins, 'From Greenland's icy mountains,' Mr. Wyatt has smeared the third verse. The Bishop wrote, as everybody knows,

> Shall we, whose souls are lighted
> 　With wisdom from on high,—
> Shall we to men benighted
> 　The lamp of life deny ?

But Mr. Wyatt substitutes *can* for the *shall* with which the first and third lines begin : a change which no man of sense can call an improvement. A hymn to which I always turn, as one that tests an editor, is Bishop Ken's incomparable one, commonly called the *Evening Hymn*. I find, with pleasure, that Mr. Wyatt has not tried to improve it : save that he has adopted an alteration which has been all but universally accepted. Bishop Ken wrote,

> All praise to Thee, my God, this night :

while most of us, from childhood, have been taught to substitute *Glory* for *All Praise*. And this is certainly an improvement. Glory, *gloria*, is certainly the right word with which to begin an ascription of praise to the Almighty. If not in itself the fittest word, the most ancient and revered associations of the Christian Church give it a prescriptive right to preference. A hymn which no man seems able to keep his sacrilegious hands off, is Charles Wesley's hymn,

Jesu, lover of my soul.

I observe Mr. Wyatt makes three alterations in the first three lines of it: each alteration for the worse. But I begin to be aware that no human being can be trusted to sit down with a hymn book and a pencil; with leave to cut and carve. There is a fascination about the work of tampering: and a man comes to change for what is bad, rather than not change at all. There are analogous cases. When I dwelt in the country, I was once cutting a little path through a dense thicket of evergreens: and a friend from the city, who was staying with us, went out with me to superintend the proceedings. Weakly, I put into my friend's hands a large and sharp weapon, called in Scotland a *scutching-knife*: and told him he might smooth off certain twigs which projected unduly on the path. My friend speedily felt the fascination of cutting and carving. And after having done considerable damage, he restored me the weapon, saying he felt its possession was a temptation too strong for him to resist. When walking about with the keen sharp steel in his hand, it was really impossible to help snipping off any projecting branch which obtruded itself upon the attention. And the writer's servant (dead, poor fellow: one of the worthiest though most unbending of men) declared, with much solemnity and considerable indignation, that in forming a walk he would never again suffer the scutching-knife to be in any other hands than his own. Now, it is a like temptation that assails the editor of hymns: and even if the editor is a competent man (and in most cases he is not), I don't think it safe to trust him with the scutching-knife. The only editor of hymns whom the writer esteems as a perfect editor, is Sir Roundell Palmer. For Sir Roundell starts with the determination to give us each hymn exactly as its author left it. It is delightful to read 'All praise to Thee, my God, this night:' and to come upon

> Jesu, lover of my soul,
> Let me to Thy bosom fly:

after 'Jesu, *Saviour* of my soul:' and 'Jesus, *refuge* of my soul.' I remark, in Sir Roundell's book, occasional signs of having taken a hymn from an early edition of the author's works: which in later editions was retouched by the author himself. Thus James Montgomery's 'Friend after friend departs,' is given as first published: not as the author left it. In the four verses, Montgomery made *five* alterations: which are not shown in Sir Roundell's work. But, as one who feels much interest in hymnal literature, and who has given some attention to it, I cannot refrain from saying that in the matter of faithfulness, Sir Roundell Palmer's book is beyond question or comparison the best.

There is nothing second, third, or tenth to it. It is first: and the rest are nowhere.

Having mentioned the best hymnal that I know, one naturally thinks of the worst. There is a little volume purporting to be *Hymns collected by the Committee of the General Assembly on Psalmody*: published at Edinburgh in 1860. It is to be remembered that the Church of Scotland has never approved this little volume: the committee have published it on their own responsibility. Mr. Wyatt, in making his collection, tells us he examined thirty thousand hymns, and took the best of them. Sir Roundell Palmer also gives us in his volume the best hymns in the language. But neither Mr. Wyatt nor Sir Roundell (both most competent judges) has seen fit to admit much of the matter contained in this little compilation. So we may conclude, either that Mr. Wyatt did not find some of these compositions among his thirty thousand: or that, having examined them, he did not think them worthy of admission to his collection of about two hundred and fifty hymns. Sir Roundell Palmer's hymns number four hundred and twelve: and he has not erred on the side of exclusion: yet he has excluded a good many of the Scotch eighty-five. Out of the first fifteen of the Scotch book, fourteen are unknown to him. And I do not think cutting and carving ever went to a length so reprehensible, as in this volume. As to the fitness of the hymns for use in church, opinions may possibly differ : but I am obliged to say that I never saw any collection of such pieces so filled with passages in execrable taste, and utterly unfit for Christian worship.

It may amuse my readers, to show them George Herbert improved. Everybody knows the famous poem, *The Elixir.* It consists of six verses. The Scotch reading consists of four. In the first verse, three verbal alterations, intended as improvements, are made on Herbert. 'Teach me, my God and king,' becomes ' Teach *us, our* God and king.' The second verse in the Scotch reading, is unknown to Herbert. It is the doing of some member of the committee. The gold has been punched out, and a piece of pinchbeck has been put in. Herbert's third verse is omitted. Then comes the well-known verse :

> All may of Thee partake :
> Nothing can be so mean,
> Which, with this tincture, FOR THY SAKE,
> Will not grow bright and clean.

This is improved as follows :

> All may of Thee partake ;
> Nothing *so small can be,*
> *But draws, when* ACTED *for Thy sake,*
> *Greatness and worth from Thee.*

You will doubtless think that Herbert pure is better than Herbert improved by the sign-painter.

But the next verse is smeared even worse. Who does not remember the saintly man's words:

> A servant with this clause,
> Makes drudgery divine:
> Who sweeps a room, as for Thy laws,
> Makes that, and the action, fine.

But, as Sam Weller remarked of Mr. Pickwick in a certain contingency, 'his most formiliar friend voodnt know him,' as thus disguised:

> If done beneath Thy laws,
> Even humblest labours shine:
> Hallowed is toil, if this the cause,
> The meanest work, divine.

Herbert's temper, we know, was angelic: but I wonder what he would have looked like, had he seen himself thus docked, and painted crimson and blue. No doubt, *The Elixir*, as the master left it, is not fitted for congregational singing. But that is a reason for leaving it alone: it is no reason for thus unpardonably tampering with the coin of the realm.

There are various pieces in this unfortunate work, whose appearance in it I can explain only on this theory. Probably, some day when the committee met, a member of committee produced a manuscript, and said that here was a hymn of his own composition; and begged that it might be put in the book. The other members read it, and saw it was rubbish: but their kindly feeling prevented their saying so: and in it went. One of the last

things many people learn, is not to take offence
when a friend declines to admire their literary
doings. I have not the faintest idea who are the
members of the committee which issued this compilation. Likely enough, there are in it some
acquaintances of my own. But that fact shall not
prevent my saying what I honestly believe : that
it is the very worst hymn-book I ever saw. I cannot believe that the persons who produced it, could
ever have paid any attention to hymnal literature :
they have so thoroughly missed the tone of all good
hymns. Indeed, many of the hymns seem to be
formed on the model of what may be called the
Scotch *Preaching Prayer*: the most offensive form
of devotion known ; and one entirely abandoned
by all the more cultivated of the Scotch clergy. I
heard, indeed, lately, an individual pray at a meeting about the Lord's day. In his prayer, he alluded
to the Lancashire distress : and informed the Almighty that the patience with which the Lancashire
people bore it was very much the result of their
being trained in Sunday schools. But, leaving this
volume, which is really not worth farther notice, let
me mention, that in the first twelve lines of ' Jesu,
lover of my soul,' there are *ten* improvements made
on Wesley. ' While the tempest still is high,' has
nigh substituted for *high.* ' Till the storm of life
is past,' is made ' Till the *storms* of life *are* past,'
Oh receive my soul at last,' has *And* substituted

for *Oh*: for no conceivable reason. And the familiar line, 'Hangs my helpless soul on Thee,' has been turned, by the wagon-painter, into '*Clings* my helpless soul *to* Thee.' I ask any intelligent reader, Is not this too bad? I am a clergyman of the Church of Scotland, for whose use these hymns have been so debased and tampered with. They never shall be sung in my church, you may rely on it. And the fact, that this cutting and carving has been done so near home, serves only to make me the more strongly to protest against it.

If it were not far too large a subject to take up now, I should say something in reprobation of the fashion in which many people venture to cut and carve upon words far more sacred than those of any poet: I mean, upon the words of Holy Scripture. Many people improve a scriptural text or phrase when they quote it: the improvement generally consisting in giving it a slight twist in the direction of their own peculiar theological views. I have heard of a man who quoted as from Scripture the following words: 'It is appointed unto all men once to die; and after death *Hell.*' It was pointed out to him that no such statement exists in Scripture: the words which follow the mention of death being, 'and after this the judgment.' But the misquoter of Scripture declined to accept the correction, declaring that he thought his own reading was better. I have heard of a revival preacher who gave out as his text the words ' Ye shall all likewise perish.' Every one will know what a wicked distortion he made of our Saviour's warning in thus clipping it. And I have heard texts of Scripture pieced together in a way that made them convey a meaning just as far from that of the inspired writers, as that conveyed by the well known mosaic, ' And Judas departed, and went and hanged himself :' ' Go thou and do likewise.'

Probably the reader is tired of the subject. I thank him for his patience in following me so far.

CHAPTER XVII.

FROM SATURDAY TO MONDAY.

HERE are great people who have seen so much, that they are not surprised by anything. There are silly people who have not seen very much, but who think it a fine thing to pretend that they are not surprised by anything. As for the present writer, he has seen so little that he feels it very strange to find himself here. And he has not the least desire to pretend that he does not feel it so.

This morning the writer awoke in a bare little chamber, curtainless and carpetless, in that great hotel at Lucerne in Switzerland which is called the *Schweizer Hof.* And having had breakfast in a very large and showy dining-room, along with two travelling companions, he is now standing at a window of that apartment, and looking out. Just in front, there spreads the green lake of Lucerne. Away to the left, is the Rigi: and to the right, beyond the lake, the lofty Pilatus, in a tarn on whose summit tradition says the banished governor of Judea drowned himself, stricken by conscience for his unjust condemnation of Christ. The town stands at this end of the lake; divided into two parts by the river Reuss, which here flows out of the lake in a swift green stream, running with almost the speed of a torrent. There is a glare of light and heat everywhere in the town: most of all on the broad level piece of ground which at this point spreads between the lake and several hotels. On a rising ground, a few hundred yards off, rising steeply from the lake, stands the Roman Catholic cathedral, a somewhat shabby building, with two lofty slender spires at its west end. There are cloisters round it: and from several openings in the wall on the side towards the lake, you have delightful peeps of the green water below and of snow-capped hills beyond. If you enter that cathedral at almost any time, you will find its plain interior filled by a large congregation; and you will hear part of the service boisterously roared out by priests of unprepossessing aspect. Why do the Roman priests so furiously bellow?

This is a Saturday morning in August: a beautiful bright morning.

There is no part of the week that is so well remembered by many people, as the period from Saturday to Monday: including both the former and the latter days. That season of time has a character of its own: and many pleasant visits and expeditions have been comprised within it. Every one can sympathize with the poet Prior, and can understand the picture he calls up, when he describes himself as 'in a little Dutch chaise on a Saturday night; on his left hand his Horace, and a friend on his right,' going out to the country to stay till Monday with the friend so situated. I fear, indeed, that Prior would not go to church on the Sunday; which I can only regret. But I am going to spend this time in a way as different as may be from that in which I am accustomed to spend it, or in which I ever spent it before.

When the writer arises on common Saturdays, the thing he has in prospect is several quiet hours spent in going over the sermons he has to preach on the following day. I suppose that most clergymen who do their work as well as they can, do on Saturday morning after breakfast walk into their study, and sit down in that still retreat to work. And if, on other days, you are thinking all the while you are at work there, of ten sick people you have to see, and of a host of other matters that must be attended to out of doors, you will much enjoy the affluent sense of abundant time for thinking, which you will have if you make it a rule that on Saturdays you shall do no pastoral nor other parochial work. Then you ought to take a long walk in the afternoon; and give the evening to entire rest, refreshing your mind by some light cheerful reading.

This advice, however, need not be prolonged; as it is addressed to a limited order of men, and to men who are not likely to take it. And to-day, instead of sitting down to work, there is something quite different to be done.

For it is time to cease looking out of the window at the Schweizer Hof, and to walk the short distance to the spot where a little steamer is preparing to start. The baggage of the three travellers is contained in three black leather bags, of modest size. The steamer departs, and leaves the town behind: but to-day, instead of sailing the length of the lake to where it ends amid the wilds of Uri, we turn to the right hand into a retired bay, which gradually shallows, till the depth of water becomes very small. Pilatus is on the right; and the place where in former days there used to be the *Slide of Alpnach.* The sides of Pilatus are covered with great forests, the timber of which would be of great use if it could be readily got hold of. And the Slide was made for the purpose of bringing down great trees from spots from which any ordinary conveyance would be impossible. So a trough of wood was formed, eight miles in length, beginning high up the mountain, and ending at the lake. It was six feet wide, and four feet deep: a stream of water was made to flow through it, to lessen friction. It wound about to suit the ground, and was carried, bridge-like, over three deep ravines. The trees intended to be sent down by it, were stripped of bark and branches; and then launched away. The biggest trees did the eight miles in six minutes; tearing down with a noise like thunder, an avalanche of wood. Sometimes a tree leapt out of the Slide, in mid career, and was instantly smashed to atoms.

The steamer stops at a rude little wharf, near which a great lumbering diligence is waiting: very clumsy, but comfortable. Six horses draw it, whose harness, made mainly of rope, is covered with bells, that keep up a ceaseless tinkle as we go. In Britain, we wish a carriage to run as quietly as possible: in Switzerland, they like a good deal of noise. We go slowly on, into the Canton of Unterwalden, by the little town of Sarnen, along a valley richly wooded. For a while, the road is level: then we begin to climb. And now, as is usual with British travellers, we get out and walk on, leaving the diligence to follow. We are entering the Brunig Pass. In former days, it could be traversed only on foot or on mules: now a carriage road has been made, a marvel of skilful engineering. We walk up a long steep ascent: on the left hand, far below, are little green lakes, and scattered châlets; on the right, rude hills. Every here and there, a little stream from the hills crosses the road. It is now a mere trickling thread of water: but acres on either side

of it, covered with huge stones, testify what a raging
torrent it must be in winter.   So we go on, till we
reach a spot where we are to witness a piece of
ingenuity combined with bad taste.   Turn out of
the highway by a little path to the right, and you
come in two hundred yards to a sawmill, driven by
an impetuous little stream.   Where does the stream
come from?   It seems to issue out of the rocky
wall, which a quarter of a mile above the sawmill
here crosses the little upland valley.   You follow
the stream towards its source.   You reach the rocky
wall.   And there, sure enough, violently rushing
out through a low-browed dark tunnel, which it
quite fills, you see the origin of the stream.   What
is on the other side of the rocky wall?

Why, there is a considerable lake, which was
once a great deal bigger.   The Lake of Lungern
was once a beautiful sheet of water, with fine wood
coming down to its margin.   But the people of the
valley thought that by partially draining the lake,
they might get some hundreds of acres of valuable
land: and all consideration of the picturesque had
to give way.   The tunnel we have seen lowered the
water in the lake by a hundred and twenty feet,
and diminished its size to half.   With great labour,
the work of nineteen thousand days given by the
peasants, the tunnel was made, beginning at its
lower end, through the rocky ridge, to within six
feet of the water at the end of the lake.   These six

feet, of friable rock, were blown up with gunpowder, fired by three daring men who instantly fled; and in a few minutes a black stream of mud and water appeared at the lower end of the tunnel. The traveller, returning by the sawmill to the road, goes on till he reaches the village: whence you may see a bare ugly tract of five hundred acres, dotted with wooden châlets, gained by spoiling the lake.

Passing through the village, you climb on and on: the diligence makes no sign of overtaking you. You reach the summit at last, 3,600 feet above the sea: whence you have a grand view of the vale of Hasli. These tremendous snowy peaks beyond are the peaks of the Wetterhorn, one of the grandest of the Alps. All this way, the road has been very lonely, but always richly wooded. Now you begin to go down. The road winds along the side of the mountain, cut out of the rock. In some places it is a mere notch, with great masses of rock hanging over far beyond its outer edge. And so, broken by a pause for some bread and wine at a little wayside inn, the day goes on towards evening.

All this while, one is trying to feel that it is Saturday; the familiar day one knows at home. For somehow it seems quite different. And in this strange country, where you are a foreigner, you feel yourself quite a different person from what you used to be at home. No doubt, by having two travelling companions from Britain, you keep a little of the British atmosphere about you. If you were walking down now into Hasli all alone, you would be much more keenly aware of the genius of the place. All your life, and your interests, at home, would grow quite shadowy and unreal. But this is one thing that makes a holiday season in a foreign country deliver you so thoroughly from your home burden of care and labour. How very lightly the charge of one's parish rests upon one, when the parish is a thousand miles away! The thing which at home is always pressing on you so heavily, grows light, at that distance, as one of those coloured air-balls of India-rubber.

And now, as the light is fading somewhat, the great diligence, running swiftly down the hill, and zigzagging round perilous corners, with little exertion of the six plump horses, but with a tremendous jingling of their bells, overtakes us: and for a mile or two you may enjoy a pleasant rest after the long walk. We stop at a place where a roofed wooden bridge crosses the river, turning sharp off to the left. Here we leave the big diligence; and climb to the top of a lesser one which is waiting, a vast height. And now, in the growing darkness, we proceed slowly up the valley, following the course of the river Aar. On the right hand, huge precipices close in the valley, from which every now and then a streak of white foam, hundreds of feet in height, shows you a waterfall. It is perfectly silent, though these seem so near: they are much farther off than you are aware. On and on, up the river: till you can see lights ahead: and you jolt along a very roughly-paved street, where in the darkness you see picturesque wooden houses on either hand. This is Meyringen: one of the most thorough and beautiful Swiss villages to be found in Switzerland. What an odd Saturday evening this seems! Our old ways of thinking and feeling are quite dislocated. We stop at the door of a large hotel, built of wood. Everything in it seems of wood, except the stone staircase. It is eight o'clock in the evening,—quite dark: they have not our long beautiful twilights there. And now we have dinner. Then we inspect a room filled with carved work in wood which is for sale: and select some little things which will pleasantly remind us of this place and time when both are far away. Finally, before ten o'clock, we climb the long stair, each to his little bare chamber; with many thoughts of those at home; and trying unsuccessfully to feel that this is Saturday night.

But the glory and beauty of Meyringen appeared the next morning: one of the sunniest, calmest, and brightest Sundays that ever shone since the creation. You go forth from the hotel, and walk down the street, with the most picturesque wooden houses on either hand: with their projecting galleries and great overhanging eaves. Above, there is the brightest blue sky; and all round, snowy peaks, dazzling white, rising into the deep blue.

Walk on till you are clear of the village, and fields of coarse grass spread round you : for you will not find there the soft green turf of Britain, but a rough harsh grass, alive with crickets and grasshoppers. We have some compensation for our uncertain climate and abundant rain. Yet, amid that scenery, so sublime, still, and bright, you do not miss anything that could be desired. And now, on the silent Sunday morning, I have no doubt that of several men whom I saw, who though arrayed in mountain dress each wore a white neckcloth, each one was thinking of his own church many hundreds of miles off, and hoping and asking that all might go well there that day.

All round Meyringen there stand those snowy Alps. Let the small critic understand that we all know that an Alp does not strictly mean a mountain, but a pasture high in the mountains. But in Britain Alps mean mountains, and nothing else. And all round are those white peaks, save in the narrow opening where the Aar comes down from above, and where it rolls away below. From great precipices on the left hand as you look up the valley, streams descend in foamy falls: and one among these has sometimes brought down, in its flood, such masses of mud and gravel, as served to overspread half the valley. Turn up this little street, at whose end you can see the church, which is a Protestant one. Eighteen feet from the pavement, there is a line drawn on the inside walls, showing the height to which the church was once filled with mud by an overflow of that torrent. Service is going on. We quietly enter, and steal to a seat by the door. A clergyman, in very ugly robes, is standing in the pulpit, which looks diagonally across the plain interior. He is reading his sermon, in a rather sleepy way. His robe is of blue, and a great white collar, turned over, is round his neck. Here is the best place to see a whole congregation, men and women, in their national dress. The men sit on one side of the church: and the women on the other. Swiss women are for the most part far from pretty. They wear here a black bodice, with white sleeves starched till they seem as stiff as boards: a yellow petticoat, and a little black hat. The church was well filled: and the people seemed to listen very attentively to their pastor's words.

But, for one thing, I do not understand them, for they are expressed in German: and for another thing I am going to worship elsewhere: so I slip quietly away. Just at the gate through which you pass into the churchyard, there is a shabby little building which I took for a school. No, it is the *Little Church*: and here, during the summer and autumn, you may join in the service of the Church of England. A succession of clergymen come, for a few weeks each. A little before the hour of worship, we enter the building. It is just like a very shabby Scotch parish school. Forms without backs occupy the floor : at one corner there is an odd little enclosure which serves as a reading-desk and a pulpit : and a little way off there is placed a very small table, which is to-day covered with white, and bears the elements of the Communion. As the congregation assembles, five-and-twenty persons, the clergyman puts on his surplice ; and entering the little desk begins the service. I cannot but admire the determination this young minister shows, even in that shabby place, to make the worship of God as decorous as may be. Although there was no organ, there was quite a musical service : even the Psalms being chanted remarkably well. Five or six young Englishwomen acted as a choir. The lessons were read by an old gentleman standing by the little communion table. But a second surplice was not forthcoming : and he was devoid of any robe. The sermon was a very decent one : not eloquent nor striking, but plain and earnest. I should have liked it better, if the clergyman had prayed, before beginning it, in the words of one of the usual collects. But he simply prefaced his discourse by the words ' In the name of the Father and of the Son and of the Holy Ghost :' and by that exceedingly silly shibboleth, conveyed to me his adherence to a decaying party, which assuredly does not consist of the wisest or

ablest of the Anglican Clergy. There are, of
course, two or three grand exceptions; but there is
something fatuous in the parade of going as near
Rome as may be, which some empty-headed youths
exhibit. Let me add, that in the evening I went
to service again. And now the sermon was so
terribly bad, so weak and silly, that I found it
hard to understand how any man who had brains
to write the former discourse, could possibly have
produced it. Yet the text was one of the noblest
in Holy Scripture.

After the forenoon service, we walk along a great
wall, built to defend the valley from floods, towards
the heights on the left hand, looking up the valley:
and in the hot afternoon toil slowly up and up, till
Meyringen is left far below. What is that distant
sound? Well, it is that of rifle-shooting: for the
men of Hasli think Sunday afternoon the best time
for practice. Let me confess that the perpetual
reports broke in very sadly on the silence of the
Holy Day. Yet there never was a nobler temple
than that on which you looked, sitting down on a
rock and gazing at the valley far below and the
snowy Alps beyond. You could not but think of
the words, chanted in that morning service, ' The
strength of the hills is His also!' And sitting here,
can one forget that at this hour the text is being
read out in the church far away: can one help
shutting out the Alps for a little, and asking that

the Blessed Spirit may carry the words that are to be spoken to many hearts, for warning, counsel, and comfort ?   It is quite true, that when at a distance of hundreds of miles, your home interests grow misty and unsubstantial: but it is likewise true that at such an hour as this, they press themselves on one with a wonderful clearness and force. My friend Smith told me that in two hours' lonely walking under Mont Blanc, on a bright clear autumn day, he felt more worried by some little perplexity which soon cleared itself up, than at any other time in his life.   And sitting down on the edge of a glacier, whence a stream broke away in thunder, with the Monarch of Mountains looking down, all he could think of was that wretched little vexation.

The Sunday dinner-hour at the *Sauvage* at Meyringen is four: so let us slowly descend from this height.   A large party dines : chiefly English. The main characteristic of dinner was the fish called *lotte*, which is caught in the river near.   There was a certain quietness becoming the day ; and it was pleasant to remark that the greater number of our countrymen seemed to make Sunday a day of rest. And indeed it is inexpressibly pleasant, after the fatigue and hurry which attend travelling rapidly on through grand scenery, to have an occasional day on which to repose.   And going to church, with a little congregation of one's countrymen and

countrywomen, to join in the familiar service in
a strange land, one felt something of that glow
which came into St. Paul's heart, when after his
voyage he was cheered by the sight of Christian
friends ; and which made him ' thank God and take
courage.'

Then to the evening service, when the congregation was less, and the sermon so extremely bad.
The setting sun was casting a rosy colour upon the
snowy peaks, as we returned to the only home one
had there. And indeed Sunday is the worst day
at an inn. There is a strongly-felt inconsistency
between the associations of the day, especially if you
live in Scotland, and the whole look of the place.
And sitting in a verandah behind the *Sauvage*, with
the fragrance of the trees in the twilight coming up
from the garden below, and looking across to the
Falls of the Reichenbach on the other side of the
valley, it was worrying to think of the weak sermon
we had just heard, where one had hoped for that
which might cheer and comfort and direct. On
another day, in a church in a grander scene than
even this, I sat beside a certain great preacher
while a poor sermon was being preached with much
attempt at oratorical effect; and thought how different it would have been had that man occupied
the pulpit. Perhaps he thought so too ; though he
did not say so. But indeed, arrayed in garments
of grey, and with a wideawake hat lying beside

him, that eminent clergyman was like a locomotive engine when the steam is not up. He could not have preached then; at least, not without two hours of previous thought. Before the best railway engine can dash away with its burden, you must fill its boiler with water, and kindle its fire. And when you may see that clergyman ascend his pulpit in decorous canonicals on a Sunday, charged with his subject, with every nerve tense, and with the most earnest purpose on his rather frightened face, to deliver his message to many hundreds of immortal beings; if you had previously seen the easy figure in the light-grey suit sitting in a pew at Chamouni, you would discern a like difference to that between the engine standing cold and powerless in the shed, and the engine coming slowly up to the platform, with the compressed strength of a thousand horses fretting for escape or employment, to take away the express train.

To-morrow morning we have to be up at half-past four: so let us go to bed. First, let us have a look at the quiet street, indistinct in the twilight; and at the outline of encircling hills.

There are places in Switzerland where you do not sleep so well as might be desired. A host of wretched little enemies scarify your skin, and drive sleep from your eyes. The *Sauvage* at Meyringen is not one of these places. It is a thoroughly clean and respectable house. Yet for the guidance of

tourists who may know even less than the writer
(which is barely conceivable), let it be said that
there is an effectual means of keeping such hostile
troops away. Procure a quantity of camphor. Wear
some of it in a bag about you; a very little bag:
and even though you sit next a disgusting, infra-
grant, unwashed person in a diligence, nothing will
assail you. And at night, rub a little of that material into powder between your palms, and sprinkle
it over your bed, having turned back the bed-clothes.
Do that, and you are safe. If you rub yourself over
with camphor besides, you are secure as though
wrapped in triple brass. You have made yourself
an offensive object to the æsthetic sensibilities of
fleas; and they will reject you with contempt.
They will do this, even though, uncamphored, you
might be (in the South Sea Island sense) *a remarkably good man.* You remember how an Englishman
once spoke to a chief of a tribe, out there. He
spoke of a certain zealous missionary. 'Ah, he
was a very good man, a very good man,' said the
Englishman, truly and heartily. 'Yes,' said the
chief, not so warmly: 'Him was a good man, but
him was very tough!' The chief spoke with the air
of one who says, critically, 'The venison at Smith's
was not so good as usual last night.' And the
Englishman forbore to enquire as to the *data* on
which the chief pronounced his judgment. No doubt
he had experimental knowledge on that subject.

It is a great deal easier to get up in the dark at half-past four in the morning in Switzerland, than it is anywhere in Britain. There is something so bracing and exhilarating in the mountain air, that you are easily equal to exertion which would knock you up elsewhere. Men who at home could not walk five or six miles without fatigue, walk their thirty miles over a Pass without difficulty: come in to dinner with a good appetite; and after dinner, without the least of that feeling of stiffness which commonly follows any unusual exertion, are out of doors again, sauntering in the twilight, or visiting some sight that is within easy reach. Yesterday was a resting day with us: so to-day, we had break-fast a little after five; and then, the three black leather bags being disposed on a black horse, that scrambled like a cat over ground that would have ruined an English steed's knees in the first quarter of a mile, we set off at six o'clock to cross the Pass of the Great Scheideck to Grindelwald.

First, along the road up the valley for a mile or so: then turn to the right and begin to climb the mountain which on that side walls the valley in. The ascent is very steep: and the path consists of smooth and slippery pieces of rock. You soon come to understand the wisdom of your guide, who requires you to walk at a very slow pace. *That* is your only chance, if you are to climb such ways for several successive hours. The inexperienced

traveller pushes on at a rapid pace, and speedily is
quite exhausted. After a little climbing, you may
turn to the right, where you will see the torrent of
the Reichenbach go down nearly two thousand feet
in a succession of rapids and falls, hurrying to the
Aar in the valley below. On, higher and higher,
till you see the huge snowy mass of the Wetterhorn
far before you on the left; and you enter a little
plain of bright green grass, dotted with many picturesque wooden châlets. On, higher and higher, till
you stop to rest and have something to eat at the
baths of Rosenlaui, a pretty inn near a rock where
the Reichenbach comes roaring out of a cleft. In
a large room here, you will be tempted to buy
specimens of wood-carving, very beautifully done.
Having rested, you determine to make a little
deviation from your way. Twenty minutes' stiff
pulling up the steep hill-side, over a very rough
path to the left: and you cross a bridge that spans
a fissure in the rock two hundred feet deep, where
a little stream foams along. Now you stand beside
the glacier of Rosenlaui: not large, but beautifully
pure. A cave has been cut out for many yards into
the beautiful blue ice; and into it you go. It is a
singular place in which to find yourself, that cave,
or rather tunnel, in the solid ice. The air is cold, the
floor is somewhat wet: a soft light comes through
the ice from without. But there is no time to linger
unduly: and we return down the rough slope to the

spot, near the inn, where the guide and packhorse are waiting. Now upwards again, by a very muddy path through a long wood of pines. But gradually the pines cease, and the ground grows bare; till you enter on a tract where the snow lies some inches deep. Parched as are your hands and your tongue, there is a great temptation to refresh both with handfuls of that snow, which in a little while will leave you more parched than ever. But after no long climbing on the snow, you reach the summit of the Pass, 6,500 feet above the sea. Here you will find a little inn, the *Steinbock*; where a simple but abundant repast awaits the travellers. Thirty or forty, almost all English, sit down to copious supplies of stewed chamois, washed down with prodigious draughts of thin claret. Here you rest an hour. And going out, you look at the Wetterhorn, which rises in a perpendicular wall of limestone rock, many thousand feet in height, beginning to rise apparently a hundred yards off. But your eye deceives you in this clear air and amid these tremendous magnitudes. The base of the precipice is more than a mile away. And when you begin to descend towards Grindelwald, the awful wall of rock seems to hang over you; though nowhere you approach within a mile of it. It is not safe to go nearer: for every now and then you hear a tremendous roar; and looking towards the Wetterhorn, you see a mass of what looks like powdery snow sliding swiftly down the rock. You are astonished that so small a thing should make such a noise. But that is an avalanche; and if you were nearer, you would know that what seemed powdery snow was indeed hundreds of tons of ice, in huge blocks and masses. And if a village of châlets had stood in the way, that slide of powdery snow would have swept it to destruction.

It is a fact, well known to students of physical philosophy, that it is incomparably easier to go down a steep hill than to ascend one. This is a result of the great and beneficial law of Gravitation; according to which all material bodies tend towards the centre of the earth. And the consequence of this law is, that when we set off to descend from this height, we do it very easily and rapidly. A horse, indeed, looks a poor and awkward figure scrambling down these paths: but if you have in your hands that long light tough staff of ash shod with iron which is called an Alpen-Stock, you will bound over the masses of rock at a great pace; doing things which in a less exhilarating air you would shrink from. All the way down, on the left, apparently close by, there is that awful wall of the Wetterhorn; and you may see other peaks, of which the most noticeable or at least the most memorable is the Schreckhorn. By-and-by, by the path, you may discern a man standing beside a great square wooden box, like a small tub, fixed on a stake of wood four or five feet high. And when the travellers approach, the man will fit to that box a wooden pipe, eight feet long: and sticking his tongue into the lesser end of the pipe, will vehemently blow into it. That rude apparatus is the Alpine Horn, of which you have heard folk talk and sing. There is nothing specially attractive to the ear, in the few notes brayed forth: but what grand echoes, doubled and redoubled, are awakened up in the breast of that huge wall, and die away in the upper air and mountain! Produce from your purse a liberal tip; and ask the mountaineer to let you try his horn. You blow with all your might, like my friend Mac Puff sounding his own trumpet: but there is dead silence, as when to such as know him well Mac Puff does so sound: a feeble hissing of air from the great tub is all that rewards your labour. And one always respects a person who can do what one cannot do. Down along the slope; till, turning a little way to the left, you approach the Upper Glacier of Grindelwald, filling up the great gulf between the Wetterhorn and the Schreckhorn. Into this glacier you enter, by an artificial tunnel: but the ice is dirty, and streams of water pour from it on your head. Thus you speedily retreat. Great belts of fir trees fringe the glacier; which, like other glaciers, comes far below the snow-line. For as the ice which forms the glacier gradually melts away at the lower extremity next the valley, the ice from above presses on and fills its place. The glacier is in fact a slowly-advancing stream of ice. And all the glaciers are gradually retreating into the mountains, as increasing cultivation and population make the lower extremity melt away somewhat faster than the waste can be supplied. Starting from far in the icy bosom of the Alps, in the region of perpetual snow, the Grindelwald glaciers come down to within a few yards of as green and rich grass as (if you were a cow) you would desire to eat.

Now we walk for an hour through meadows in the valley; pausing at a châlet to have some Alpine strawberries, small, and flavourless: and so at five o'clock on Monday afternoon enter Grindelwald. The inns are filled with travellers; but we are lucky in finding space at the *Adler*, whose windows look full on the Lower Glacier, at the distance of a mile. From a great black-looking cave at the end of the glacier, a river breaks away; of the dirty whity-brown water that comes from glaciers. It is a curious thing to see a river starting, full grown from the first. Look to the left of the lower end of the glacier; the ground meets the ice. Look to the right, and there a pretty big river, that looks as if it had burst out from the earth, is flowing away as if it had run a score of miles.

Let the traveller refresh himself by much-needed ablution: they give you pretty large basins here.

And then descending, sit down to dinner at the *table-d'hôte.* A large party: almost all Germans. So are the waiters. Thus, if you express to a neighbour your conviction that something presented to you as chamois, is in truth a portion of a very tough and aged goat, no offence is given.

Shall it be recorded how, after dinner, we sat in the twilight on a terrace hard by, looking at the glacier and the Alps: how, as it darkened down, we entered the dining-room again, and there beheld, seated at tea, a certain great Anglican prelate? Shall it be recorded how, if one had never seen nor heard of him before, you might have learned something of his eloquence, geniality, and tact, transcending those of ordinary men, even from that hour and a half before he retired to rest? Shall it be recorded how, having begun to tell a story to his own party, he gradually and easily, as he discerned others listening with interest, addressed himself to them, till he ended his story in the audience of all in that large chamber? And shall it be recorded how two pretty young English girls sat and gazed with rapt and silent admiration on the great man's face? Two or three young fellows who had sought, during that day, to commend themselves to these fair beings, felt themselves (you could see) hopelessly eclipsed and cut out; and regarded the unconscious Bishop with looks of fury. Happily, he did not know: so it did him no harm.

My friend Mac Spoon recently dilated, in my hearing, on the advantages of Pocket Diaries; which (as wise men know) are not records of passing and past events, but memoranda of engagements. You note down in these, said he, all you have to do; while yet if your book should be lost, and so fall into the hands of a stranger, he could not for his life understand the meaning of your inscriptions. Thus (he went on) you see how under the head of Thursday, April 32nd, 1864, I have marked *Jericho, Train at* 10·30. Now if *that* were to fall into a stranger's possession, he could make nothing of it: he would not know what it meant at all. But as for me, the moment I look at it, I know that it means that on Thursday, April 32nd, 1864, I am to go to Jericho by the 10·30 train. Such were the individual's words. And now, for the sake of those readers who could not understand that mysterious inscription, I think it expedient distinctly to declare, that the reason why this History is called *From Saturday to Monday* is, that it gives an account of historical events, beginning with Saturday and ending on Monday. And thus, having reached Monday evening (for soon after the Bishop's story, everybody went to bed), my task is done. It can never transpire, what happened on the Tuesday. Perhaps something happened of great public interest. But if I were to record it here, then it would appear as if what occurred on Tuesday occurred between Saturday and Monday; which is absurd.

The remembrance of foreign travel is pleasanter than the travel itself. For in remembrance there are none of the hosts that are dispelled by copious camphor: no wear of the muscles, nor of the lungs and heart: no eyes hot and blinded with the sunshine on the snow; no parched throat and leathery tongue; no old goat's flesh disguised as chamois venison. The little drawbacks are forgot; but the absence of care and labour, the blue sky and the bright sun, glacier and cataract, and the snowy Alps remain.

CHAPTER XVIII.

CONCERNING THINGS WHICH CANNOT GO ON.

OF course, in the full meaning of the words, Ben Nevis is one of the Things that cannot Go On. And among these, too, we may reckon the Pyramids. Likewise the unchanging ocean : and all the everlasting hills, which cannot be removed, but stand fast for ever.

But it is not such things that I mean by the phrase : it is not such things that the phrase suggests to ordinary people. It is not things which are passing, indeed ; but passing so very slowly, and with so little sign as yet of their coming end, that to human sense they are standing still. I mean things which even we can discern have not the element of continuance in them : things which press it upon our attention as one of their most marked characteristics, that they have not the element of continuance in them. And you know there are such things. Things too good to last

very long.   Things too bad to be borne very long.
Things which as you look at, you say to yourself,
Ah, it is just a question of time ! We shall not have
you long!

This, as it appears to me, my reader, is the essential quality which makes us class anything among
the Things which cannot Go On : it is that the thing
should not merely be passing away, or even passing away fast; but that it shall bear on its very
face, as the first thing that strikes us in looking at
it, that it is so.   There are passing things that have
a sort of perennial look: things that will soon be
gone, but that somehow do not press it upon us that
they are going.   If you had met Christopher North,
in his days of affluent physical health, swinging
along with his fishing-rod towards the Tweed, you
might, if you had reflected, have thought that in
truth all *that* could not go on.   The day would
come when that noble and loveable man would be
very different: when he would creep along slowly,
instead of tearing along with that springy pace:
when he would no longer be able to thrash pugna-
cious gipsies, nor to outleap flying tailors : when
he would not sit down at morning in his dusty
study, and rush through the writing of an article
as he rushed through other things, impetuously,
determinedly, and with marvellous speed, and
hardly an intermission for rest: when mind and
body, in brief, would be unstrung.   But *that* was

not what you thought of, in the sight of that pro-
digal strength and activity. At any rate, it was
not the thought that came readiest. But when you
see the deep colour on the cheek of a consumptive
girl, and the too bright eye: when you see a man
awfully overworking himself: when you see a
human being wrought up to a frantic enthusiasm
in some cause, good or bad: when you find a lady
declaring that a recently-acquired servant, or a
new-found friend, is absolute perfection: when you
see a church, crowded to discomfort, passages and
all, by people who come to listen to its popular
preacher: when you go to hear the popular
preacher for yourself, and are interested and carried away by a sermon, evincing such elaborate
preparation as no man, with the duty of a parish
resting upon him, could possibly find time for in
any single week,—and delivered with overwhelming vehemence of voice and gesture: when you hear
of a parish in which a new-come clergyman has set
a-going an amount of parochial machinery which
it would need at least three and probably six clergymen to keep working: when you see a family,
living a cat-and-dog life: when you see a poor
fellow, crushed down by toil and anxiety, setting
towards insanity: when you find a country gentleman, with fifteen hundred a year, spending five
thousand: when you see a man submitting to an insufferable petty tyranny, and commanding himself

by a great effort, repeated several times a day, so far as not just yet to let fly at the tyrant's head: when you hear of King Bomba gagging and murdering his subjects, amid the reprobation of civilised mankind: when you see the stoker of an American steamer sitting upon his safety-valve, and observe that the indicator shows a pressure of a hundred and fifty pounds on the square inch of his boiler: —then, my friend, looking at such things as these, and beholding the end impending and the explosion imminent, you would say that these are Things which cannot Go On.

And then, besides the fact that in the case of very many of the Things which cannot Go On, you can discern the cause at work that must soon bring them to an end; there is a further matter to be considered. Human beings are great believers in what may be called the doctrine of Average. That is a deep conviction, latent in the ordinary mind, and the result of all its experience, that anything very extreme cannot last. If you are sitting on a winter evening in a chamber of a country house which looks to the north-east; and if a tremendous batter of wind and sleet suddenly dashes against the windows with a noise loud enough to attract the attention of everybody; I am almost sure that the first thing that will be said, by somebody or other, in the first momentary lull in which it is possible to hear, will be, ' Well, *that* cannot last long.' We have in our minds, as regards all things moral and physical, some idea of what is the average state of matters: and whenever we find any very striking deviation from *that*, we feel assured that the deviation will be but temporary. When you are travelling by railway, even through a new and striking country, the first few miles enable you to judge what you may expect. The country may be very different indeed from that which you are accustomed to see, day by day: but still, a little observation of it enables you to strike an average, so to speak, of that country. And if you come suddenly to anything especially remarkable: to some enormously lofty viaduct, whence you look down upon the tops of tall trees and upon a foaming stream: or to some tunnel through a huge hill: or to some bridge of singular structure: or to some tract wonderfully wooded or wonderfully bare: you involuntarily judge that all this is something exceptional; that it cannot last long; that you will soon be through it, and back to the ordinary jog-trot way.

And now, my friend, let me recall to mind certain facts connected with the great order of Things which cannot Go On: and let us compare our experience with regard to these.

Have you a residence in the country, small or great? Have you ever had such a residence? If you have one, or ever have had one, I have no doubt at all but there is or was a little gravelled walk, which you were accustomed often to walk up and down. You walked there, thinking of things painful and things pleasant. And if nature and training made you the human being for a country life, you found that that little gravelled path could do you a great deal of good. When you went forth, somewhat worried by certain of the little cares which worry at the time but are so speedily forgotten, and walked up and down; you found that at each turn you took, the path, with its evergreens at either hand, and with here and there a little bay of green grass running into the thick masses of green boughs and leaves, gently pressed itself upon your attention; a patient friend, content to wait your time. And in a little space, no matter whether in winter or in summer, the path with its belongings filled your mind with pleasant little thoughts and cares; and smoothed your forehead and quieted your nervous system. I am a great believer in grass and evergreens and gravelled walks. Was it not pleasant, when a bitter wind was blowing outside your little realm, to walk in the shelter of the yews and hollies, where the air felt so snug and calm: and now and then to look out beyond your gate, and catch the bitter East on your face, and then turn back again to the warm, sheltered walk! Beautiful in frost, beautiful in snow, beautiful in rain, beautiful in sunshine, are clumps of evergreens : is green grass : and cheerful and healthful to our whole moral nature is the gravelled walk that winds between!

But all this is by the way. It is not of gravelled walks in general that I am to speak: but of one special phenomenon concerning such walks; and bearing upon my proper subject. If you are walking up and down a path, let us say a hundred and fifty yards long, talking to a friend, or holding conversation with yourself; and if at each turn you take, you have to bend your head to pass under an overhanging bough : here is what will happen. To bend your head for once, will be no effort. You will do it instinctively, and never think about the matter. To stoop even six times, will not be much. But if you walk up and down for an hour, that constant evading of the overhanging bough will become intolerably irksome. For a little, it is nothing: but you cannot bear it if it is a thing that is to go on. Here is a fact in human nature. You can stand a very disagreeable and painful thing for once: or for a little while. But a very small annoyance, going on unceasingly, grows insufferable. No annoyance can possibly be slighter, than that a drop of cold water should fall upon your bare head. But you are aware that those ingenious persons, who have investigated the constitution of man with the design to discover the sensitive places where man can feel torture, have discovered what can be got out of that falling drop of water. Continue it for an hour; continue it for a day: and it turns to a refined agony. It is a thing which cannot go on long, without driving the sufferer mad. No one can say what the effect might be, of compelling a human being to spend a week, walking, through all his waking hours, in a path where he had to bend his head to escape a branch every minute or so. You, my reader, did not ascertain by experiment what would be the effect. However pretty the branch might be, beneath which you had to stoop, or round which you had to dodge, at every turn; that branch must go. And you cut away the blossoming apple-branch: you trained in another direction the spray of honeysuckle: you sawed off the green bough, beautiful with the soft beechen leaves. They had become things which you could not suffer to go on.

Have you ever been misled into living in your house, during any portion of the time in which it was being painted? If so, you remember how you had to walk up and down stairs on planks, very steep and slippery: how, at early morning, a sound pervaded the dwelling, caused by the rubbing your doors with stones, to the end of putting a smoother surface upon the doors: how your children had to abide in certain apartments under ground, to be beyond the reach of paint, and brushes, and walls still wet. The discomfort was extreme. You

could not have made up your mind to go on
through life, under the like conditions : but you
bore it patiently, because it was not to go on. It
was as when you shut your eyes, and squeeze
through a thicket of brambles, encouraged by the
hope of reaching the farther side. So when you
are obliged to ask a man to dinner, with whom you
have not an idea or sympathy in common. Sup-
pressing the tendency to yawn, you force yourself
to talk about things in which you have not the
faintest interest: and you know better than to say
a word upon the subjects for which you really care.
You could not stand this : were it not that from
time to time you furtively glance at the clock, and
think that the time of deliverance is drawing near.
And on the occasion of a washing-day, or a change
of cook, you put up without a murmur with a dinner to which you could not daily subdue your
heart. We can go on for a little space, carried by
the impetus previously got, and by the hope of
what lies before us. It is like the dead points in
the working of a steam-engine. You probably
know that many river steamboats have but a single
engine : and that there are two points, each reached
every few seconds, at which a single engine has no
power at all. The paddle-wheels continue to turn,
in virtue of the strong impetus already given them.
Now, it is plain to every mind, that if the engine
remained for any considerable period at the point

where it is absolutely powerless, the machinery driven by the engine would stop. But in practice, the difficulty is very small: because it is but for a second or two that the engine remains in this state of paralysis. It does quite well for a little: but is a state that could not go on.

Any very extreme feeling, in a commonplace mind, is a thing not likely to go on long. Very extravagant likes and dislikes: very violent grief, such as people fancy must kill them: will, in most cases, endure not long. In short, anything that flies in the face of the laws which regulate the human mind: anything which is greatly opposed to Nature's love for the Average: cannot, in general, go on. I do not forget, that there are striking exceptions. There are people, who never quite get over some great grief or disappointment: there are people who form a fixed resolution, and hold by it all through life. I have seen more than one or two men and women, whose whole soul and energy were so devoted to some good work, that a stranger, witnessing their doings for a few days, and hearing their talk, would have said, ' *That* cannot last. It must soon burn itself out, zeal like that!' But if you had made enquiry, you would have learned that all *that* had gone on un-flagging, for ten, twenty, thirty years. There must have been sound and deep principle there at the first, to stand the wear of such a time: and you may well believe that the whole nature is now confirmed irretrievably in the old habit; you may well hope that the good Christian and philanthropist who has gone on for thirty years, will go on as long as he lives;—will go on for ever. But, as a general rule, I have no great faith in the stability of human character: and I have great faith in the law of Average. People will not go on very long, doing what is inconvenient for them to do. And I will back Time against most feelings and most resolutions in human hearts. It will beat them in the end. You are a clergyman, let us suppose. Your congregation are fond of your sermons. They have got into your way: and if so, they probably like to hear you preach, better than anybody else; unless it be the two or three very great men. A family, specially attached to you, moves from a house near the church, to another two or three miles away. They tell you, that nothing shall prevent their coming to their accustomed places every Sunday still: they would come, though the distance were twice as great. They are perfectly sincere. But your larger experience of such cases makes you well aware that time, and distance, and mud, and rain, and hot sunshine, will beat them. Coming to church over that inconvenient distance, is a thing that cannot go on. It is a thing that ought not to go on: and you make up your mind to the fact. You cannot vanquish the laws of Nature. You may make water run up hill, by laborious pumping. But you cannot go on pumping for ever: and whenever the water is left to its own nature, it will certainly run down hill. All such declarations as 'I shall never forget you:' 'I shall never cease to deplore your loss:' 'I can never hold up my head again:' may be ethically true: but time will prove them logically false. The human being may be quite sincere in uttering them: but he will change his mind.

I do not mean to say that it is very pleasant to have to think thus: or that much good can come of dwelling too long upon the idea. It is a very chilling and sorrowful thing, to be reminded of all this in the hard, heartless way in which some old people like to drive the sad truth into the young. It is very fit and right that the girl of twenty, broken-hearted now because the young individual she is fond of is gone off to Australia, should believe that when he returns in five years he will find her unchanged: and should resent the remotest suggestion that by that time she will probably think and feel quite differently. It is fit and right that she should do all this, even though a prescient eye could discern that in two years exactly she will be married to somebody else: and married, too, not to some old hunx of great wealth whom her parents have badgered her

into marrying against her will; but (much worse
for the man in Australia, who has meanwhile taken
to drinking) married with all her heart to some
fine 'young fellow, very suitable in age and all
other respects. Yet, certain though the general
principle may be, a wise and kind man or woman
will not take much pleasure in imparting the sad
lesson, taught by experience, to younger hearts.
No good can come of doing so. Bide your time,
my friend: and the laws of nature will prevail.
Water will not long run up hill. But while the
stream is quite happy and quite resolute in flowing up an incline of one in twenty, there is no
good in standing by it, and in roaring out that in
a little while it will get tired of *that.* Experience
tells us several things, which are not quite to the
credit of our race: and it is wrong to chill a hopeful and warm heart with these. We should be
delighted to find that young heart falsifying them
by its own history: let it do so if it can.

And it is chilling and irritating to be often reminded of the refrigerating power of Time upon
all warm feelings and resolutions. I have known a
young clergyman, appointed early in life to his first
parish; and entering upon his duty with tremendous
zeal. I think a good man, however old, would rejoice at such a sight: would delightedly try to
direct and counsel all that hearty energy, and to
turn all that labour to the best account. And even

if he thought within himself that possibly all this might not quite last, I don't think he would go and tell the young minister so. And the aged man would thankfully remember, that he has known instances in which all that *has* lasted; and would hope that in this instance it might last again. But I have known a cynical, heartless, time-hardened old man (the uncle, in fact, of my friend Mr. Snarling), listen with a grin of mingled contempt and malignity to the narration of the young parson's doings; and explain the whole phenomena by a general principle, inexpressibly galling and discouraging to the young parson. 'Oh,' says the cynical, heartless old individual, 'new brooms sweep clean!' That was all. The whole thing was explained and settled. I should like to apply a new knout to the old individual, and see if it would cut smartly.

And then we are to remember, that though it be only a question of time with the existence of anything, *that* does not prove that the thing is of no value. A great part of all that we are enjoying, consists of Things which cannot Go On. And though the wear that there is in a thing be a great consideration in reckoning its worth; and more especially, in the case of all Christian qualities, be the great test whether or not they are genuine; yet things that are going, and going very fast, have their worth. And it is very fit that we should enjoy them while they last; without unduly overclouding our enjoyment of them by the recollection of their evanescence. 'Why,' said an eminent divine,— 'why should we pet and pamper these bodies of ours, which are soon to be reduced to a state of mucilaginous fusion?' There was a plausibility about the question: and for about half a minute it tended to make you think, that it might be proper to leave off taking your daily bath, and brushing your nails and teeth : likewise that instead of patronising your tailor any further, it might be well to assume a horse-rug : and also that it might be unworthy to care for your dinner, and that for the future you should live on raw turnips. But of course, anything that revolts common sense, can never be a part of Christian doctrine or duty. And the natural reply to the rhetorical question I have quoted would of course be, that after these mortal frames are so fused, we shall wholly cease to care for them : but that meanwhile we shall suitably tend, feed, and clothe them, because it is comfortable to do so ; because it is God's manifest intention that we should do so : because great moral and spiritual advantage comes of our doing so : and because you have no more right to disparage and neglect your wonderful mortal frame, than any other talent or gift confided to you by God. Why should we neglect, or pretend to neglect, these bodies of ours, with which we are commanded to glorify God : which are bought with Christ's blood : which, even through the last lowliness of mortal dissolution, even when turned to dust again, are 'still united to Christ:' and which are to rise again in glory and beauty, and be the redeemed soul's companion through eternity? And it is a mere sophism to put the shortness of a thing's continuance, as a reason why it should not be cared for while it lasts. Of course, if it last but a short time, all the shorter will be the time through which we shall care for it. But let us make the best of things while they last: both as regards our care for them and our enjoyment of them.

That a thing will soon be done with: that the cloud will soon blow by: is a good reason for bearing patiently what is painful. But it is very needless to thrust in this consideration, to the end of spoiling the enjoyment of what is pleasant. I have seen people, when a little child, in a flutter of delighted anticipation, was going away to some little merrymaking, anxious to put down its unseemly happiness by severely impressing the fact, that in a very few hours all the pleasure would be over, and lessons would begin again. And I have seen, with considerable wrath, a cloud descend upon the little face at the unwelcome suggestion. What earthly good is to come of this piece of stupid, well-meant malignity? It originates, doubtless, in that great fundamental belief in many narrow minds, that the more uncomfortable you are, the likelier

you are to be right: and that God is angry when
he sees people happy. Unquestionably, most of
the little enjoyments of life are very transient. All
pleasant social gatherings: all visits to cheerful
country houses: all holidays: are things which
cannot go on. No doubt, that is true: but that is
no reason why we should sulkily refuse to enjoy
them while they last. There is no good end
secured, by persisting in seeing 'towers decayed
as soon as built.' It is right, always latently, and
sometimes expressly, to remember that they must
decay: but meanwhile, let us be thankful for their
shelter and their beauty. Sit down, happily, on a
July day, beneath the green shade of your beeches:
do not needlessly strain what little imagination you
have, to picture those branches leafless, and the
winter wind and clouds racking overhead. Enjoy
your parcel of new books when it comes, coming
not often: cut the leaves peacefully, and welcome
in each volume a new companion: then carefully
decide the fit place on your shelves where to dis-
pose the pleasant accession to your store: and do
not worry yourself by the reflection that when you
die, the little library you collected may perhaps
be scattered; and the old, friendly-looking volumes
fall into no one knows whose hands: perhaps be
set forth on out-door bookstalls; or be exhibited
on the top of a wall, with a sack put over them
when it begins to rain, as in a place which I have

seen. 'What is the use of washing my hands?' said a little boy in my hearing: 'they will very soon be dirty again!' Refuse, my reader, to accept the principle implied in the little boy's words: however specious it may seem. Whitewash your manse, if you be a Scotch minister, some time in April: paint your house in town, however speedily it may again grow black. Write your sermons diligently: write them on the very best paper you can get, and in a very distinct and careful hand: and pack them with attention in a due receptacle. It is, no doubt, only a question of time how long they will be needed, before the day of your departure shall make them no more than waste paper. Yet, though things which cannot go on, you may hope to get no small use out of them, to others and to yourself, before the time when the hand that travelled over the pages shall be cold with the last chill; and the voice that spoke these words shall be hushed for ever. We know, obscurely, what we shall come to: and by God's grace we are content, and we hope to be prepared: but there is no need to overcast all life with the ceaseless anticipation of death. You may have read how John Hampden's grave was opened, at the earnest desire of an extremely fat nobleman who was his injudicious admirer. The poor wreck of humanity was there: and, as the sexton said, 'We propped him up with a shovel at his back, and I cut off a lock of his hair.' I hold with Abraham, who 'buried his dead from his sight;' I hold with Shakspeare, who desired that no one should disturb him in his lowly bed, till He shall awaken him whose right it is to do so. Yet I read no lesson of the vanity of Hampden's life, in that last sad picture of helplessness and humiliation. He had come to *that*: yet all this does not show that his life was not a noble one while it lasted, though now it was done. He had his day: and he used it: whether well or ill let wiser men judge. And if it be right to say that he withstood tyranny, and helped to lay the foundation of his country's liberties, the whim of Lord Nugent and the propping up with the shovel can take nothing away from that.

You understand me, my friend. You know the kind of people who revenge themselves upon human beings who meanwhile seem happy, by suggesting the idea that it cannot last. You see Mr. A., delighted with his beautiful new church: you know how Miss B. thinks the man to whom she is to be married next week, the handsomest, wisest, and best of mankind: you behold the elation of Mr. C. about that new pair of horses he has got: and if you be a malicious blockhead, you may greatly console yourself in the spectacle of the happiness of those individuals, by reflecting, and perhaps by saying, that it is all one of those things that cannot go on.   Mr. A. will in a few months find no end of worry about that fine building: Miss B.'s husband, at present transfigured to her view, will settle into the very ordinary being he is: and Mr. C.'s horses will prove occasionally lame, and one of them a permanent roarer.   Yet I think a wise man may say, I am aware I cannot go on very long; yet I shall do my best in my little time.   I look at the right hand which holds my pen.   The pen will last but for a short space; yet that is no reason why I should slight it now.   The hand may go on longer. Yet, warm as it is now, and faithfully obeying my will as it has done through all those years, the day is coming when it must cease from its long labours. And, for myself, I am well content that it should be so.   Let us not strive against the silent current, that bears us all away and away.   Let us not quarrel with the reminders we meet on many country gravestones, addressed to us who are living from the fathers who have gone before.   Yet you will think of Charles Lamb.   He said (but nobody can say when Elia meant what he said), 'I conceive disgust at those impertinent and unbecoming familiarities, inscribed upon your ordinary tombstones. Every dead man must take upon himself to be lecturing me with his odious truism, that "Such as he now is I must shortly be."   Not so shortly, friend, perhaps as thou imaginest.   In the meantime I am alive.   I move about.   I am worth twenty of thee. Know thy betters!'

You may look on somewhat farther, in a sweet country burying-place. Dear old churchyard, once so familiar: with the old oaks and the gliding river, and the purple hills looking over: where the true heart of Jeanie Deans has mouldered into dust: I wonder what you are looking like to-day! Many a time have I sat, in the quiet summer day, on a flat stone: and looked at the green graves: and thought that they were Things that could not Go On! *There* were the graves of my predecessors: the day would come when old people in the parish would talk, not unkindly, of the days, long ago, when some one was minister whose name is neither here nor there. But it was a much stranger thing to think, in that silent and solitary place, of the great stir and bustle there shall be in it some day! Here it has been for centuries: the green mossy stones and the little grassy undulations. But we know, from the best of all authority, that 'the hour is coming' which shall make a total change. This quiet, this decay, this forgetfulness, are not to Go on!

We look round, my reader, on all our possessions, and all our friends: and we discern that there are the elements of change in all. 'I am content to stand still,' says Elia, 'at the age to which I am arrived: I, and my friends: to be no younger, no richer, no handsomer: I do not want to be weaned by age; or drop, like mellow fruit, into the grave.'

There are indeed moods of mind, in which all thoughtful men have possibly yielded to a like feeling: but I never heard but of one other man whose deliberate wish was just to go on in this round of life for ever. Yet, though content to be in the wise and kind hands in which we are, we feel it strange to find how all things are going. Your little children, my friend, are growing older: growing out of their pleasant and happy childhood: the old people round you are wrinkling up, and breaking down. And in your constitution, in your way of life, there are things which cannot go on. There is some little physical malady, always rather increasing: and you cannot always be enlarging the doses of the medicine that is to correct it, or the opiates which make you sleep. I confess, . with sorrow, that when I see an extraordinarily tidy garden, or a man dressed with special trimness, I cannot help looking forward to a day when all that is to cease: when the man will be somewhat slovenly; when the garden will be somewhat weedy. I think especially of the garden: and the garden which comes most home to me is the manse garden. It was a marvel of exquisite neatness and order: but a new minister comes, who does not care for gardening: and all *that* goes. And though rejoicing greatly to see a parish diligently worked, yet sometimes I behold the parochial machinery driven with such a pressure of steam, that I cannot but think it never will last. I have known men who never could calmly think: who lived in a hurry and a fever. There are places where it costs a constant effort, not always a successful effort, to avoid coming to such a life: but let us strive against it. Let us not have constant push, and excitement, and high pressure. I hate to feel a whirl around me, as of a huge cotton mill. Let us 'study to be quiet!' And I have observed that clergymen who set that feverish machinery a-going, generally find it expedient to get away from it as speedily as may be, so as to avoid the discredit of its breaking down in their hands: being well aware that it is a thing which cannot go on. We cannot always go at a tearing gallop, with every nerve tense. Probably we are doing so, a great deal too much. If so, let us definitely moderate our pace, before the pace kills us.

'It's a long lane that has no turning,' says the proverb, testifying to the depth of human belief in the Average: testifying to our latent conviction that anything very marked is not likely to go on. A great many people, very anxious and unhappy and disappointed, cherish some confused hope that surely all this has lasted so long, things must be going to mend. The night has been so long, that morning must be near: even though there be not the least appearance of the dawn as yet. If you have been a briefless barrister, or an unemployed physician, or an unbeneficed clergyman, for a pretty long time; even though there be no apparent reason now, more than years since, why success should come, you are ready to think that surely it must be coming now, at last. It seems to be overdue, by the theory of Average. Yet it is by no means certain that there is a good time coming, because the bad time has lasted long. Still, it is sometimes so. I have known a man, very laborious, very unfortunate, with whom everything failed: and after some years of this, I have seen a sudden turn of fortune come. And with exactly the same merit and the same industry as before, I have beheld him succeed in all he attempted, and gain no small eminence and reputation. 'It behoved him to dree his weird,' as was said by Meg Merrilies: and then the good time came. If you are happy, my reader, I wish your happiness may last. And if you are meanwhile somewhat down and depressed, let us hope that all this may prove one of the Things which cannot Go On!

CONCLUSION.

IT is the way of Providence, in most cases, gradually to wean us from the things which we must learn to resign. And it has been so with this holiday-time, now all but ended. It is not now what it was when we came here. The leaves wore their summer green when we came: now they have faded into autumn russet and gold. The paths are strewn deep with those that have fallen; and even in the quiet sunshiny afternoon, some bare trees look wintry against the sky. Like the leaves, the holiday-time has faded. It is outgrown. The appetite for work has revived: and all of us now look forward with as fresh interest to going back to the city to work, as we once did to coming away from the city to rest and play.

We have been weaned, by slow degrees. Nature is hedging us in. The days are shortening fast: the breeze strikes chill in the afternoons, as they darken. The sea sometimes feels bitter, even though you enter it head foremost. Nor have there lacked days of ceaseless rain, and of keen north wind. Two lighthouses, one casting fitful flashes across the water, and one burning with a steady light, become great features of the scene by seven o'clock in the evening. A little later, there is a line of lights that stretches for miles at the base of the dark hills along the opposite shore : indoor occupations have supplanted evening walks. Yet a day or two, and those lights will no more be seen. The inhabitants of the dwellings they make visible will have returned to the great city; and very many of the pretty cottages and houses will remain untenanted through the long winter-time.

As these last days are passing, one feels the vague remorse which is felt when most things draw to an end. One feels as if we might have made more of this time of quiet amid these beautiful hills. Surely we ought to have enjoyed the place and the time more! Thus we are disposed to blame ourselves ; but to blame ourselves unjustly. You would be aware of the like tendency, parting from almost anything; no matter how much you had made of it. You will know the vague remorse when dear friends die, thinking you ought to have been kinder to them : you will know it, though you did for them all that could be done by mortal. And when you come to die, my friend, looking back on the best-spent life, you will think how differently you would spend it were it to be spent again : you will feel as if your talent had been very poorly occupied. And doubtless with good reason, here.

Last night, there was a magnificent sunset. You saw the great red ball above the mountains, visibly going down. It was curious, to watch the space between the sun and the dark ridge beneath it lessening moment by moment, till the sun slowly sunk from sight. Of course, he had been approaching his setting just as fast all day, as in those last minutes above the horizon; but there was something infinitely more striking about the very end. At broad noonday, it is not so easy to fully take in the great truth which Dr. Johnson had engraved on the dial of his watch, that he might be often re-reminded of it,—the solemn Νὺξ γὰρ ἔρχεται. It is in the last minutes that we are made to think that we ought to have valued the sun more when we had him; and valued more the day he measured out.

Day by day this volume has grown up through this holiday-time. In its earlier portion, the author diligently revised the chapters you have read. And by-and-by, the leisurely postman brought the daily pages of pleasing type, in which things look so different from what they look in the cramped magazine printing. Great is the enjoyment which antique ornaments and large initial letters afford to a simple mind.

E E

And now it is the forenoon of our last day here: we go early to-morrow morning. Play-time is past; and work-time is to begin. I hear voices outside, and the pattering of little feet: there are the sea and the hills; and all the place is pervaded by the sound of the waves. On no day through our time here, did the place look as it does now: it wears the peculiar aspect which comes over places from which you are parting. How fast the holidays have slipped away! And what a beautiful scene this is! What a pretty little Gothic church it is, in which for these Sundays that are gone the writer has taken part of the duty: how green the ivy on the cliffs, and the paths through the woods; what perpetual life in that ceaseless fluctuation of which you seldom lose sight for long! But we must all set our faces to the months of work once more, thankful to feel fit for them: not without some anxiety in the prospect of them; looking for the guidance and help of that kindest Hand which has led through the like before.

www.ingramcontent.com/pod-product-compliance
Lightning Source LLC
Chambersburg PA
CBHW021335110726
47900CB00005B/1474